Spelling

John R. Pescosolido, Ph.D.
Professor Emeritus
Central Connecticut State University
New Britain, Connecticut

Consultants

Felice M. Rockoff
Reading Teacher
New York City Public Schools
New York, New York

Theodore J. Thibodeau
Assistant Superintendent
Attleboro Public Schools
Attleboro, Massachusetts

Anna L. Ulrich
Adjunct Professor
College of Santa Fe
Albuquerque, New Mexico

Anita Uphaus
Coordinator of Early Childhood Programs
Austin Independent School District
Austin, Texas

STECK-VAUGHN
COMPANY
ELEMENTARY • SECONDARY • ADULT • LIBRARY

Acknowledgments

Executive Editor: Diane Sharpe
Project Editor: Amanda Johnson
Design Manager: Richard Balsam
Designers: Jim Cauthron
Danielle Szabo

Product Development: Cottage Communications
Typesetting: Publishers' Design and Production Services, Inc.

Writers: Linda Ekblad (pp. 62, 140, 152); Kathleen Fischer (p. 126); Bobbi Katz (pp. 158, 190); Susan Katz (pp. 38, 108); Jackie Podhaizer (p. 30); Stuart Podhaizer (Etymologies); Gena Reisner (pp. 12, 44, 70, 82, 94); Joan Rosenblatt (pp. 24, 56, 88, 114, 120, 134, 146, 166, 178); Linda Rogers (pp. 102, 172); Lorraine Sotiriou (pp. 6, 18, 50, 76, 184)

Artists: Andrea Baruffi, Maxie Chambliss, Brian Cody, Holly Cooper, Arlene Dubanevich, Julie Durrell, Allan Eitzen, Jon Friedman, John Gamache, Jon Goodell, David Griffin, Carol Grosvenor, Konrad Hack, Meryl Henderson, Pamela Higgins, Joan Holub, Will Kefauver, Tom Leonard, Susan Lexa, Shelly Matheis, Carolyn McHenry, Kimble Pendleton Mead, Linda Miyamoto, Marcy Ramsey, Jerry Smath, Joel Snyder, Arvis Stewart, Pat Traub, John Wallner, Kay Wilson

---

ISBN 0-8114-9274-5

Contents

Lesson 1 Words with /ă/

Listen for /ă/ in each word.

rapid

traffic

magnet

act

magic

chapter

rabbit

snack

plastic

crack

program

planet

crash

salad

factory

sandwich

half

calf

aunt

laughter

1. Write the two words that begin with a vowel.

_____ _____

2. Write the three words that begin with the letter p.

_____ _____

_____

3. Which word begins and ends like market?

_____

4. Which word begins and ends like funny? _____

5. Write one word that begins with the letters ch and one that ends with ch.

_____ _____

6. Which word ends with the letters sh? _____

7. Write the two words that end with the letter d.

_____ _____

8. Which five words end with /k/? Circle the letters that spell /k/. _____ _____

_____ _____

_____

9. Which two words have /f/ in the middle? Circle the letters that spell /f/.

_____ _____

10. In which word is /b/ spelled bb? _____

11. Write the two words in which you see the letter l but don't hear /l/. _____ _____

12. Which two words have the same spelling of /ă/ as laugh

_____ _____

13. Write the word in which you hear /j/ but don't see the letter j. _____

4

Checkpoint

Write a spelling word for each clue.
Then use the Checkpoint Study Plan on page 224.

1. Moving cars and trucks are ____.

2. One of two equal parts is a ____.

3. Another word for hare is ____.

4. The opposite of crying is ____.

5. Every play has a last ____.

6. A narrow opening or break is a ____.

7. In a house is a room, in a book is a ____.

8. A list of events is a ____.

9. Elroy is his uncle, Gertrude is his ____.

10. Workers make things in a ____.

11. A small meal is a ____.

12. The magician's trick seemed to be ____.

13. The opposite of slow is ____.

14. A mixture of uncooked vegetables is a ____.

15. A car accident may be called a ____.

16. A horse has a colt, a cow has a ____.

17. Many toys are made of ____.

18. The earth is a ____.

19. Something that attracts metal is a ____.

20. This mystery word comes from the title of an English earl of the 18th century. The Earl was fond of games, especially cards. He loved games so much that he didn't allow meals to interrupt them. While he played, he had his servants bring him a slice of meat between two pieces of bread. This food soon became popular. Today we call two slices of bread with some filling by the title of this earl. His title was the Fourth Earl of ____.

5

Use each list word once.

How Not to Buy Skis

George Ira Pshaw handed the driver the bus fare and jumped aboard. Even with all the _____, the bus was able to make _____ progress to the airport. If the bus arrived early, George would have time for lunch. He thought about what he would eat.

"Maybe I'll have a peanut butter _____, or a lettuce and tomato _____," he thought. "I want to eat a light _____."

When George checked his luggage at the airport, a tall stranger spoke to him. "Skiing the North Slope tomorrow?"

George was flattered to be taken for an experienced skier. The North Slope was hard.

"Allow me to introduce myself," the stranger said. "My name is Yul B. Sawrey. Here's my card."

"Oh, you sell ski equipment," said George.

"That's right. Maybe you've seen my skis advertised on your local TV _____," Yul said. "My skis are the only ones on the _____ Earth that won't break. They are so good that they are crash-proof."

"That sounds too good to be true. It's almost like _____," George said.

"Almost," said Sawrey slyly. "My skis are made in my own _____ from a new, light _____. They push you away from anything into which you might _____. They _____ like a reverse _____."

"I'll buy a pair!" George shouted. "A beginner can certainly use magic skis."

At the ski slope the next day, George decided he didn't need skiing lessons. With his new skis, he could take on the hardest run. He didn't even finish reading the first _____ in his book, How to Ski. He began down the North Slope as fast as a _____. CRASH! He hit a rock. His new skis broke in _____ with a loud _____. The next thing he knew, he was in the hospital wearing a cast from his _____ to his hip.

George's _____ came to see him in the hospital. She felt sorry for George. He told his aunt, "I should have known better than to buy skis from a man named 'Yul B. Sawrey.'"

His aunt answered, "Well, now we can call you 'G. I. Pshaw Was!'"

George's _____ could be heard down the hall.

7

rapid
traffic
magnet
act
magic
chapter
rabbit
snack
plastic
crack
program
planet
crash
salad
factory
sandwich
half
calf
aunt
laughter

Alphabetical Order

Words are listed in alphabetical order in a dictionary. Words that begin with a come first, then words that begin with b, and so on. It is simple to find a word in a dictionary if you know about alphabetical order. To put words in alphabetical order, look at the first letter of each word.

<u>a</u>bout
<u>b</u>uild

When words begin with the same letter, look at the second letter to put the words in alphabetical order.

a<u>b</u>out
a<u>r</u>ound

When the first two letters are the same, look at the third letter.

ab<u>l</u>e
ab<u>o</u>ut

When the first three letters are the same, look at the fourth letter.

abo<u>a</u>rd
abo<u>u</u>t

⭐ Write the words in each group in alphabetical order.

1. traffic   factory   half   snack

_____

_____

_____

_____

2. calf   aunt   chapter   act

_____

_____

_____

_____

3. sandwich rabbit rapid salad

_____

_____

_____

_____

4. crack magnet magic crash

_____

_____

_____

_____

Challenge Yourself

candid   landslide   javelin   jabber

Write what you think each underlined Challenge Word means. Check your Spelling Dictionary to see if you were right. Then write sentences showing that you understand the meaning of each Challenge Word.

1. Having nothing to hide, the girl gave candid answers to the questions her teacher asked.

2. Heavy rains on the steep mountainside resulted in a landslide.

3. The athlete threw the javelin so that the point landed first.

4. Sometimes when I'm nervous, I jabber on with nobody listening.

Write to the Point

Did you ever make a mistake that seems funny now when you think about it? Maybe you took some bad advice, forgot to do something important, or tried to do something that was too hard for you. Write a story about what happened. Use spelling words from this lesson in your story.

Challenge Use one or more of the Challenge Words in your story.

Proofreading

Use the proofreading marks to show the errors in the paragraph below. Write the five misspelled words correctly in the blanks.

⬭	word is misspelled
⊙	period is missing
≡	letter should be capitalized

Skiing along at a rapud speed, kim suddenly landed with a krash. Nothing was hurt but the egg salad samwitch she had brought as a snak. it was squashed flat in its plastic wrapping Kim burst into laugter at the sight

1. _____

2. _____

3. _____

4. _____

5. _____

9

Lesson 2   Words with /ā/

Listen for /ā/ in each word.

brain

explain

remain

raise

complain

container

paid

scale

male

parade

escape

snake

female

weigh

weight

neighbor

holiday

delay

break

bakery

1. Which word begins with the letters ex?

_____

2. Write the two words that begin with the letters br.

_____

3. Which word begins with the letters re?

_____

4. Write the two words that begin with /k/.

_____

5. Which word begins and ends with a vowel?

_____

6. Which two words begin with /p/ and end with /d/?

_____

7. Which word begins and ends like rake? _____

8. Which word begins and ends like fence? _____

9. Which word begins and ends like mile? _____

10. Write the two words that begin with the letter s and end with the letter e. _____

11. Write the three words that have three syllables.

_____

_____

12. Which word has the same spelling of /ā/ as steak?

_____

13. Which three words have the same spelling of /ā/ as eight?

_____   _____

14. Which two words have the same spelling of /ā/ as ray?

_____   _____

Checkpoint

Write a spelling word for each clue.
Then use the Checkpoint Study Plan on page 224.

1. To measure in pounds or kilograms is to ____.

2. Another word for the mind is ____.

3. When the money was given, the bill was ____.

4. The person who lives next door is your ____.

5. To describe means to ____.

6. You run in a race, you march in a ____.

7. Another word for woman is ____.

8. To find fault is to ____.

9. One kind of reptile is a ____.

10. The opposite of fix is ____.

11. Weight can be measured on a ____.

12. The opposite of to leave is to ____.

13. Pounds or kilograms are a measure of ____.

14. A jar is a kind of ____.

15. Bread, cake, and pastry are sold in a ____.

16. The opposite of to lower is to ____.

17. Another word for man is ____.

18. Labor Day is a September ____.

19. To put off doing something is to ____.

20. This mystery word comes from two Latin words, *ex* and *cappa*. *Ex* meant out of. *Cappa* meant cape. Ancient Romans wore capes. When one Roman citizen wanted to arrest another, he grabbed the other by the cape. To get free, the arrested man would slip out of his cape and run away. The mystery word, which means to get free, comes from *ex cappa*. Can you guess the mystery word? Be sure to notice how the spelling of this word has changed. ____

11

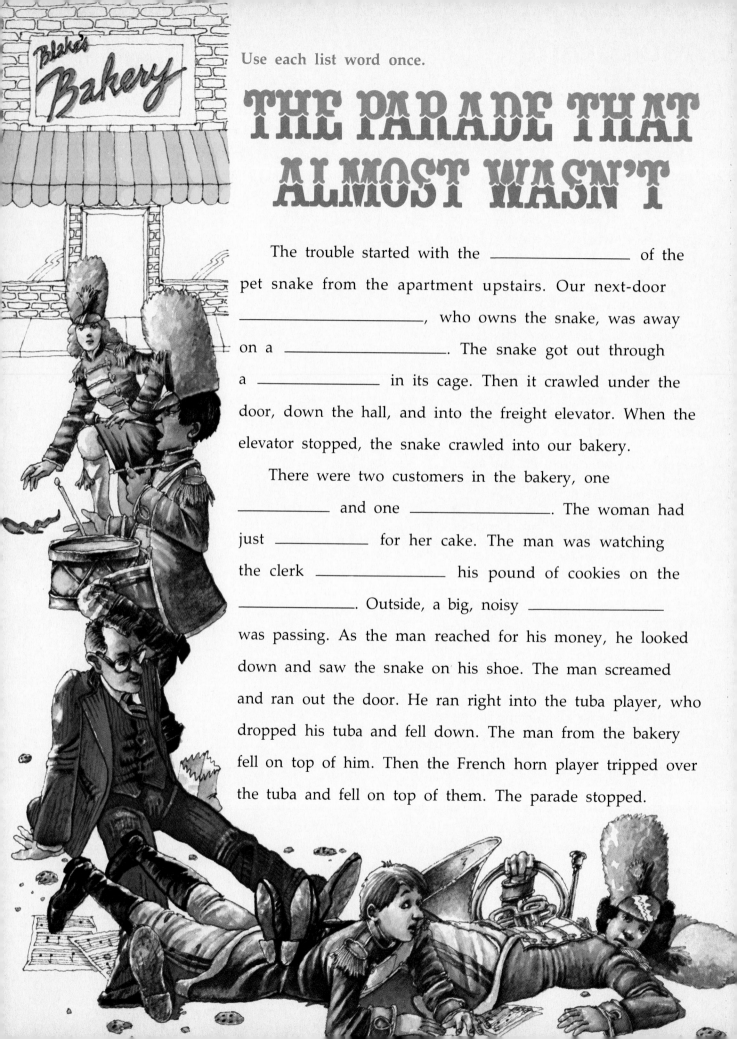

Use each list word once.

THE PARADE THAT ALMOST WASN'T

The trouble started with the _____ of the pet snake from the apartment upstairs. Our next-door _____, who owns the snake, was away on a _____. The snake got out through a _____ in its cage. Then it crawled under the door, down the hall, and into the freight elevator. When the elevator stopped, the snake crawled into our bakery.

There were two customers in the bakery, one _____ and one _____. The woman had just _____ for her cake. The man was watching the clerk _____ his pound of cookies on the _____. Outside, a big, noisy _____ was passing. As the man reached for his money, he looked down and saw the snake on his shoe. The man screamed and ran out the door. He ran right into the tuba player, who dropped his tuba and fell down. The man from the bakery fell on top of him. Then the French horn player tripped over the tuba and fell on top of them. The parade stopped.

While this was happening, the other customer in the
_____ had dropped her cake and grabbed what
she thought was an empty bucket. But it was a large
_____ full of sugar. The heavy
_____ of the full bucket was too much. She
dropped it, spilling all the sugar. Then she tried to catch the
_____ in the empty bucket. But she slipped on
the sugar and fell to the floor. The snake crawled out the
door and into the parade.

The drummer was the first to see the snake. He began
to yell so loudly that a vein stood out on his forehead.
Finally the drum majorette saw the snake. She used her
_____. She shouted and told everyone to
_____ in line. Then she picked up the snake.

"Let's not _____ the parade any longer," she
said. "Start marching when I _____ my baton."
Holding the snake high in the air with her left hand, she
raised her baton and began to march.

The French horn player got up and picked up her
French horn. The man from the bakery left and got lost in
the crowd. The tuba player got up slowly and began to
_____ about an ache in his back. The
parade began to move.

The next day, a picture of the drum majorette holding
the snake was in all the papers. Everyone said how brave
she was.

She said, "Let me _____. When
I was little, three snakes lived in a hole next to my house.
Nothing can erase my memory of those snakes, and no
silly old milk snake will ever scare me!"

13

brain
explain
remain
raise
complain
container
paid
scale
male
parade
escape
snake
female
weigh
weight
neighbor
holiday
delay
break
bakery

Capitals and Punctuation

A sentence begins with a capital letter.

A sentence that tells something ends with a period.

I like chicken soup.

A sentence that asks something ends with a question mark.

Do you like chicken soup?

A sentence that shows strong feeling or surprise ends with an exclamation point.

This chicken soup tastes terrible!

★ From the story below, write the words that should be capitalized. Then find the words that should be followed by a period, a question mark, or an exclamation point. Write the words with the correct punctuation.

during the school year, our class decided to take a break from our studies we took a holiday trip to the mountains our leader, Mr. Peterson, explained to us the purpose of the trip we were to scale a mountain six thousand feet high after hearing this, most of the males and females in the group decided to remain at home how could Mr. Peterson expect us to do this and not complain

however, Mr. Peterson finally persuaded us to go we looked like a parade climbing up the mountain we hiked for a long time and finally reached the mountain top after a brief rest, we began our trip down at this rate we surely would lose weight

suddenly, we heard a scream we looked just in time to see a snake escape from the area by slithering away that was a close one

Capitals Needed		Words Before Punctuation

Checkpoint

Write a spelling word for each clue.
Then use the Checkpoint Study Plan on page 224.

1. To think of and make for the first time is to ____.

2. A seat in the park for two or more persons is a ____.

3. Your street number and town name are your ____.

4. The new boy hopes his classmates will be ____.

5. Hidden gold may be a ____.

6. Wide is to width as deep is to ____.

7. You sew with a needle and ____.

8. When you're sick, you don't feel like your normal ____.

9. Take a deep ____ of clean air.

10. Great riches means great ____.

11. A feeling of enjoyment is ____.

12. The opposite of answers is ____.

13. To have in mind is to ____.

14. If you feel chilly, you may need a ____.

15. In place of or rather than means ____.

16. Parcheesi, chess, and ____ are games.

17. To be free of disease is to be ____.

18. If it's raining, it is wet ____.

19. To find the size of something is to ____.

20. We often see this mystery word in our grammar books.
    It is defined as a group of words that expresses
    complete thought. Did you know that it comes from a
    word that meant thought? The mystery word comes
    from the Latin word *sententia*. *Sententia* meant a thought,
    opinion, or idea. Can you guess the mystery word ____

17

Use each list word once.

THE CHESS GAME

"How about a game of _____ or chess?" Freda asked. Dr. Wilson sat down beside her on the park _____.

"A game of chess would be a _____, Freda. We haven't played chess since I moved to my new _____ on Clinton Street," Dr. Wilson said. He looked down at the _____ tied around his finger. He wondered why he had tied it there.

"Isn't this beautiful fall _____?" Freda took a deep _____ of air. "It makes you feel so strong and _____."

"My mother always called it _____ weather because it's too warm for a coat." Dr. Wilson paused after his _____, as if in the _____ of thought.

"What is it, Doctor?" Freda asked.

"I was just wondering about this thread. It's to remind me of something. But what? Well, never mind. I'll remember sooner or later. But now, a surprise."

"You're always making things in your laboratory. Did you _____ something new?" asked Freda.

"And you're still your usual curious _____, always asking _____," laughed Dr. Wilson. Then he carefully pulled something from his pocket. He held it as if it were a valuable _____ that would bring him great _____.

"You wanted to play a game of chess with me. Why not play with my mini-robot _____? I call it I-1."

"What a great idea!" Freda cried. "It's so tiny. Did you ever _____ just how tall your robot is?"

"I-1 is five centimeters tall," Dr. Wilson answered.

"Trying to beat a robot is going to be quite difficult. But I _____ to do it," Freda said.

"Pawn to Knight 4," said I-1.

"Pawn to Queen 3," countered Freda.

"About this thread . . ." wondered Dr. Wilson.

An hour later, Freda yelled, "Checkmate. I won!"

FIZZ!   FIM!!   FOOSH!!!

I-1 threw a fit, and sparks flew everywhere.

"I-1 won! I-1 won!" it screamed.

"I-1 certainly isn't very _____, Dr. Wilson," said Freda.

Dr. Wilson yelled, "I remember now! I-1 must <u>always</u> be allowed to win."

FIZZ!   FIM!!   FOOSH!!!

healthy
thread
wealth
weather
instead
measure
pleasure
breath
sweater
treasure
bench
intend
invent
sentence
self
questions
address
checkers
depth
friendly

Guide Words

Guide words are the two words in heavy type at the top of each dictionary page. Guide words make it easy to locate a word in a dictionary because the first guide word is the first word on the page, and the second guide word is the last word on the page. The other words come between in alphabetical order. When searching for a word in a dictionary, always check the guide words first to see if a word is on a particular page.

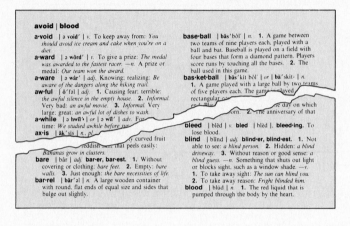

avoid | blood

a·void | ə void' | v. To keep away from: *You should avoid ice cream and cake when you're on a diet.*

a·ward | ə wôrd' | v. To give a prize: *The medal was awarded to the fastest racer.* —n. A prize or medal: *Our team won the award.*

a·ware | ə wâr' | adj. Knowing; realizing: *Be aware of the dangers along the hiking trail.*

aw·ful | ô'fəl | adj. **1.** Causing fear; terrible: *the awful silence in the empty house.* **2.** *Informal.* Very bad: *an awful movie.* **3.** *Informal.* Very large; great: *an awful lot of dishes to wash.*

a·while | ə hwīl' | *or* | ə wīl' | adv. For a time: *We studied awhile before sup...*

ax·is | ăk'sĭs | n. pl. ...

... reddish ... that peels easily: *Bananas grow in clusters.*

bare | bâr | adj. **bar·er, bar·est. 1.** Without covering or clothing: *bare feet.* **2.** Empty: *bare walls.* **3.** Just enough: *the bare necessities of life.*

bar·rel | băr'əl | n. A large wooden container with round, flat ends of equal size and sides that bulge out slightly.

base·ball | bās'bôl' | n. **1.** A game between two teams of nine players each, played with a ball and bat. Baseball is played on a field with four bases that form a diamond pattern. Players score runs by touching all the bases. **2.** The ball used in this game.

bas·ket·ball | băs'kĭt bôl' | *or* | bă'skĭt- | n. **1.** A game played with a large ball by two teams of five players each. The game is played rectangular ...

... day on which ... **2.** The anniversary of that ...

bleed | blēd | v. **bled** | blēd |, **bleed·ing.** To lose blood.

blind | blīnd | adj. **blind·er, blind·est. 1.** Not able to see: *a blind person.* **2.** Hidden: *a blind driveway.* **3.** Without reason or good sense: *a blind guess.* —n. Something that shuts out light or blocks sight, such as a window shade. —v. **1.** To take away sight: *The sun can blind you.* **2.** To take away reason: *Fright blinded him.*

blood | blŭd | n. **1.** The red liquid that is pumped through the body by the heart.

★Write the following words in alphabetical order. Then look them up in the Spelling Dictionary and write the guide words for each word.

bench	address	depth	healthy	measure	pleasure
breath	sentence	instead	checkers	wealth	friendly

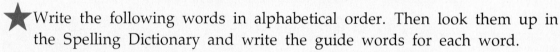

Word   Guide Words

1. _____   _____
2. _____   _____
3. _____   _____
4. _____   _____
5. _____   _____
6. _____   _____
7. _____   _____
8. _____   _____
9. _____   _____
10. _____   _____
11. _____   _____
12. _____   _____

WORDS AT WORK

Challenge Yourself

endeavor   concept   identical   meddle

Write what you think each underlined Challenge Word means. Check your Spelling Dictionary to see if you were right. Then write sentences showing that you understand the meaning of each Challenge Word.

1. Because of the team's <u>endeavor</u> to improve, they now have a trophy.

2. The government of the United States is based on the <u>concept</u> that all people are equal.

3. People often called Anita by her sister's name because the girls were <u>identical</u> twins.

4. I'd give her advice, but I don't want to <u>meddle</u>.

Write to the Point

Imagine that you have a friend visiting you at your house. Your friend wants to learn how to play a new game. Think of a game you know that is fun to play but simple enough to explain in a few sentences. Then write instructions telling how to play it. Be sure to explain each part of the game clearly and in the correct order. Use spelling words from this lesson in your instructions.

Challenge Use one or more of the Challenge Words in your instructions.

Proofreading

Use the proofreading marks to show the errors in the paragraph below. Write the five misspelled words correctly in the blanks.

◯	word is misspelled
≡	letter should be capitalized
∧	word is missing

The whether was bad, so i decided invent a new indoor game insted of playing cheakers. First, i hid a tresure. Then my little sister asked ten qestions about what it was and where to find.

1. _____

2. _____

3. _____

4. _____

5. _____

21

Lesson 4 Words with /ĕ/

Listen for /ĕ/ in each word.

pledge

remember

elephant

gentle

metal

petal

else

exercise

energy

length

extra

desert

wreck

expert

special

century

metric

excellent

selfish

vegetable

1. Which four words begin with the letters ex?

   _____   _____

   _____   _____

2. Which three words begin with /s/? _____

   _____   _____

3. Which four words begin and end with a vowel?

   _____   _____

   _____   _____

4. Which two words are spelled the same except for the

   first letter? _____   _____

5. Which word begins and ends like racer?

   _____

6. Which word ends with the letters th? _____

7. Write the word that ends with the letters sh.

   _____

8. Write the word in which /sh/ is spelled ci.

   _____

9. Which two words end with /k/? Circle the letters that

   spell /k/. _____   _____

10. Write the four words in which you hear /j/ but don't see

    the letter j. _____

    _____   _____

11. Which word has /z/ in the middle? _____

12. Which two words have /f/ in the middle? Circle the

    letters that spell /f/. _____

13. Write the word in which you see the letter w but don't

    hear /w/. _____

14. In which word is /l/ spelled ll? _____

22

Checkpoint

Write a spelling word for each clue.
Then use the Checkpoint Study Plan on page 224.

1. One hundred years is a ____.

2. A dry place with sand and rocks is a ____.

3. Part of a flower is a ____.

4. Something not ordinary or usual is ____.

5. Another word for promise is ____.

6. The opposite of forget is ____.

7. Someone who knows a lot about a thing is an ____.

8. It is not here, but somewhere ____.

9. Sun, wind, water, and coal are sources of ____.

10. Our system of measurement may change to ____.

11. Broccoli is a ____.

12. Wide is to width as long is to ____.

13. Generous is the opposite of ____.

14. Another word for destroy is ____.

15. The opposite of harsh is ____.

16. Silver and iron are kinds of ____.

17. For good health, get enough ____.

18. Something over and above is ____.

19. Something very good is ____.

20. This mystery word is the name of an animal. Like some other names for animals, it originally described something about the animal. Squirrel, for example, meant shadow tail in Greek. Spider meant spinner in Old English. The mystery word comes from the Greek word for ivory, *elephas*. It names an animal with ivory tusks. Can you guess the mystery word? ____

23

Use each list word once.

THE CIRCUS TRAIN

Carlo's whole family had been with the circus for more than a _____. They all loved the circus. Carlo's mother was an _____ animal trainer. Carlo's job was to feed the animals and walk them around to give them their _____. But Carlo wanted something _____. He made a _____ that soon he would show everyone he was ready to learn to train animals himself.

One night, the circus train was speeding across the _____. It was on its way to Los Angeles. The train was making _____ time. If things went smoothly, the circus would arrive in Los Angeles by dawn. But things did not go smoothly. The train hit something on the track, and tons of _____ screeched to a halt. The train shook along its entire _____. In the car where the animals were, a door flew open. A frightened _____ headed quickly through this exit. She ran across a bare stretch of desert and disappeared.

Now this was no ordinary elephant. Flower, as she was called, was very _____. She liked to work. She always had plenty of _____ for raising the huge circus tent. And she wasn't _____. She would gladly share her food.

Carlo and Flower were good friends. Carlo would always _____ to give Flower _____ water and food. And even though Flower weighed three _____ tons, she was very _____ with Carlo and would sometimes tickle him with her trunk.

When Carlo saw that Flower was gone, he started to worry. He went to the ledge at the back of the train to look for her. He saw only a trail of large footprints leading off into the darkness. Carlo got one of the tumbler's motorcycles. He pointed it in the direction of the footprints and stepped on the gas pedal.

He drove across the desert looking for Flower. He followed her footprints until he came to a little town. He saw Flower sitting in a _____ garden, quietly eating some carrots. The rest of the garden was already a _____. Flower had even destroyed all the roses on the edge of the garden. A bright red rose _____ was still stuck to her trunk. Just then the police arrived, and Carlo explained what had happened. The police helped Carlo get Flower out of the garden and watched him as he led Flower back to the train.

When they got back, everyone was cheering. With Carlo's encouragement, Flower led all the other elephants in pulling the train back onto the tracks.

As the train was starting again, Carlo overheard his mother tell the circus manager that her son was ready to learn to be an animal trainer.

pledge
remember
elephant
gentle
metal
petal
else
exercise
energy
length
extra
desert
wreck
expert
special
century
metric
excellent
selfish
vegetable

Nouns

A noun is a word that names a person, place, thing, or idea.

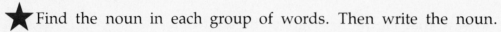

woman	park	pumpkin	happiness
child	zoo	apple	beauty
man	city	pear	peace

★ Find the noun in each group of words. Then write the noun.

1. metal   remember   until

2. across   complain   energy

3. paid   elephant   invent

4. erase   century   about

5. was   petal   excellent

6. vegetable   weigh   remain

★ Unscramble and write each sentence. Then underline the nouns.

7. drove desert week We the last through

8. The down swam wreck the to divers

9. exercise likes of get Jill lots to

10. class said of Allegiance Pledge Our the

11. ran field length Andy the of the

WORDS AT WORK

Challenge Yourself

compel   **condemn**
     dedication   **pendulum**

Use your Spelling Dictionary to answer these questions. Then write sentences showing that you understand the meaning of each Challenge Word.

1. Do school rules <u>compel</u> you to walk backwards and wear gloves on your feet?

2. Should laws <u>condemn</u> cruel actions against people and animals?

3. Does a person who naps during a job show great <u>dedication</u> to his or her work?

4. Is a <u>pendulum</u> a part on some clocks?

Write to the Point

Imagine you are a newspaper reporter in Carlo's town. Your boss has sent you to cover the circus train story. Write a brief news article telling what happened to the circus train. Start with the headline "Elephant Escapes from Circus Train!" Remember to include the most important details. Use spelling words from this lesson in your article.

Challenge Use one or more of the Challenge Words in your article.

Proofreading

Use the proofreading marks to show the errors in the paragraph below. Write the five misspelled words correctly in the blanks.

⬭	word is misspelled
⊙	period is missing
⤴	take out word

To become an expurt circus acrobat like Ms. Chung, rember to practice every day and get the right kind of of exerize Get plenty of rest, too, or else you won't have the enerjy to give a an excellant performance.

1. _____
2. _____
3. _____
4. _____
5. _____

27

Lesson 5   Words with Capitals

Say each word.

Sunday

Monday

Tuesday

Wednesday

Thursday

Friday

Saturday

January

February

March

April

May

June

July

August

September

October

November

December

St.

1. Which three words begin with the letter <u>m</u>?

   _____ _____

   _____

2. Write the three words that begin with a vowel.

   _____ _____

   _____

3. Write the two words that begin with the letter <u>t</u>.

   _____ _____

4. Which two days and one month begin with the letter <u>s</u>?

   _____ _____

5. Which three words begin with the letter <u>j</u>? Circle the word that has one syllable. _____

   _____ _____

6. Which two words begin with the letter <u>f</u>? Circle the word that has four syllables.

   _____ _____

7. Write the three words that end with the same five letters. _____ _____

   _____

8. Write the day of the week that has three syllables.

   _____

9. Write the word in which you see the letter <u>d</u> but don't hear /d/. _____

10. Write the word in which the letter <u>r</u> appears twice.

    _____

11. What is the abbreviation of the word <u>Street</u>?

Checkpoint

Write a spelling word for each clue.
Then use the Checkpoint Study Plan on page 224.

1. The day after Saturday is ____.

2. The third month of the year is ____.

3. Avenue is to Ave. as Street is to ____.

4. The calendar year begins on the first of ____.

5. When the school week begins it is ____.

6. The last month of the year is ____.

7. Sunday is before Monday, Monday is before ____.

8. The day after Tuesday is ____.

9. Thanksgiving falls on the last Thursday in ____.

10. The month that has only three letters is ____.

11. School usually starts in the month of ____.

12. Summer begins in the month of ____.

13. The last school day in the week is ____.

14. The day before Friday is ____.

15. The fourth month of the year is ____.

16. The month after September is ____.

17. The day named for Saturn is ____.

18. The shortest month is ____.

19. These two mystery words are names for months. Both come from the names of great Romans. In one of these months, the great Roman general Julius Caesar was born. *Julius* Caesar had the Roman people name this month for him. Can you guess this month's name? ____

20. The other month was named for Julius Caesar's nephew. When the nephew became emperor, he was called Caesar Augustus. *Augustus* meant the great man. Can you guess which month was named for him? ____

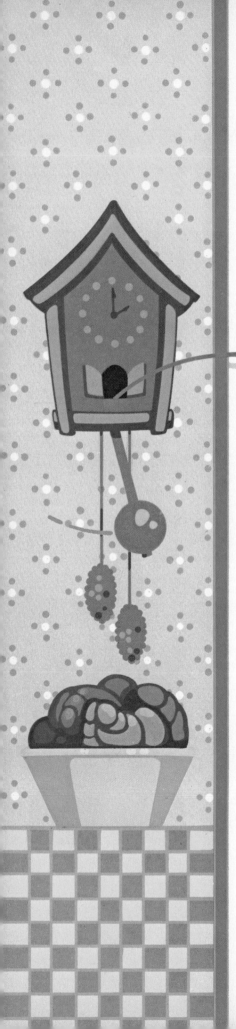

Use each list word once.

TIMELY PUZZLES

Write the name of a month in each blank.

Cuckoo, Cuckoo!

What do you do?

In April

I open my bill.

In _____

I sing night and day.

In _____

I change my tune.

In _____

Away I fly.

In _____

Away I must.

Some people think it is dangerous to eat fresh oysters in certain months. They say the oysters are not good during these months and can make a person very sick. They suggest following their rule for eating fresh oysters. Their rule is: EAT FRESH OYSTERS ONLY IN MONTHS WITH THE LETTER R IN THEIR NAMES.

Write the names of the months in which you can eat fresh oysters safely.

_____ _____

_____ _____

_____ _____

_____ _____

Write the name of the day that matches each meaning.

_____ This day takes its name from the same word as <u>thunder</u>.

_____ This day's name comes from a word meaning <u>moon</u>.

_____ This day was named for the <u>sun</u>.

_____ This day was named for the Norse goddess <u>Fria</u>, the goddess of beauty and love.

_____ This day's name comes from <u>Tiw</u>, a Norse god of war.

_____ This day was named for the Roman god of agriculture, <u>Saturn</u>.

_____ The chief Norse god <u>Woden</u>, ruler of the sky, gave his name to this day.

Write the abbreviation that corresponds to this sign. _____

Monday
Tuesday
Wednesday
Thursday
Friday
Saturday
Sunday
January
February
March
April
May
June
July
August
September
October
November
December
_St._

Capitals

Use a capital letter to begin names of the days and months.

Sally was born on a Friday in December.

★ Unscramble the sentences below. Capitalize the names of the days and months. Remember to put a period at the end of each sentence.

1. is april balmy In the weather

_____

2. my birthday in is Don't forget february that

_____

3. field is in class trip november Our

_____

4. School in september begins

_____

5. on august We vacation in go july and

_____

★ Roy made a list of the things he has to do. He made mistakes in spelling and capitalizing the days of the week. Write the seven words correctly.

Days		Things to Do
sonday	_____	visit grandparents
munday	_____	brush dog
teusday	_____	return library book
wenesday	_____	go to baseball practice
thrusday	_____	study for test
fryday	_____	take spelling test
saterday	_____	go to baseball game

WORDS AT WORK

Challenge Yourself

Blvd.   **Jupiter**

  North Pole   **Memorial Day**

Decide which Challenge Word fits each clue. Check your Spelling Dictionary to see if you were right. Then write sentences showing that you understand the meaning of each Challenge Word.

1. This is when you might see a parade and remember those who died for their country.

2. It isn't a street, avenue, lane, or highway, but cars travel on it.

3. Because of its size, this place was named after the ancient Roman ruler of the gods.

4. You'll need your warmest clothes if you travel there.

Write to the Point

An itinerary lists places you will visit on a trip and the dates when you will arrive. Here is an example:

> Monday, January 5—Disney World
>
> Friday, February 11—Grand Canyon

Imagine you can take a yearlong trip. Plan one stop for each month. Write an itinerary for your trip. Use spelling words from this lesson.

Challenge Use one or more of the Challenge Words in your itinerary.

Proofreading

Use the proofreading marks to show the errors in the paragraph below. Write the five misspelled words correctly in the blanks.

◯	word is misspelled
≡	letter should be capitalized
⋏	exclamation point is missing

This may I started studying piano. Every Wenesday I go to my teacher's house on forest st. On Munday, Jully 31, I give my first recital. How glad I'll be on Teusday, Awgust 1, to wake up and know that the recital is over

1. _____

2. _____

3. _____

4. _____

5. _____

33

Lesson 6 Words in Review

A. factory

half

laughter

sandwich

B. neighbor

break

bakery

escape

holiday

complain

scale

C. friendly

measure

metric

length

wealth

energy

vegetable

treasure

special

★ You will need a piece of paper for these review activities.

1. In Lesson 1 you studied two different ways to spell /ă/:
a, au. Write the words in list A.

_____   _____

_____   _____

2. In Lesson 2 you studied six different ways to spell /ā/:
ai, a__e, ei, ay, ea, a. Write the words in list B.

_____   _____

_____   _____

_____

★ **3.** Use each review word from lists A and B in a sentence.

4. In Lessons 3 and 4 you studied three different ways to
spell /ĕ/: **ea, e, ie.** Write the words in list C.

_____   _____

_____   _____

_____   _____

★ **5.** Look up each review word from list C in the Spelling
Dictionary. Write the guide words.

★ **6.** Write all 20 review words in alphabetical order.

Your teacher may give you a test. Answer these questions
when you have finished.

7. Did you spell all the words correctly? _____

8. Did you leave out a letter? _____

9. Did you write the wrong letter? _____

10. Did you miss the spelling of a vowel sound? _____

Writer's Workshop

A Personal Narrative

In a personal narrative, a writer tells a true story about his or her own life. The story captures a memory that is special to the writer because of something good, bad, funny, or important that happened. The writer uses first-person words such as I and me because he or she is the person telling the story. Here is part of Michiko's personal narrative about the time her cat disappeared.

The Search for Star

When my cat Star didn't show up for dinner on Friday, I wasn't too worried. Star likes to wander, and I knew he would be home by morning. But when he didn't show up for breakfast or lunch the next day, I began to worry.

I walked all over the neighborhood calling him. I looked on the playground and behind the corner store where the trash cans are. Since Star had gotten stuck in a tree three times, I checked out all the tall trees. By evening I had nearly lost hope.

To write her personal narrative, Michiko followed the steps in the writing process. She used a chain of events chart as a **Prewriting** activity. The chart helped her to remember what happened. It also helped her to put the events in the order in which they happened. Part of Michiko's chain of events chart is shown here. Study what Michiko did.

1	2	3
Star didn't show up for meals.	I walked in the neighborhood calling him.	I looked in the tall trees.

Get ready to write your own personal narrative. Choose a special memory that you would enjoy sharing. After you have decided what to write about, make a chain of events chart. Then follow the other steps in the writing process—**Writing, Revising, Proofreading,** and **Publishing.**

Lesson 7 Words with /ē/

Listen for /ē/ in each word.

delivery

hobby

angry

tardy

fancy

merry

pretty

penalty

ugly

liberty

empty

shady

busy

complete

theme

athlete

trapeze

evening

compete

believe

1. Write the two words that begin with /k/.

   _____ _____

2. Which three words begin with the letter <u>t</u>? Circle the word that has one syllable. _____

   _____ _____

3. Which word begins with the letters <u>sh</u>?

   _____

4. Which word begins and ends like <u>factory</u>?

   _____

5. Which four words begin and end with a vowel?

   _____ _____

   _____ _____

6. Which word begins with a vowel and ends with a consonant? _____

7. Which word has the same spelling of /ē/ as <u>relieve</u>?

   _____

8. Which two words contain the /z/ sound?

   _____ _____

9. Write the two words that have three syllables.

   _____ _____

10. Write the word that has four syllables.

    _____

11. Write the three words in which a double consonant letter spells one sound.

    bb _____ rr _____

    tt _____

12. Which two words contain the letters <u>th</u>?

    _____ _____

36

Checkpoint

Write a spelling word for each clue.
Then use the Checkpoint Study Plan on page 224.

1. If he is mad, he is ＿＿.

2. If your day is filled with activity, you are ＿＿.

3. Discover is to discovery as deliver is to ＿＿.

4. After sundown, it is ＿＿.

5. The opposite of full is ＿＿.

6. Jolly, happy, and ＿＿ go together.

7. A subject or topic may be called a ＿＿.

8. Another word for late is ＿＿.

9. The opposite of plain is ＿＿.

10. Under the trees we found a ＿＿ spot.

11. If I break a rule, I must pay a ＿＿.

12. Collecting stamps is a ＿＿.

13. She is ＿＿ enough to win a beauty contest.

14. Something with no part left out is ＿＿.

15. An acrobat might do stunts on a ＿＿.

16. The opposite of beautiful is ＿＿.

17. If you are free, you have ＿＿.

18. To pretend is to make ＿＿.

19. To take part in a contest is to ＿＿.

20. The ancient Greeks were enthusiastic sports fans. They held many contests in running, boxing, and wrestling. The winner of these contests was given a prize. The prize was called the *athlon* in Greek. The contest for the prize was called the *athlos*. The name for a person who competed for the prize comes from these words. We use the word today to describe someone who participates in sports. Can you guess it? ＿＿

37

Use each list word once.

The Ambassadors

Samantha waited for the ambassadors from the planet Ixod to arrive. It was a hot day, so she waited on the _____ side of the landing pad. Samantha had made sure she was on time to greet the visitors. The Ixodians did not like anyone to be _____.

What a sight the Ixodians were as they left their ship. They were tall and rainbow-colored. Each Ixodian uniform came _____ with a red helmet. Samantha thought the ambassadors looked very _____.

"Welcome," Samantha said. "I have planned lots of fun for you. I hope you will have a very _____ time. I thought you would like to rest while you wait for the _____ of your things. Then this _____ we will go to a magic show."

Xio, the Ixodian leader said, "Samantha, please feel at _____ to show us what you think we will like." However, the Ixodians were very quiet during the show. They never seemed surprised by the magic.

"Circus clowns" was the _____ for the next day's entertainment. Samantha took her guests to a store that sold clown puppets. There were puppets with sad faces and puppets with mean, _____ faces. There were clown dolls with colorful, _____ costumes. The Ixodians seemed to have seen the puppets before. Later, at the circus, the ambassadors didn't bat an eyelash at the funny clown on the tightrope. Even the man on the flying _____ didn't excite the Ixodians.

Samantha did not want to be upset or _____. She decided to ask Xio what the problem was. She found him watching TV.

"Xio! What are you doing?" she asked.

"I'm watching a football game," he explained. "I have always been an _____, and football has long been a _____ of mine. I love it so much I don't even wear my future-predicting helmet while I watch the game."

Samantha could not _____ her ears. "Do you mean your helmet tells you everything that is going to happen before it happens? That's why your people seem so lifeless and _____. Now I know how to make your people enjoy their visit more."

Xio listened. Then Xio and Samantha gathered the Ixodians together.

"Today," Samantha said, "you are going to learn to play football. But first, please remove your red helmets and put on these football helmets instead."

The Ixodians did as asked. They learned how to make a goal and how not to cause a _____. They were kept _____ cheering each other on.

When it was time to go, Xio said to Samantha, "Someday Ixod may _____ against Earth in an intergalactic football game. But for now, you have taught my people that life is much more interesting when you don't always know what lies ahead."

delivery
hobby
angry
tardy
fancy
merry
pretty
penalty
ugly
liberty
empty
shady
busy
complete
theme
athlete
trapeze
evening
compete
believe

Parts of a Dictionary Entry

The words that are listed in alphabetical order under the guide words in a dictionary are called entry words. They are printed in dark type with a dot between the syllables. A dictionary entry includes the entry word, the sound spelling, the part of speech, the definition or meaning of the word, and anything else important about the word.

Entry Word ——

Entry ——

Other Forms ——

be·lieve |bĭ lēv'| *v.* **be·lieved, be·liev·ing. 1.** To accept as true or real: *Everyone in the club believed that Dinky had seen a monster.* **2.** To have confidence or faith: *I believe her. I don't believe in her.* **3.** To have faith, especially religious faith; *believe in God.* **4.** To have confidence in the value, worth, existence, etc., of: *He believes in getting plenty of sleep.* **5.** To expect; think or suppose: *I believe it will snow tomorrow.*
be·liev'a·ble *adj.* **—be·liev'er** *n.*
Idiom. make believe. To pretend.

—— Sound Spelling
—— Part of Speech (Verb)

—— Definitions

Many words have more than one meaning. To decide how a word is used in a sentence, a dictionary and context clues must be used.

★ Read the above entry and answer these questions.

1. What is the entry word in the above entry? _____

2. How many meanings does the dictionary show for this entry

 word? _____

★ Write the number of the definition used in each of these sentences.

3. Our teacher believes in homework. _____

4. I believe everything Grandma tells me. _____

5. Ted believes the rain will stop before the game. _____

★ Write the following words in alphabetical order. Then look them up in the Spelling Dictionary. Write the number of meanings each word has.

shady   angry   trapeze   complete   fancy

Word	Number of Meanings
6. _____	_____
7. _____	_____
8. _____	_____
9. _____	_____
10. _____	_____

WORDS AT WORK

Challenge Yourself

canopy	recede	utility	siege

Write what you think each underlined Challenge Word means. Check your Spelling Dictionary to see if you were right. Then write sentences showing that you understand the meaning of each Challenge Word.

1. Marta's bed has a white lace canopy over it.

2. If we have a drought, the water in the river will recede.

3. We get utility bills for water, telephone, and electricity.

4. The enemy held the town under siege, so no one was allowed to leave.

Write to the Point

Imagine that you are directing a movie about aliens from outer space who have landed on Earth. Write a paragraph describing these beings. Create a name for these unusual beings and their home planet. What do the aliens look like? How do they move? How do they communicate? Use spelling words from this lesson in your description.

Challenge Use one or more of the Challenge Words in your description.

Proofreading

Use the proofreading marks to show the errors in the paragraph below. Write the five misspelled words correctly in the blanks.

Can you believe it Friday evning I was in the library, buzy reading about life other planets. Suddenly, to my compleet surprise, a Martian sat down in the emty seat beside me. He pretty uggly but seemed quite nice.

	word is misspelled
? ∧	question mark is missing
∧	word is missing

1. _____

2. _____

3. _____

4. _____

5. _____

41

Lesson 8   Words with /ē/

Listen for /ē/ in each word.

greet

speech

asleep

needle

steep

sheet

agree

degree

freeze

weak

defeat

reason

wheat

beneath

peace

increase

breathe

ski

piano

pizza

1. Write the two words that begin with the letter b.

_____   _____

2. Write the two words that begin with the letter w.

_____   _____

3. Which two words begin with the letters de?

_____   _____

4. Write the four words that begin with the letter s.

_____   _____

_____   _____

5. Write the three words that begin with a vowel.

_____

_____

6. Which three words begin with /p/? Write the word with one syllable first. Then write the word with two syllables. Write the word with three syllables last.

_____   _____

_____

7. Which word ends with /z/? _____

8. In which word does the same letter spell both /t/ and /s/?

_____

9. Write the other two words that have the same spelling of /ē/ as pizza. _____

10. Which word begins and ends like great? _____

11. Which word begins and ends like noodle?

_____

12. Which word begins and ends like raisin?

_____

13. Write the word in which you hear /hw/.

42

Checkpoint

Write a spelling word for each clue.
Then use the Checkpoint Study Plan on page 224.

1. A large musical instrument with a keyboard is a ____.

2. Powerless means ____.

3. To have the same opinion is to ____.

4. It was so cold, I thought I would ____.

5. The opposite of war is ____.

6. A piece of paper may be called a ____.

7. Another word for under is ____.

8. You use your nose to ____.

9. In water you swim, on snow you ____.

10. The opposite of decrease is ____.

11. The opposite of awake is ____.

12. A unit of temperature is a ____.

13. How you talk makes up your ____.

14. The opposite of victory is ____.

15. On a farm you may grow ____.

16. To sew, you need a sharp ____.

17. A hill with a sharp slope is ____.

18. Why you did something is the ____.

19. To welcome is to ____.

20. The origin of this mystery word is uncertain. But we know it came to English from Italian. It may have come from the Italian word *pizzicare*. *Pizzicare* means to pluck or pinch something. When dough is kneaded and patted, it is plucked and pinched. So the word came to be used for something made out of dough. That is what we use it for today. Can you guess the word? ____

43

Use each list word once.

The Homework Assignment

Here I sit staring at this piece of paper. Mr. Costa has given everyone in class a writing assignment for tomorrow. He wants us to write a story about what we would like to be doing ten years from now. I can never think of anything. I start daydreaming right away. . . .

I am on a _____ *ski slope. The hill must be at least a forty-five-* _____ *angle. The snow on the hill is covered with a thin sheet of ice because there was a big* _____ *last night. I know the hill is dangerous, but I'm not afraid. I can* _____ *better than anyone I know. I take a deep breath, forcing myself to* _____ *slowly and evenly. I concentrate on the* _____ *and quiet here on the mountain. I count down very slowly and push off. The ice feels slippery* _____ *my skis. I am flying down the hill, faster, faster, faster . . .*

My best friend wrote her story this afternoon. She invited me to share a _____ with her for supper this evening, but Mom says I can't go anywhere until I finish my homework. . . .

I am sitting at the grand _____. *I have just finished playing Beethoven's "Moonlight Sonata." The crowd is going wild. I take one bow, two bows, three bows. They are still clapping. Finally I* _____ *to play one more piece. The crowd is quiet as I raise my hands to begin . . .*

Maybe I'll just sneak into the kitchen for a slice of Mom's freshly baked whole _____ bread. All this homework sure makes me hungry! . . .

As I enter the auditorium, the President smiles and stands up to _____ me. I begin to give my _____. Several people in the back of the hall begin to scream because they disagree with my opinions. I see that I will have to give them a good _____ to vote for me or else they will _____ me in this election. . . .

Yawn! I'm getting tired. I think I'll take a little nap. I may even get a good idea from a dream while I'm _____. I can't think of what to write about yet. . . .

I am in the operating room. The patient is covered with a _____. He was very _____ when they brought him in, and he is getting weaker every minute. The nurse put a bandage on his arm so that his wound wouldn't bleed. There is only one way to _____ his chances of living. I ask the nurse for the _____ and give him the injection that will put him to sleep. I am the best doctor in the country. If anyone can save him, I can. . . .

I've wasted an hour. And I still don't have an idea for that story! I guess I just don't have a good imagination.

greet
speech
asleep
needle
steep
sheet
agree
degree
freeze
weak
defeat
reason
wheat
beneath
peace
increase
breathe
ski
piano
pizza

Verbs

A verb is a word that describes action.

Alex <u>walked</u> to the fair with me.

★ Complete each sentence below with one of these verbs.

greet   **agree**   **freeze**   **needle**   **defeat**
reason   **breathe**   **increase**   **ski**

1. That team is difficult to _____ .

2. Mother said that Mrs. Hatch will _____ us at the door.

3. Robert likes to tease the dog and _____ his little brother.

4. We need oxygen in order to _____ .

5. At what temperature does milk _____ ?

6. We all _____ that Merin is the most talented piano player.

7. Gloria will _____ from the snowy mountain's summit.

8. Jay's family fed him six times a day to _____ his weight.

9. Alice can _____ with even the most unreasonable people.

★ Unscramble and write each sentence. Then underline the verbs. Don't forget to put the correct punctuation at the end of each sentence.

10. climbed We steep hill the

_____

11. and ate Tom the pizza all Mary

_____

12. gave speech her yesterday She

_____

13. Jones wheat Farmer raises

_____

14. the beneath crushed feet I my grass

_____

WORDS AT WORK

Challenge Yourself

easel   **tweed**   **meager**   **safari**

Decide which Challenge Word fits each clue. Check your Spelling Dictionary to see if you were right. Then write sentences showing that you understand the meaning of each Challenge Word.

1. Clothing made of this would help keep you warm in winter.

2. If painters don't have one, they won't have anything to stand their latest work on.

3. If you like wild animals but don't like zoos, try going on this with a camera.

4. This might describe a serving of food that leaves you hungry.

Write to the Point

What kind of career would you like to have someday? Perhaps it's one you read about in "The Homework Assignment." Write a paragraph about your dream career. Describe the kind of work you would do. Explain why you would find this work exciting or satisfying. Use spelling words from this lesson in your paragraph.

Challenge Use one or more of the Challenge Words in your paragraph.

Proofreading

Use the proofreading marks to show the errors in the paragraph below. Write the five misspelled words correctly in the blanks.

When i enter to Uncle Al's bakery and breath in, lovely odors greet me. That is one reazon why I am want to be a baker. I also like to help Uncle Al toss the wheet dough for pitza or roll it into a sheat for cookies. A baker's life is the life for me!

	word is misspelled
≡	letter should be capitalized
✗	take out word

1. _____

2. _____

3. _____

4. _____

5. _____

47

Lesson 9   Words with /ĭ/

Listen for /ĭ/ in each word.

since

riddle

bridge

disease

wrist

divide

discuss

different

quickly

quit

chimney

except

equipment

relax

review

enough

expect

built

guilty

guitar

1. Which two words begin with the letters <u>ex</u>?

_____ _____

2. Write the two words that begin with the letters <u>re</u>.

_____ _____

3. Which three words have /kw/ in them?

_____ _____

_____

4. Which word begins and ends with /s/?

_____

5. Which word begins and ends with /d/?

_____

6. Which word begins with the letters <u>ch</u>?

_____

7. Which word ends with /j/? _____

8. Which word ends with /f/? Circle the letters that spell /f/.

_____

9. Which word ends with /ks/? Circle the letter that

spells /ks/. _____

10. Which word ends with /z/? _____

11. Which three words have the same spelling of /ĭ/ as

<u>building</u>? (Remember, <u>qu</u> spells /kw/.) _____

_____ _____

12. Write the word in which you see the letter <u>w</u> at the

beginning but don't hear /w/. _____

13. Write the words in which a double consonant spells

one sound.

dd _____   ff _____

ss _____

48

Checkpoint

Write a spelling word for each clue.
Then use the Checkpoint Study Plan on page 224.

1. He stopped working when he ____ his job.

2. The musician played the ____.

3. Today I build, yesterday I ____.

4. To separate into parts is to ____.

5. She wears a watch on her ____.

6. The opposite of innocent is ____.

7. Smoke goes up a ____.

8. The opposite of the same is ____.

9. Something hard to answer or understand is a ____.

10. As much as you need is ____.

11. You may go over a river by walking on a ____.

12. Another word for sickness is ____.

13. To go over or to see again is to ____.

14. The opposite of stiffen up is ____.

15. To look forward to means to ____.

16. A word for apart from is ____.

17. Tents and sleeping bags are camping ____.

18. It has rained steadily ____ early morning.

19. The opposite of slowly is ____.

20. When we speak, we do more than move our lips and make sounds. We also use our minds. Before words are said, the mind has separated out the ideas it wants to express. The origin of the mystery word reflects this process. The word means to speak. But its base word has nothing to do with speaking. Its base is the Latin word *discutio*, meaning to shake apart. Because we shake apart or separate our thoughts when we speak, the word came to mean speak. Can you guess it? ____

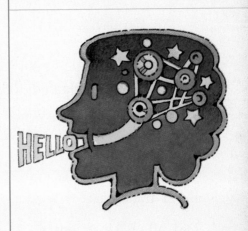

49

THE GARDEN

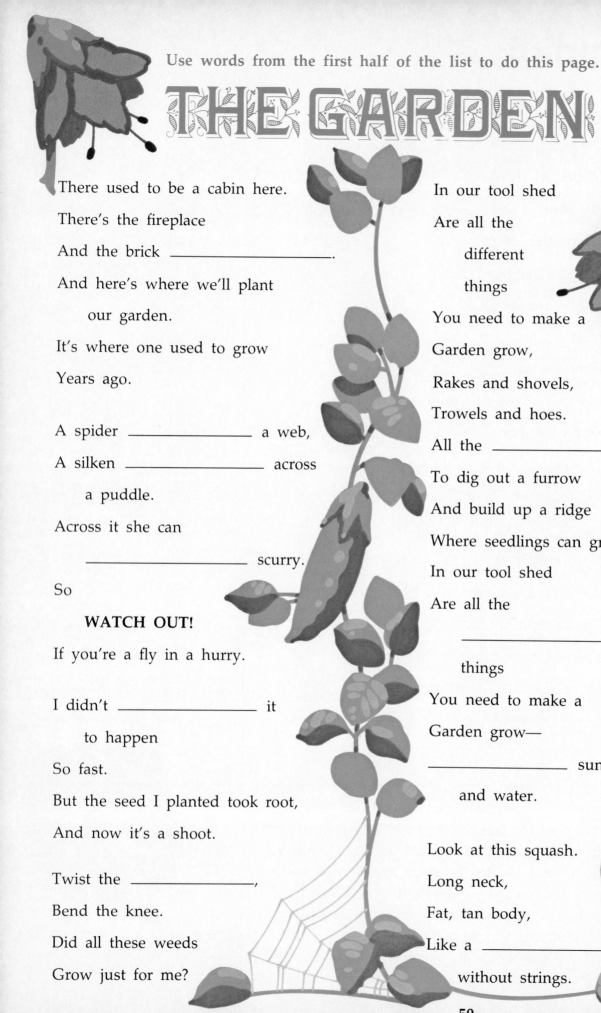

There used to be a cabin here.

There's the fireplace

And the brick _____.

And here's where we'll plant

    our garden.

It's where one used to grow

Years ago.

A spider _____ a web,

A silken _____ across

    a puddle.

Across it she can

    _____ scurry.

So

WATCH OUT!

If you're a fly in a hurry.

I didn't _____ it

    to happen

So fast.

But the seed I planted took root,

And now it's a shoot.

Twist the _____,

Bend the knee.

Did all these weeds

Grow just for me?

In our tool shed

Are all the

    different

    things

You need to make a

Garden grow,

Rakes and shovels,

Trowels and hoes.

All the _____

To dig out a furrow

And build up a ridge

Where seedlings can grow.

In our tool shed

Are all the

    _____

    things

You need to make a

Garden grow—

_____ sun and earth

    and water.

Look at this squash.

Long neck,

Fat, tan body,

Like a _____

    without strings.

50

Use words from the second half of the list to do this page.

I feel terrible, really guilty,

Because the potatoes are sick.

They've caught a _____

Called a blight.

Maybe if I had watered them _____,

Or maybe if I hadn't _____ weeding them,

They'd be all right.

I wish I could just take it easy and _____.

But I feel terribly _____.

I think that tonight

I'll _____ it with Dad.

Together we'll _____

What we can do

To get rid of the blight

And make the spuds all right.

I always _____ my vegetables

Evenly among my neighbors,

Because

I've had a green thumb

Ever _____ I was young.

And it's never been a puzzle

Or a _____ to me at all

How to make my plants grow

TALL

51

quickly
equipment
wrist
built
different
guitar
except
expect
chimney
bridge

since
riddle
disease
divide
discuss
quit
relax
review
enough
guilty

Parts of Speech

A dictionary lists the part of speech for each entry word. The part of speech tells if a word is one of the following:

noun *n.*	adjective *adj.*	pronoun *pron.*	conjunction *conj.*
verb *v.*	adverb *adv.*	preposition *prep.*	interjection *interj.*

★ Write the following words in alphabetical order. Then look up each word in the Spelling Dictionary and write its part of speech.

wrist   disease   divide   expect

Word   Part of Speech

1. _____   _____

2. _____   _____

3. _____   _____

4. _____   _____

★ Some words are used as more than one part of speech. A dictionary lists the most commonly used part of speech first. Then the other parts of speech and definitions follow.

> **e·nough** |ĭ nŭf'| *adj.* Sufficient to meet a need or satisfy a desire: *There is enough food for everybody. Will $10 be enough to pay for the tickets?* —*n.* An adequate quantity: *He ate enough for two.* —*adv.* **1.** To a satisfactory amount or degree; sufficiently: *Are you warm enough?* **2.** Very; fully; quite: *We were glad enough to leave.* **3.** Tolerably; rather: *She sang well enough, but the show was a failure.*

— adjective
— noun
— adverb

5. What is the entry word of the above entry? _____

6. How many parts of speech are listed? _____

7. What are they? _____

★ What part of speech is <u>enough</u> used as in each of these sentences?

8. We ate enough to last us a week! _____

9. There are enough tickets for everyone in the class.

_____

10. Is this table big enough for our art project? _____

52

WORDS AT WORK

Challenge Yourself

quizzical   bliss   commit   pinnacle

Use your Spelling Dictionary to answer these questions. Then write sentences showing that you understand the meaning of each Challenge Word.

1. When people are puzzled, do their faces sometimes show a <u>quizzical</u> look?

2. Do most people feel <u>bliss</u> if they do badly on a test?

3. Is it a detective's job to catch people who <u>commit</u> crimes?

4. If you were climbing a steep mountain, would you start at the <u>pinnacle</u>?

Write to the Point

Think of something you know how to make, grow, fix, or clean. Then write a paragraph or two explaining how you do it. Describe each step in the process from start to finish, and be sure to present the steps in their correct order. Use spelling words from this lesson in your explanation.

Challenge Use one or more of the Challenge Words in your explanation.

Proofreading

Use the proofreading marks to show the errors in the paragraph below. Write the five misspelled words correctly in the blanks.

> Mr. Hertz's tomatoes had grown quikly since last month All exept a few of them were ripe enugh to eat, so he gave me some. Wow I didn't expeck them to be so good and so diffrent from the ones at the store

	word is misspelled
⊙	period is missing
!	exclamation point is missing

1. _____

2. _____

3. _____

4. _____

5. _____

Lesson 10 Words with /ĭ/

Listen for /ĭ/ in each word.

film

skill

chicken

arithmetic

timid

insist

insect

pitch

sixth

kitchen

picnic

damage

village

garbage

cottage

message

package

mystery

system

business

1. Which two words begin with /k/? Circle the letter that spells /k/. _____ _____

2. Which two words end with /k/? Circle the letter that spells the final /k/.

    _____ _____

3. Which two words begin with the letter i and end with the letter t? _____ _____

4. Which word begins and ends like farm? _____

5. Which word begins and ends like tied? _____

6. Write one word that begins with the letters ch, one that ends with ch, and one that has ch in the middle.

    _____ _____

    _____

7. Write the six words in which you hear /j/ but don't see the letter j.

    _____ _____

    _____ _____

    _____ _____

8. Which two words have y as the second letter?

    _____ _____

9. Which word has /ks/ in the middle? Circle the letter that spells /ks/. _____

10. Which word has /z/ in the middle? _____

11. Write the words in which a double consonant spells one sound.

    ll _____ ll _____

    ss _____ ss _____

    tt _____

Checkpoint

Write a spelling word for each clue.
Then use the Checkpoint Study Plan on page 224.

1. To throw a ball to the batter in baseball is to ____.

2. Mind your own ____.

3. A community smaller than a town is a ____.

4. Another word for shy is ____.

5. A small house is a ____.

6. We add, subtract, multiply, and divide in ____ class.

7. The ability to do something well is a ____.

8. Spoken or written words make up a ____.

9. A bee is a type of ____.

10. An orderly way is a ____.

11. Another word for parcel is ____.

12. Another word for movie is ____.

13. Let's eat outdoors and have a ____.

14. After fifth comes ____.

15. At the dump there is a lot of ____.

16. A kind of fowl is a ____.

17. To hurt or harm is to ____.

18. The place to cook is in the ____.

19. To take a strong stand is to ____.

20. This word comes from the Greek word *mystes*. *Mystes* meant close-mouthed or silent. The Romans borrowed the word and changed it to *mysterium*. Today we use the word to mean something people don't know and therefore don't talk about. Can you guess what it is? ____

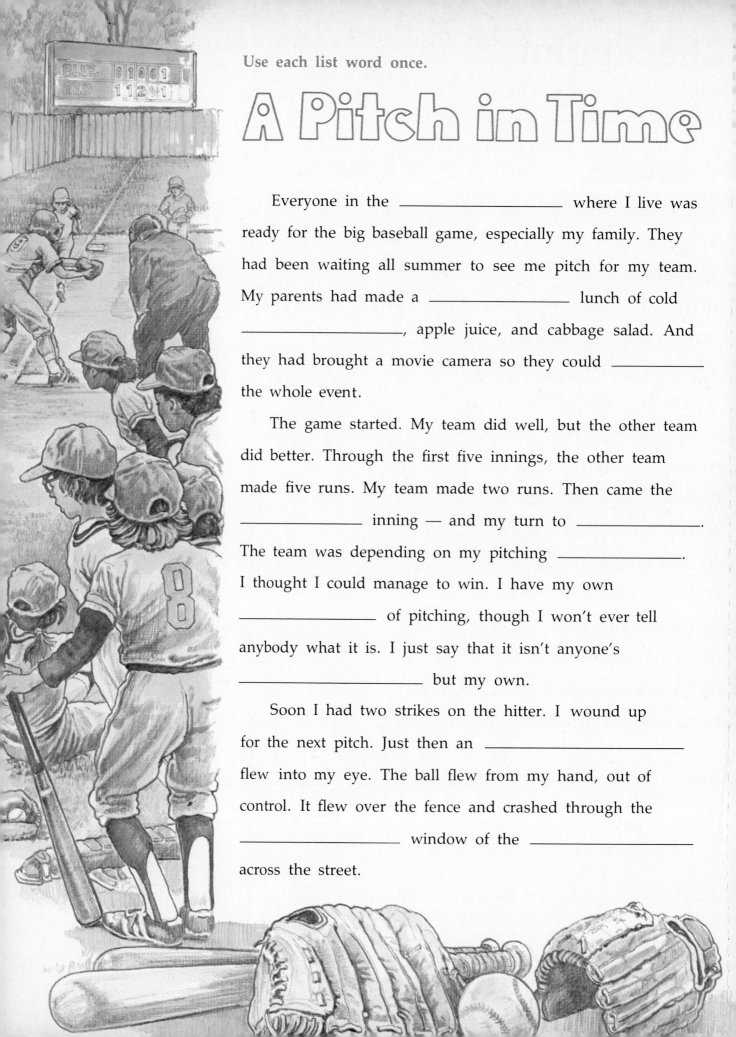

Use each list word once.

A Pitch in Time

Everyone in the _____ where I live was ready for the big baseball game, especially my family. They had been waiting all summer to see me pitch for my team. My parents had made a _____ lunch of cold _____, apple juice, and cabbage salad. And they had brought a movie camera so they could _____ the whole event.

The game started. My team did well, but the other team did better. Through the first five innings, the other team made five runs. My team made two runs. Then came the _____ inning — and my turn to _____. The team was depending on my pitching _____. I thought I could manage to win. I have my own _____ of pitching, though I won't ever tell anybody what it is. I just say that it isn't anyone's _____ but my own.

Soon I had two strikes on the hitter. I wound up for the next pitch. Just then an _____ flew into my eye. The ball flew from my hand, out of control. It flew over the fence and crashed through the _____ window of the _____ across the street.

Stops Crime

I was so embarrassed I wanted to hide. All the players ran across the street. The door of the cottage was open, so we went in to see how much _____ had been done. The window was broken, of course, and the ball had knocked over the _____ can. As I was picking up the garbage, I came across a _____ written in big print. It said:

> Sept. 20
> Pick up the _____ in two days.
> Meet me behind the store at the regular time.
> S.C.

I was always good at adding, so I did some quick _____ in my head and realized that the note meant today. I figured that the police could solve this _____, so I took the note to them.

The man at the desk made me feel _____ and unsure of myself. He tried to dismiss me; he didn't even want to listen to me. I had already been embarrassed once that day. I wasn't going to let it happen again. I found the courage to _____ he look at the note. And then I left.

Well, we lost the game. But several days later, the police chief called to congratulate me. The police had arrested several people in a robbery ring. I was a hero after all!

57

film
skill
chicken
arithmetic
timid
insist
insect
pitch
sixth
kitchen
picnic
damage
village
garbage
cottage
message
package
mystery
system
business

Commas

Use a comma to separate a series of words or word groups in a sentence.

Bill had a sandwich, a piece of pie, and a glass of milk.
Then he gathered up his baseball glove, bat, and ball.

Write the sentences below, adding commas where they are needed. Correct the misspelled word in each sentence.

1. I need a pencil eraser and paper to do my arithmatick.

2. Chicen can be fried broiled or baked.

3. I can't decide whether spiders ants or beetles are my favorite insecks.

4. We brought ham eggs chicken and brownies for our piknik.

5. The timmid elephant was afraid of mice snakes and his own shadow!

6. In the vilaje were a bakery a post office and a town hall.

7. The kitchin was a mess with pots pans and dishes everywhere.

8. Lynn wanted to study bizness teaching and medicine.

WORDS AT WORK

Challenge Yourself

rummage   symptom   abyss   lyrics

Decide which Challenge Word fits each clue. Check your Spelling Dictionary to see if you were right. Then write sentences showing that you understand the meaning of each Challenge Word.

1. You might hum a song because you can't remember these.

2. When someone is getting a cold, the first one might be a sore throat, sneezing, or a cough.

3. You might have to do this to find a pencil or eraser in a messy desk drawer.

4. If you drop something into this, you will probably never see it again.

Write to the Point

Think of a time when you made an embarrassing mistake. What did you learn from your mistake? Did the lesson you learned help you later? Write a paragraph about your embarrassing mistake and the lesson you learned. Use spelling words from this lesson in your paragraph.

Challenge Use one or more of the Challenge Words in your paragraph.

Proofreading

Use the proofreading marks to show the errors in the paragraph below. Write the five misspelled words correctly in the blanks.

⬭	word is misspelled
∧	word is missing
=	letter should be capitalized

At our family picnic, we all ensist on playing baseball by our own sistum. Mom likes to pich with eyes closed. once Aunt Rita let the sixt strike go by before she called me out. And it's mistery who wins, because my brother forgets to keep score.

1. _____

2. _____

3. _____

4. _____

5. _____

Lesson 11 Plurals

Say each word.

benches

sandwiches

branches

speeches

crashes

wishes

businesses

skis

athletes

neighbors

vegetables

exercises

degrees

stories

parties

companies

hobbies

penalties

calves

wives

Solve these plural puzzles.

cartwheel + s = <u>cartwheels</u>

1. ski + s = _____

2. vegetable + s = _____

3. athlete + s = _____

4. degree + s = _____

5. exercise + s = _____

6. neighbor + s = _____

peach + es = <u>peaches</u>

7. bench + es = _____

8. crash + es = _____

9. branch + es = _____

10. sandwich + es = _____

11. speech + es = _____

12. wish + es = _____

13. business + es = _____

body − y + i + es = <u>bodies</u>

14. story − y + i + es = _____

15. hobby − y + i + es = _____

16. company − y + i + es = _____

17. penalty − y + i + es = _____

18. party − y + i + es = _____

wolf − f + v + es = <u>wolves</u>

19. calf − f + v + es = _____

Find the word that forms its plural the way <u>life</u> does.

life ⟶ <u>lives</u>

20. _____ ⟶ _____

60

Checkpoint

Write a spelling word for each clue.
Then use the Checkpoint Study Plan on page 224.

1. The plural form of wife is ____.

2. Another word for tales is ____.

3. Cows give birth to ____.

4. Activities for fun may be ____.

5. If I go to work out, then I want to do my ____.

6. Formal talks in front of an audience are ____.

7. In a factory are workers, on a ball field are ____.

8. Fruits and ____ are part of a good diet.

9. You need bread to make ____.

10. A tree has a trunk and many ____.

11. Hopes and dreams are like ____.

12. Race-cars may have ____.

13. Long seats in parks are called ____.

14. Social gatherings are ____.

15. Ice is for skates, snow is for ____.

16. The people who live nearby are your ____.

17. Another word for fines is ____.

18. Water freezes at 32 ____.

19. More than one company is ____.

20. This word comes from the word <u>busy</u>. It originally meant the state of being engaged in any activity that made one busy. Later it came to mean an activity of a serious and important kind. Today when we use this word by itself, we usually mean someone's job or occupation. Can you make this word plural and guess the word? ____

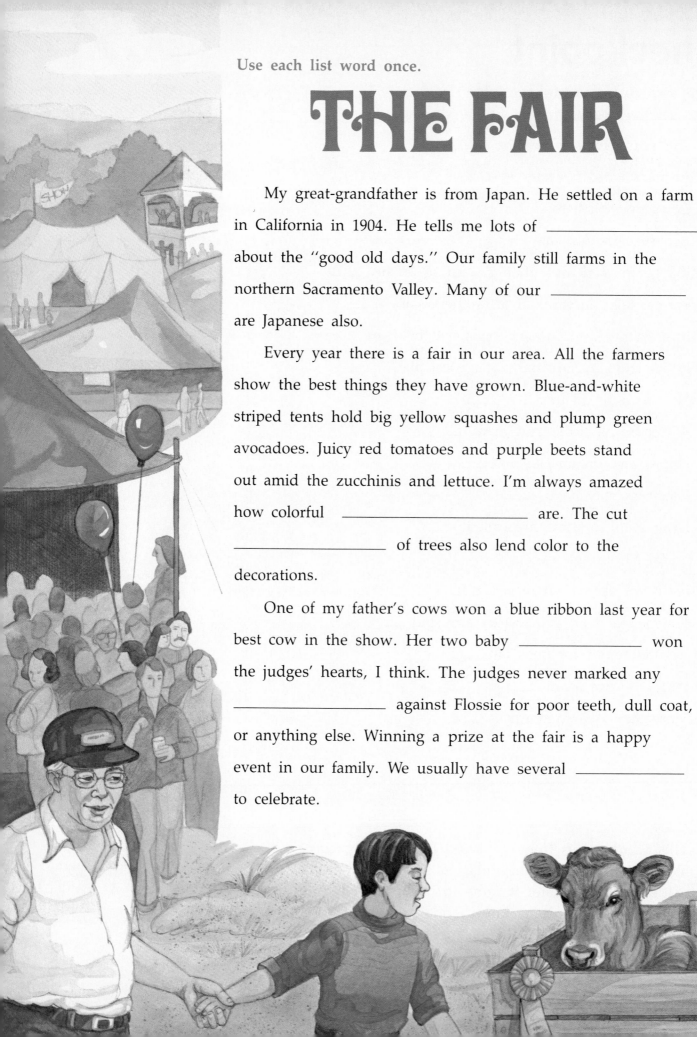

Use each list word once.

THE FAIR

My great-grandfather is from Japan. He settled on a farm in California in 1904. He tells me lots of _____ about the "good old days." Our family still farms in the northern Sacramento Valley. Many of our _____ are Japanese also.

Every year there is a fair in our area. All the farmers show the best things they have grown. Blue-and-white striped tents hold big yellow squashes and plump green avocadoes. Juicy red tomatoes and purple beets stand out amid the zucchinis and lettuce. I'm always amazed how colorful _____ are. The cut _____ of trees also lend color to the decorations.

One of my father's cows won a blue ribbon last year for best cow in the show. Her two baby _____ won the judges' hearts, I think. The judges never marked any _____ against Flossie for poor teeth, dull coat, or anything else. Winning a prize at the fair is a happy event in our family. We usually have several _____ to celebrate.

The Chamber of Commerce always has a tent at the fair. Local _____ show people what they sell. Small businesses and big _____ all participate. There is also a tent for crafts. People show the beautiful things they make in their spare time. Their _____ range from woodcarving to rugmaking.

This year there is going to be a sports tent. High school _____ will show people how to do _____. Equipment dealers are going to display everything from fishing poles to _____.

Children get lost and look for parents. Husbands look for _____, and wives look for husbands. Friends look for friends. Amid the confusion, politicians give _____ and people lounge on wooden _____ to listen to folk musicians play their banjos. Children throw pennies into the goldfish pond and make _____. You can hear laughter and shouts as one bumper car _____ into another. You can smell the aroma of spicy meatball _____.

The fair is my favorite week of the year. It doesn't matter whether it rains or shines, and I never care if it's freezing or 90 _____. It makes me feel good to be part of farming and the fair.

benches
sandwiches
branches
speeches
crashes
wishes
businesses
skis
athletes
neighbors
vegetables
exercises
degrees
stories
parties
companies
hobbies
penalties
calves
wives

Plurals

A dictionary lists the plural form of a noun when the plural is formed in a special way. Some dictionaries list plural forms of all nouns.

---

bench | běnch | *n., pl.* **bench·es.** **1.** A long seat: *park bench.* **2.** A heavy work table: *the carpenter's bench.* **3.** The seat for judges in a court of law. —*v.* To take a player out of a game: *The referee benched the player for bad conduct.*

half | hăf | *or* | häf | *n., pl.* **halves** | hăvz | *or* | hävz |. **1.** One of two equal parts. **2.** One of two equal periods of time in certain games: *the first half of the football game.*
   Idioms. **in half.** Into two equal parts. **not half bad.** Good.

de·gree | dǐ grē′ | *n., pl.* **de·grees.** **1.** A unit used in measuring temperature. **2.** A unit used in measuring angles: *a 90-degree angle.* **3.** A title given by a college or university. **4.** Amount, extent: *a high degree of skill.*

par·ty | pär′tē | *n., pl.* **par·ties.** **1.** An entertainment or social gathering: *a birthday party.* **2.** A group of people acting together: *A search party was sent out to find the missing child.* **3.** A political organization: *In an election, each party has a candidate.*

★ Read the entries above and answer these questions.

1. What is the plural of the noun bench? _____

   How is the plural of bench formed? _____

2. What is the plural of the noun degree? _____

   How is the plural of degree formed? _____

3. What is the plural of the noun half? _____

   How is the plural of half formed? _____

4. What is the plural of the noun party? _____

   How is the plural of party formed? _____

★ Write the following nouns in alphabetical order. Then write the plural form next to each word. Check your answers in the Spelling Dictionary.

    ski   **wife**   **sandwich**   **business**   **company**

        Word   Plural

5. _____   _____

6. _____   _____

7. _____   _____

8. _____   _____

9. _____   _____

WORDS AT WORK

Challenge Yourself

cosmetics   scarves   apologies   actresses

Decide which Challenge Word fits each clue. Check your Spelling Dictionary to see if you were right. Then write sentences showing that you understand the meaning of each Challenge Word.

1. They can be long or square, plain or fancy, woolly or silky.

2. You will never see them in the sky at night, but some of them are well-known stars.

3. They can change what you see when you look in the mirror.

4. When you have made a serious mistake, sometimes you need to make these, too.

Write to the Point

Is there a special event that you look forward to every year? It might be a holiday, a festival, a sports event, or even your birthday. At what time of the year does the event happen? Write a paragraph telling what happens on the occasion and why you enjoy it. Use spelling words from this lesson in your paragraph.

Challenge Use one or more of the Challenge Words in your paragraph.

Proofreading

Use the proofreading marks to show the errors in the paragraph below. Write the five misspelled words correctly in the blanks.

In july my neighbores hold a Summer street party. everyone enjoys these partys. The kids play or sit on picnic benchs and eat sandwichs. The adults share funny storys or talk about their businesses. Some show off their hobbies.

⬭	word is misspelled
/	letter should be lower case
≡	letter should be capitalized

1. _____

2. _____

3. _____

4. _____

5. _____

Lesson 12 Words in Review

A. piano

complete

speech

believe

empty

evening

reason

liberty

breathe

freeze

B. damage

mystery

except

insist

business

discuss

message

different

guilty

review

★ You will need a piece of paper for these review activities.

1. In Lessons 7 and 8 you studied seven different ways to spell /ē/: **y, e___e, ie, ee, ea, ea___e, i.** Write the words in list A.

_____

_____

_____

★ 2. Look up each review word from list A in the Spelling Dictionary. Write the first definition of each word.

3. In Lessons 9 and 10 you studied six different ways to spell /ĭ/: **i, e, ui, a, y, u.** Write the words in list B.

_____ _____ _____

_____ _____

_____

★ 4. Use each review word from list B in a sentence.

★ 5. Write all 20 review words in alphabetical order.

Your teacher may give you a test. Answer these questions when you have finished.

6. Did you spell all the words correctly? _____

7. Did you leave out a letter? _____

8. Did you write the wrong letter? _____

9. Did you miss the spelling of a vowel sound? _____

Writer's Workshop

A Narrative

A narrative is a story. Every good story has a beginning, a middle, and an end. In the beginning the main character and the problem that the main character must solve are introduced. In the middle of the story, the main character tries to solve the problem. The end of the story tells how the problem is solved. Notice how Diego introduces the main character and the problem in the beginning of his story "The Hardest Race."

The Hardest Race

Luke knew he should be training for the big race next week, but he didn't feel like it. Usually he loved to race. He spent all his free time getting into shape. This time it was different, though, because Luke would be racing against his best friend, Carlos. Luke knew how much Carlos wanted to win. After all, Luke had helped Carlos practice for a whole year. Winning against Carlos wouldn't be any fun, but losing might feel even worse.

To write his story, Diego followed the steps in the writing process. First he decided what kind of story he wanted to write and who the main character would be. Then he used a story map as a **Prewriting** activity. The map helped Diego plan the three main ingredients of the plot of his story—the beginning, the middle, and the end. The map also helped him put the events of his story in an order that made sense. Diego's story map is shown here. Study what Diego did.

Beginning
Luke must race against his best friend, Carlos.

Middle
Luke wins the race.

End
Carlos is a good sport.

Get ready to write your own story. You can write a realistic story like Diego's, a mystery, a fairy tale, or any kind of story you wish. After you have decided what to write about, make a story map. Then follow the other steps in the writing process—**Writing, Revising, Proofreading,** and **Publishing.**

Lesson 13 Words with /ī/

Listen for /ī/ in each word.

mild

grind

climb

blind

ninth

tried

remind

science

idea

library

pirate

island

quite

knife

invite

awhile

polite

decide

revise

guide

1. Which word begins with /kw/? Circle the letters that spell /kw/. _____

2. Write the word in which you see the letter k but don't hear /k/. _____

3. Write the three words that begin and end with a vowel.

   _____ _____

   _____

4. Write the two words that begin with the letter g.

   _____ _____

5. Write the two words that begin with the letter p.

   _____ _____

6. Which word begins and ends with /s/?

   _____

7. Which six words end with the letter d?

   _____ _____

   _____ _____

   _____ _____

8. Which word ends with /z/? _____

9. Which word ends with the letters th? _____

10. Write the word in which you see the letter s but don't hear /s/ or /z/. _____

11. Write the word in which you see the letter b but don't hear /b/. _____

12. Write the word in which the letter r appears twice.

   _____

13. Which word has /s/ in the middle? _____

14. Write the word in which /hw/ is spelled wh.

Checkpoint

Write a spelling word for each clue.
Then use the Checkpoint Study Plan on page 224.

1. Another word for gentle is _____.

2. After seventh and eighth comes _____.

3. Another word for sightless is _____.

4. Today I try, yesterday I _____.

5. To crush into fine particles is to _____.

6. To lead means to _____.

7. Spoon, fork, and _____ go together.

8. To change something is to _____.

9. Land surrounded by water is an _____.

10. A public place for books and magazines is a _____.

11. To ask someone to come or go to a place is to _____.

12. A sea thief is a _____.

13. Another word for very is _____.

14. Biology is one kind of _____.

15. To reach a decision means to _____.

16. For a short time is the same as _____.

17. The opposite of cause to forget is _____.

18. To go up a tree is to _____.

19. Another word for a thought is an _____.

20. Very often two languages have similar expressions. In English, if we say that a person is polished, we usually mean well-mannered. The Romans had a similar expression. In Latin, the word *politus* means polished. Like the English word <u>polished</u>, it was used to refer to someone with good manners. The mystery word comes from the Latin word *politus*. It means well-mannered. Can you guess it? _____

Use each list word once.

Lost at Sea

June 6, 1843

I have always wanted to be a sailor. When I had a chance to sign on board the ship Fairweather, I did!

We have been at sea for eight months, and all that time the weather has been pleasant and _____. Once, we were almost attacked by a _____ ship. But we got away. The rest of our trip has been peaceful.

I like my life as a sailor. Each day, after I finish my work, I _____ to the top of the main mast and watch the sea. I am _____ happy.

July 1, 1843

This is the first day of the _____ month of our voyage, and the weather has changed. The sky is growing very dark and a great wind is blowing. The waves are getting bigger. . . .

July 3, 1843

The storm got worse and worse. A huge wave crashed over the deck and threw me into the sea. I grabbed an empty barrel. Then I watched in horror as the ship sailed on without me.

This morning I found myself washed up on the shore of an

_____. All I had were the clothes I was wearing and

the diary that I had put in my pocket. I _____ to

discover where I was. But without a compass or a map, I had no

_____. I could not _____ what to do.

Then I saw a boy about my own age walking toward me. I wanted

to be _____, so I bowed to him. He bowed back

and offered to _____ me through the forest to his

family's hut. Although we didn't speak the same language, we were able

to understand each other by using a kind of sign language.

When we got to the hut, he introduced me to his family. I signaled

that I was hungry. They pointed to a cooking pot, and I understood

that they wanted to _____ me to eat with them. They

used a stone to _____ some spices into a fine powder.

Then they sliced some vegetables with a _____. They fried

all this in some oil and added rice. It was the most delicious meal I

have ever eaten. Whenever I taste a certain rare spice in the future, it

will _____ me of that meal.

May 10, 1844

Today a ship sailed into the bay. I can't believe I'm going home.

My island friends have asked me to stay _____ longer.

But I explained that I have to return to my family.

I have had plenty of time to _____ my opinion of

a sailor's life. How could I have been so _____ to the

dangers of a life at sea? When I reach home, perhaps I will study

_____ and spend my life in a laboratory. Or

perhaps I'll just read about the sea in a quiet _____.

I will definitely not be a sailor.

mild
grind
climb
blind
ninth
tried
remind
science
idea
library
pirate
island
quite
knife
invite
awhile
polite
decide
revise
guide

Punctuation

Put quotation marks around the exact words of a speaker. Notice the position of the quotation marks and commas in the following:

> Lisa asked, "Will you come to the parade with us?"
> Bob said, "I would love to go with you."

A comma follows the word that introduces a quotation. The first word in a direct quotation begins with a capital letter. The end punctuation comes inside the final quotation marks.

⭐ Write the following sentences. Add quotation marks, commas, and other punctuation where needed.

1. Mr. Perry said My job is getting to be a grind

_____

2. Mrs. Perry asked Why don't you decide to take a vacation

_____

_____

3. Mr. Perry answered We could go to a deserted island

_____

_____

Sometimes a speaker's exact words are at the beginning of a sentence. Notice the position of the quotation marks and punctuation marks now.

> "Will you come to the parade with us?" Lisa asked.
> "I would love to go with you," said Bob.

⭐ Write the following sentences. Add quotation marks, commas, and other punctuation where needed.

4. Don't you think it would be fun to climb a mountain asked Mrs. Perry

_____

_____

5. We should take a guide so we won't get lost added Mr. Perry

_____

WORDS AT WORK

Challenge Yourself

rightful   recycle   prior   exile

Use your Spelling Dictionary to answer these questions. Then write sentences showing that you understand the meaning of each Challenge Word.

1. Does a person who buys a new or used car become the car's <u>rightful</u> owner?

2. Does it hurt the environment to <u>recycle</u> old newspapers or glass bottles?

3. Were you in fourth grade <u>prior</u> to being in fifth grade?

4. Could a person in <u>exile</u> go back home to see friends?

Write to the Point

Write an adventure story in the form of a diary. Imagine you're in a dangerous situation, and write three diary entries telling what happens. Begin each entry with a date so that the reader will know how much time has passed. Use spelling words from this lesson in your diary.

Challenge Use one or more of the Challenge Words in your diary.

Proofreading

Use the proofreading marks to show the errors in the paragraph below. Write the five misspelled words correctly in the blanks.

The stars were the sailor's giude, but the night had a grown quite foggy. The sailor had no iddea where he was, and he couldn't deside what to do. Should he drop the boat's anchor and wait for awile, or would the that just invite a pyrate attack

◯	word is misspelled
?∧	question mark is missing
⤴	take out word

1. _____

2. _____

3. _____

4. _____

5. _____

Lesson 14 Words with /ŏ/

Listen for /ŏ/ in each word.

shock

copper

bottom

comma

solid

hospital

common

problem

lobster

promise

bother

collar

dollar

closet

object

honor

honest

wander

quantity

watch

1. Write the two words that begin with the letter p.

   _____ _____

2. Which word begins with the letters sh?

   _____

3. Which word begins with /kw/? Circle the letters that spell /kw/. _____

4. Write the two words in which you see the letter h at the beginning of the word but don't hear /h/.

   _____ _____

5. Which other word begins with the letter h that is pronounced /h/? _____

6. Which word begins and ends like sand? _____

7. Which word begins and ends like later? _____

8. Write the three words that end with the letter t.

   _____ _____

   _____

9. Write the two words that end with the letters ar.

   _____ _____

10. Which three words have the same spelling of /ŏ/ as quality? _____ _____

    _____

11. Write the word that has the letters th in the middle.

    _____

12. Write the words in which a double consonant spells one sound.

    ll _____ ll _____

    mm _____ mm _____

    pp _____ tt _____

Checkpoint

Write a spelling word for each clue.
Then use the Checkpoint Study Plan on page 224.

1. The opposite of top is ____.

2. Ten dimes make one ____.

3. Another word for vow is ____.

4. Water is a liquid, ice is a ____.

5. Another word for look at or be careful is ____.

6. If frightened suddenly, you may feel a ____.

7. Foods go in the refrigerator, clothes go in the ____.

8. To roam means to ____.

9. Another word for amount is ____.

10. A sea animal with claws is a ____.

11. A thing that has shape and can be seen is an ____.

12. One kind of metal is ____.

13. A word for medical center is ____.

14. The opposite of rare is ____.

15. Another word for tease is ____.

16. If you tell the truth, you are ____.

17. Something you try to solve is a ____.

18. A part of your shirt is the ____.

19. To show respect is to ____.

20. The words <u>period</u> and <u>colon</u> are names of punctuation marks. They come from ancient Greek words. This is odd because the ancient Greeks did not use punctuation marks in their writing. In ancient Greek, these words did not name marks. They were grammar terms that named certain groups of words. This mystery word comes from the Greek word *komma*, which meant clause. Now the mystery word names the punctuation mark that often follows a clause. Can you guess it? ____

75

THE QUARK GIFT BOOK

Greetings, people from Earth!

Welcome to this light-year's new and better Quark Gift Book. We _____ that you will never have to _____ around trying to find a gift for that important person or thing on your holiday shopping list. Now you can order gifts in the _____ you need without any trouble or _____. We _____ all major space cards.

Down in the dumps? Wear a Liftoff rocket _____ around your neck and things will be looking up. It comes in the choicest Earth tones, _____ red, and sky blue. Small or Large.

750 Bloteems

The last word in getting rid of garbage! Just throw an unwanted _____ into the Black Hole and POOF! You can _____ it disappear. And it won't harm the ecology either!

120,000 Bloteems

We must be _____ with you. This does not come gift wrapped.

76

Do you have a sick friend in the _____?
Finding the right gift for a shut-in is not an unusual
problem. In fact, it's very _____. But don't
worry. Give the Intergalactic Environmental Unit. By setting
the buttons, you can feel as if you have _____
earth under your feet. Or, if you like, it can make you feel
like you are living at the _____ of the ocean.
No more dusty feelers! No more sticky bimnuls! And the
IEV is easy to store in a _____. It comes in a
silver or _____ case.

7000 Bloteems

Tired of bumping around while flying through space? Try our
new _____ absorbers. They will get rid of that
awful _____.

Set of 4, only 150 Bloteems

To order a gift from this book, please use your space card
number. And don't forget the _____ between the
planet and galaxy in your address. Remember, three Bloteems
equal one _____ ($1.00).

shock
copper
bottom
comma
solid
hospital
common
problem
lobster
promise
bother
collar
dollar
closet
object
honor
honest
wander
quantity
watch

Subject of a Sentence

The subject of a sentence tells who or what is doing the action or is being talked about. A subject can be more than one word.

That little boy won the race.
Judy is best at hopscotch.

★ Read the sentences above and answer these questions.

1. What is the action verb in the first sentence? _____

2. Who or what won something? _____

   That little boy is the subject of the first sentence.

3. Who is being talked about in the second sentence? _____

   Judy is the subject of the second sentence.

★ Write the subject of each sentence below.

4. The hospital was a busy place on Saturday. _____

5. Lobster is a tasty treat. _____

6. The dog collar was lying in the mud. _____

7. A comma is a punctuation mark. _____

8. Debbie saw the deer through the trees. _____

9. Our cat can jump very high. _____

10. A dollar doesn't buy very much. _____

11. Susan wandered aimlessly around the house. _____

12. The problem can be solved easily. _____

13. The object of the game is simple. _____

14. Jack saw the sunset. _____

15. My watch can't be fixed. _____

16. That closet is a mess. _____

17. The woman waiting for the bus looked dismayed. _____

_____

Challenge Yourself

solitude   jot   jostled   dislodge

Write what you think each underlined Challenge Word means. Check your Spelling Dictionary to see if you were right. Then write sentences that show the meaning of each Challenge Word.

1. The author needed <u>solitude</u> to write her book, so she spent hours alone, working in her room.

2. You had better <u>jot</u> this address down in case you forget it.

3. The people <u>jostled</u> one another as they tried to get off the crowded bus.

4. I shook the piggy bank to <u>dislodge</u> the coin that was stuck in the slot.

Write to the Point

Think of an idea for a fantastic new product that you would like to invent. Then write an advertisement for the product. Explain what it does and why it would make an excellent gift. Give the price, too. Use spelling words from this lesson in your advertisement.

Challenge Use one or more of the Challenge Words in your advertisement.

Proofreading

Use the proofreading marks to show the errors in the paragraph below. Write the five misspelled words correctly in the blanks.

⬯	word is misspelled
!⋏	exclamation point is missing
≡	letter should be capitalized

Help Does the catalog promis to return my money if I can't use an objikt I bought? i don't want my dog to wandur when I walk him on Mars, so I ordered a coller and leash to fix the problum. But I didn't bother to check if they make space suits in his size.

1. _____
2. _____
3. _____
4. _____
5. _____

79

Lesson 15 Words with /ō/

Listen for /ō/ in each word.

known

throw

bowl

follow

arrow

elbow

grown

borrow

swallow

tomorrow

zone

vote

telephone

code

alone

microscope

suppose

chose

sew

owe

1. Which word begins with the letters <u>th</u>?

   _____

2. Write the four words that begin with a vowel.

   _____   _____

   _____   _____

3. Which word begins with /k/? _____

4. Write one word that begins with /z/ and two that end with /z/. _____   _____

   _____

5. Which word begins with the letter <u>v</u>? _____

6. Which word begins and ends like <u>boil</u>?

   _____

7. Which word begins and ends like <u>given</u>?

   _____

8. Which word begins and ends like <u>male</u>?

   _____

9. In which word is /ō/ spelled <u>ew</u>? _____

10. Write the word whose pronunciation is made up of one vowel sound. _____

11. Write the word in which you see the letter <u>k</u> but don't hear /k/. _____

12. In which two words do you hear /f/? Circle the letters that spell /f/. _____   _____

13. Write the words in which a double consonant spells one sound.

    ll _____   ll _____

    pp _____   rr _____

    rr _____   rr _____

80

Checkpoint

Write a spelling word for each clue.
Then use the Checkpoint Study Plan on page 224.

1. A needle and thread are used to ____.

2. Today I grow, before that I had ____.

3. Another word for toss is ____.

4. The opposite of to lead is to ____.

5. In an election you cast your ____.

6. The day following today will be ____.

7. To be with no one else is to be ____.

8. If you're in debt, you ____ a bill.

9. A secret message may be in ____.

10. Hit the target by using a bow and ____.

11. I know, I knew, I had ____.

12. Another word for guess is ____.

13. The opposite of lend is ____.

14. A certain area is a ____.

15. After you chew, you ____.

16. As dinner is to plate, soup is to ____.

17. Picked out or selected means ____.

18. As knee is to leg, ____ is to arm.

19. When scientists invent things, they like to give them Greek names. The two mystery words name scientific inventions. The first word names an instrument that allows us to see small things. It comes from the Greek words for small (*micros*) and for see (*skŏpeō*). Can you guess this word? ____

20. The second mystery word names something that allows you to make sounds that can be heard far away. It comes from two Greek words. *Telos* meant far away. *Phoneo* meant to make a sound. What is this word? ____

81

Letter from the Science Fair

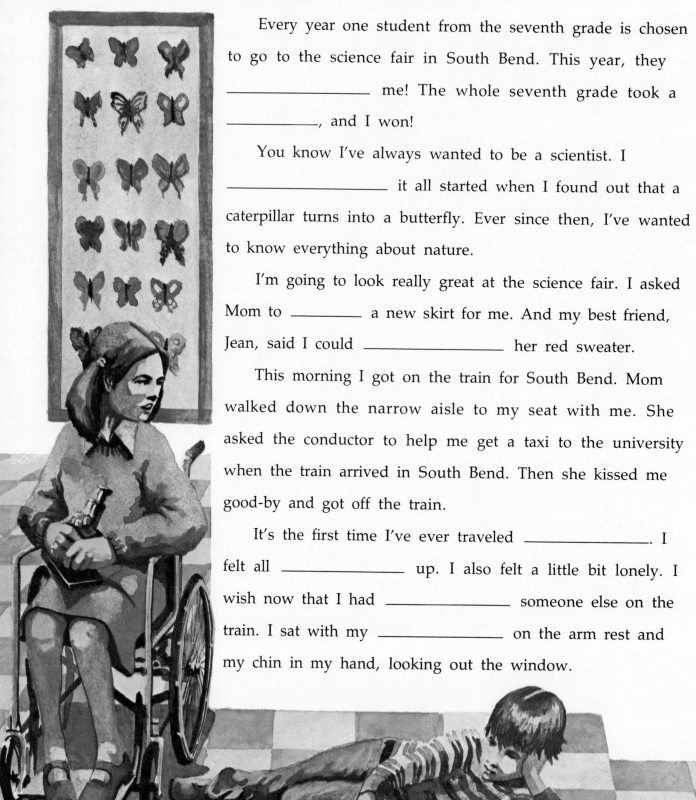

Dear Susie,

Every year one student from the seventh grade is chosen to go to the science fair in South Bend. This year, they _____ me! The whole seventh grade took a _____, and I won!

You know I've always wanted to be a scientist. I _____ it all started when I found out that a caterpillar turns into a butterfly. Ever since then, I've wanted to know everything about nature.

I'm going to look really great at the science fair. I asked Mom to _____ a new skirt for me. And my best friend, Jean, said I could _____ her red sweater.

This morning I got on the train for South Bend. Mom walked down the narrow aisle to my seat with me. She asked the conductor to help me get a taxi to the university when the train arrived in South Bend. Then she kissed me good-by and got off the train.

It's the first time I've ever traveled _____. I felt all _____ up. I also felt a little bit lonely. I wish now that I had _____ someone else on the train. I sat with my _____ on the arm rest and my chin in my hand, looking out the window.

When we got to the train station in South Bend, the conductor told me to _____ him to a taxi. Then he folded my wheelchair and put it in the taxi for me. The taxi took me to the main building of the university. Just inside the front door I saw an _____ pointing to a large room. A sign read TO THE SCIENCE FAIR. I wheeled right into the room.

A woman met me at the door, gave me a name tag, and pointed to where my table was. She explained that the room was divided into several zones. My table is in the special _____ reserved for seventh graders. I began to unpack my exhibit immediately. I was especially worried about the _____ and slides, but they were fine. I set up the microscope and looked at one of my slides. Then I set up the rest of my exhibit.

When I was finished with my exhibit, I found a _____ and called home. I dialed my area _____ and the number. Mom answered. She and Dad were glad to hear I had arrived safely.

I bought a sandwich on the train, but I was so excited that I could hardly _____ a bite. Now I'm hungry. When I finish this letter, I think I'll just _____ on my coat and join some of the other kids in the cafeteria for a _____ of chili.

Well, _____ is the big day! I feel so great to be at the science fair on my own. I guess I really _____ it all to that caterpillar!

Your friend,

Anne

known
throw
bowl
follow
arrow
elbow
grown
borrow
swallow
tomorrow
zone
vote
telephone
code
alone
microscope
suppose
chose
sew
owe

Predicate

The predicate is the part of a sentence that tells what the subject does or did, or what the subject is or was. In these sentences Jason is the subject.

Jason jogs to school every day.
Jason is a very good athlete.

Read the sentences above and answer these questions.

1. What words tell what Jason does or did in the first sentence?

_____

2. What words tell what Jason is or was in the second sentence?

_____

★ Write each sentence below, correcting the misspelled words. Then underline the complete predicate.

3. Becky will telefone you after school.

_____

4. Jack wants to borow my bike.

_____

5. You ow me a dime.

_____

6. I like to so my own clothes.

_____

7. Kim and Evan arrive tommorow.

_____

8. Anne has groan an inch this year.

_____

9. Jesse couldn't swalow when he was sick.

_____

10. I suppoze I should study now.

WORDS AT WORK

Challenge Yourself

disclose   wallow   stowaway   brooch

Decide which Challenge Word fits each clue. Check your Spelling Dictionary to see if you were right. Then write sentences showing that you understand the meaning of each Challenge Word.

1. This person might hide in a car trunk or on a ship in the hope of getting a free ride.

2. You do this to a secret when you tell it to someone.

3. You could pin one on the collar of a blouse or jacket to dress it up.

4. Pigs do this in mud to cool themselves off.

Write to the Point

Do you have a friend or relative whom you haven't seen in a while? Write a letter telling that person some of the news in your life that you would like to share. If you wish, share some of your thoughts and feelings, too. Use spelling words from this lesson in your letter.

Challenge Use one or more of the Challenge Words in your letter.

Proofreading

Use the proofreading marks to show the errors in the paragraph below. Write the five misspelled words correctly in the blanks.

> Tommorrow I will give my report called "The Amazing microscope." I choze this topic because have grone very interested in studying nature. I have already learned quite a lot about nature, but I suppoze there much more to be knoan.

	word is misspelled
≡	letter should be capitalized
∧	word is missing

1. _____

2. _____

3. _____

4. _____

5. _____

85

Lesson 16 Words with /ō/

Listen for /ō/ in each word.

notice

tornado

hotel

scold

echo

hero

control

clothing

poem

yolk

float

throat

coast

oak

coach

groan

boast

roast

though

dough

1. Which word begins with /sk/? Circle the letters that spell /sk/. _____

2. Write the two words that begin with the letters <u>th</u>.

   _____   _____

3. Which word has the letters <u>th</u> in the middle?

   _____

4. Which word begins and ends like <u>flat</u>? _____

5. Which word begins and ends like <u>coal</u>? _____

6. Which word begins and ends like <u>hospital</u>?

   _____

7. Which word begins with the letter <u>p</u>? _____

8. Write the three words that end with the letter <u>o</u>.

   _____   _____

   _____

9. Which word ends with the letters <u>ch</u>?

   _____

10. Write the two words that end with the letter <u>k</u>.

    _____   _____

11. Write the three words that end with the letters <u>st</u>.

    _____   _____

    _____

12. Which word ends with /s/? _____

13. Which two words have the same spelling of /ō/ as <u>thorough</u>? _____   _____

14. In which word do the letters <u>ch</u> spell /k/?

    _____

15. Which word sounds exactly like <u>grown</u>?

    _____

Checkpoint

Write a spelling word for each clue.
Then use the Checkpoint Study Plan on page 224.

1. To cook with dry heat in an oven is to _____.

2. A repeated sound is an _____.

3. Another word for see or pay attention to is _____.

4. The opposite of to sink is to _____.

5. A kind of trainer is a _____.

6. At the edge of the sea is the _____.

7. Socks, pants, and shirts are _____.

8. To talk to harshly is to _____.

9. To have power over is to _____.

10. Someone who likes to brag likes to _____.

11. Part of an egg is the _____.

12. Another word for however is _____.

13. The opposite of coward is _____.

14. An acorn grows into an _____.

15. The front part of the neck is the _____.

16. A sound of dismay or pain is a _____.

17. A baker makes bread from _____.

18. Another word for inn is _____.

19. A piece of writing that rhymes is a _____.

20. This mystery word names a violent wind. The wind takes on a funnel shape and whirls about. It spins at up to 300 miles per hour. This wind can cause much damage. It takes its name from the Spanish word *tronada*. *Tronada* means thunderstorm. It probably got this name because thunder often comes with funnel-shaped winds. Can you guess the mystery word? _____

87

Use each list word once.

HURRICANE

Marie's father was the head cook at Casa Grande, the most famous seaside _____ on the western _____ of the island. Marie often helped in the kitchen. Today was no different. While her father kneaded _____ for bread and put a _____ in the oven, she broke an egg and stirred the _____ into the cake batter.

When she was finished, she changed from her work _____ to her swimsuit. It had been hot in the kitchen. Now she was ready to _____ on the gentle waves of the sea. On her way down to the beach, she saw Juan, the hotel manager. He was posting a _____ on the bulletin board. It was a storm warning. She ran to alert the hotel guests.

One guest, a softball trainer and _____, didn't seem afraid. In fact, she began to _____. "No hurricane or _____ can scare me," she bragged.

A second guest began to moan and _____ when he heard the news. "I'm not brave. I'm no _____," he said.

Just then, Juan announced over a loudspeaker that everyone should take shelter in the hotel. They listened to his voice _____ up and down the beach for a long moment. Then Marie led them to the hotel's kitchen, which was in the basement. They would be safe there.

Even in the basement, they could hear the wind roaring and the huge waves crashing over the beach. The guests tried hard to _____ their rising fears. Even the brave coach felt her _____ become so tight that she couldn't swallow. She began to _____ herself for being so afraid.

Marie decided she had to do something to take their minds off the storm. She grabbed some paper and pencils. "May I have your attention?" she shouted above the noise of the storm. "Even _____ we're stuck in the kitchen until the storm blows over, there's no reason we can't have a good time. Let's all sit around the big _____ table and make believe that we are poets. There will be a prize for the best _____ about the storm." Everyone scrambled for seats and began to write.

Marie breathed a deep sigh as she heard the storm die down. Everyone was safe. Juan announced that the prize for the writing contest would be a free dinner. Then he thanked Marie for entertaining the guests and keeping them busy during the storm.

Marie often helped in the kitchen. Today had been no different from any other.

notice
tornado
hotel
scold
echo
hero
control
clothing
poem
yolk
float
throat
coast
oak
coach
groan
boast
roast
though
dough

Capitals

Use a capital letter to begin a person's first or last name. Also, use a capital letter to begin a title that goes with someone's name. Always capitalize the word I.

My neighbor, Mrs. Allison, and I enjoy each other's company.
Her son, Tom, is very friendly, too.

★ Write the sentences below. Correct the misspelled words and capitalize where necessary.

1. I'll never forget our class trip to the cost with mr. and mrs. lane.

2. Adam and i packed our clotheing, and justin packed the food.

3. We knew mr. lane would never skold us for packing too much.

4. Our track coch, mr. wallace, came to see us off.

5. Coach wallace is everyone's hiro.

6. He cleared his troat and said good-by to us and good luck to mr. and mrs. lane.

7. After driving most of the day, mrs. lane asked us to notise signs for a place to stay.

8. With a cheer, justin, scott, and i spotted a sign for a hotell.

WORDS AT WORK

Challenge Yourself

loathe   nomad   token   smolder

Use your Spelling Dictionary to answer these questions. Then write sentences showing that you understand the meaning of each Challenge Word.

1. Would the coals from a fire <u>smolder</u> if you didn't put the fire out completely?

2. Would someone who is a <u>nomad</u> stay in one place all her life?

3. Could a flower or a photograph be a <u>token</u> of a special day?

4. If you care for someone very much, do you <u>loathe</u> that person?

Write to the Point

Some emergencies, like hurricanes, can't be prevented. Others, such as accidents, can often be prevented. Write a list of rules telling what to do in a certain kind of emergency or how to prevent such an emergency from happening. Use spelling words from this lesson in your rules.

Challenge Use one or more of the Challenge Words in your rules.

Proofreading

Use the proofreading marks to show the errors in the paragraph below. Write the five misspelled words correctly in the blanks.

⬭	word is misspelled
⊙	period is missing
/	letter should be lower case

We stayed in our hotell during the storm and listened to the wind grown. Along the coste the wind made waves crash on the Beach We saw a boat come untied and flote away. The wind seemed out of controll. We weren't afraid, though We were very careful.

1. _____

2. _____

3. _____

4. _____

5. _____

Lesson 17 Media Words

Say each word.

studio

director

producer

commercial

television

broadcast

musician

prime time

network

camera

recorder

cassette

tape deck

earphones

newspaper

columnist

masthead

by-line

editorial

headline

1. Which word begins with the letter <u>h</u>? _____

2. Which word begins and ends like <u>cafeteria</u>?

   _____

3. Write one word that begins with the letters <u>st</u> and two
   words that end with <u>st</u>. _____

   _____

4. Which word has the letters <u>st</u> in the middle?

   _____

5. Write the word in which you hear /zh/.

   _____

6. Which two words end with /k/? Circle the letters that
   spell /k/. _____

7. Which three words have /k/ in the middle?

   _____

8. Write the three words that end with the letters <u>er</u>.

   _____

   _____

9. Which word ends with the letters <u>or</u>? _____

10. Which word has /f/ in the middle? Circle the letters that
    spell /f/. _____

11. Which word has a hyphen? _____

12. In which two words do you hear /sh/ but don't see the
    letters <u>sh</u>? _____ _____

13. Which word has two pairs of double consonants?

    _____

14. Which word has five syllables? _____

15. Which word is made up of two words that rhyme?

    _____

Checkpoint

Write a spelling word for each clue.
Then use the Checkpoint Study Plan on page 224.

1. A listing of people who work on a newspaper is a ____.

2. An advertisement on radio or television is a ____.

3. You can play a cassette on a ____.

4. The time when the most people watch TV is ____.

5. To put on the air is to ____.

6. Many TV stations belong to a ____.

7. Pictures are taken with a ____.

8. Stereo is to album as tape deck is to ____.

9. The one who manages the show is the ____.

10. Someone who writes or plays music is a ____.

11. The writer of a newspaper column is a ____.

12. I record songs on my tape ____.

13. The line giving an author's name is a ____.

14. Daily or weekly news is found in the ____.

15. Many shows are taped in a ____.

16. The one who guides the show is a ____.

17. The title of a news article is a ____.

18. A journalist writes his or her opinion in an ____.

19. Another name for headsets is ____.

20. New inventions are usually given Greek or Latin names. Sometimes an invention gets an odd name that is half Greek and half Latin. This mystery word has such a name. The mystery word names an electronic device that turns radio waves into sight and sound. It comes from two words, *telos* and *video*. *Telos* is Greek. It means far away. *Video* comes from Latin and means see. The mystery word names a device that lets us see things that happen far away. Can you guess the word? ____

Use words from the first part of the list to do this page.

MULTIMEDIA

My mother works for a television _____.
She is a producer. As a _____, she plans
each show. She gets to choose all the people who work on
it. One of the most important people she chooses is the
_____. He directs people in the show.

Mother's show is _____ at
nine every Wednesday evening, during prime time. Every
weekday evening from eight o'clock to eleven is called
_____.

Every morning at eight, my mother goes to the
_____ where the show is filmed. Yesterday, I
went with her. First she met with the director and the
_____ who is in charge of the music. The
music for each show is recorded on a _____
tape. This is done in a studio where they have the best tape
_____. I had thought that the musician
would just put his _____ on his ears,
put the tape into the _____, and push
"PLAY." It wasn't that simple.

The musician, the director, and Mother went over the
script for the show. Together they decided which
_____ would be used to film each scene. They
also had to decide where they would break for a
_____.

I stayed at work with Mother until nine that night. I
was surprised to find out how much work it takes to put
together one half-hour _____ show.

Use words from the second part of the list to do this page.

My father works at the Daily Times. Dad writes a daily column about television. He is a _____. His name appears after his column. This is called his _____. Dad's name also appears on the masthead followed by his title, Television Editor. Dad's boss is also listed on the _____ of the paper. His boss is the Managing Editor.

Last week I visited my father at his office. He showed me a copy of the _____ from the day he started work there. Then we watched the program that he was going to write about in his column. We watched it on a video cassette recorder. The show was about a woman who was lost in the desert for five days. After Dad wrote his column, I helped him write the _____ for it. We finally decided on "One Woman's Fight for Life."

Then we went out to a coffee shop for lunch. Dad's best friend, Morty, went with us. Morty works on the _____ page where all of the editorials and letters to the editor appear.

I really enjoyed the day with Dad. I felt important because I had helped to write the headline. The next day, when I saw Dad's by-line, I was proud.

studio
director
producer
commercial
television
broadcast
musician
prime time
network
camera
recorder
cassette
tape deck
earphones

newspaper
columnist
masthead
by-line
editorial
headline

Capitals

Names of places such as cities, states, countries, bodies of water, mountains, and streets are capitalized.

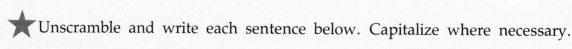

Larry visited San Francisco, California, last summer.
He saw the Pacific Ocean.

★ Unscramble and write each sentence below. Capitalize where necessary.

1. was broadcast The new york from

_____

2. team camera to johnson street rushed A

_____

3. the was commercial rocky mountains The filmed in

_____

4. a hollywood We studio visited

_____

5. said newspaper miami, florida The was held in concert the

_____

_____

6. lives director paris in The of that film

_____

7. often the is washington, d.c. headlines in

_____

8. music of and georgia We played a tennessee cassette about the tape

_____

_____

9. The show atlantic ocean television was about the

_____

10. editorial london The about was

_____

96

WORDS AT WORK

Challenge Yourself

Use your Spelling Dictionary to answer these questions. Then write sentences showing that you understand the meaning of each Challenge Word.

1. Would a person who likes writing about people and events enjoy a job in journalism?

2. Is a magazine an example of a periodical?

3. In a newspaper, is front-page news usually important?

4. Is a newsstand a place where newspapers are printed?

Write to the Point

Some people think young people watch too much TV. What do you think? Write a paragraph giving your opinion of television. What is good about it? What is bad? Give reasons and examples to support your opinions. Use spelling words from this lesson in your paragraph.

Challenge Use one or more of the Challenge Words in your paragraph.

Proofreading

Use the proofreading marks to show the errors in the paragraph below. Write the five misspelled words correctly in the blanks.

> word is misspelled
>
> letter should be capitalized
>
> take out word

At primetime my grandfather he does more than just watch telavision. he sometimes pops a casette into the tape deck. Then he puts on on the earfones and settles in his favorite chair. Then he opens the newspapper in his lap to the front page and starts to read.

1. _____

2. _____

3. _____

4. _____

5. _____

97

Lesson 18 Words in Review

A. decide

guide

science

island

library

B. quantity

common

hospital

promise

honest

C. control

sew

throat

echo

though

yolk

owe

grown

groan

telephone

★ You will need a piece of paper for these review activities.

1. In Lesson 13 you studied three different ways to spell /ī/: **i, i__e, ui__e.** Write the words in list A.

_____   _____

_____

2. In Lesson 14 you studied two different ways to spell /ŏ/: **o, a.** Write the words in list B.

_____   _____

_____   _____

★ **3.** Use each review word from lists A and B in a sentence.

4. In Lessons 15 and 16 you studied seven different ways to spell /ō/: **ow, o__e, ew, owe, o, oa, ou.** Write the words in list C.

_____   _____

_____   _____

_____   _____

_____

★ **5.** Look up each review word from list C in the Spelling Dictionary. Write the part of speech for each word. (Hint: Some words may be more than one part of speech.)

★ **6.** Write all 20 review words in alphabetical order.

Your teacher may give you a test. Answer these questions when you have finished.

7. Did you spell all the words correctly? _____

8. Did you leave out a letter? _____

9. Did you write the wrong letter? _____

10. Did you miss the spelling of a vowel sound? _____

A Business Letter

Suppose that you read a great book and wanted to write a letter to the author to tell him or her how much you liked the book. You would need the author's address. One way to get the address is to write a business letter to the publisher of the book. Here is a business letter that Leah wrote to a publisher.

> 27 Palm Road
> Jacksonville, FL 32216
> April 3, 1996
>
> Hall Publishing Company
> 157 Madison Avenue
> New York, NY 10023
>
> Dear Hall Publishing Company:
>
> I really enjoyed the book <u>South Pacific Adventure</u> by Kate Rossini. Please send me Ms. Rossini's address so that I can tell her how much I liked the book. Thank you.
>
> Sincerely,
> **Leah Yu**
> Leah Yu

To write her business letter, Leah followed the steps in the writing process. She used a list as a **Prewriting** activity. The list helped her make sure that she did not forget to include any important information in the letter. Leah's list is shown here. Study what Leah did.

> My address
>
> Address of publishing company
>
> Name of book: South Pacific Adventure
>
> Author: Kate Rossini

 Get ready to write your own business letter. Choose a company that sells books or games through a catalog. Write a letter to the company, asking for a copy of the catalog. When you have decided what company to write to, make a list like Leah's. Then follow the other steps in the writing process—**Writing, Revising, Proofreading,** and **Publishing.**

Lesson 19 Words with /ŭ/

Listen for /ŭ/ in each word.

judge

husband

pumpkin

crush

hundred

jungle

knuckle

instruct

tongue

monkey

onion

dozen

compass

among

wonderful

rough

country

touch

blood

flood

1. Write the three words that begin with a vowel.

_____ _____

_____

2. Which word begins and ends like <u>watchful</u>?

_____

3. Which word begins and ends like <u>pin</u>?

_____

4. Which two words begin and end like <u>hurried</u>?

_____ _____

5. Which word begins with a letter <u>k</u> that you don't hear?

_____

6. Write one word that begins with /f/ and one that ends with /f/. Circle the letters that spell /f/.

_____

7. Which two words begin with the letter j? Circle the word that ends with /j/.

_____ _____

8. Write the word that has the same spelling of /ŭ/ as <u>flood</u>. _____

9. Write the word that ends with the letters <u>sh</u>.

_____

10. Which two words end with /ē/?

_____ _____

11. Which word ends with the letters <u>ch</u>? _____

12. In which word is /s/ spelled <u>ss</u>? _____

13. Which word contains the letter <u>z</u>? _____

14. In which word do you see the letters <u>gue</u> but hear only /g/? _____

Checkpoint

Write a spelling word for each clue.
Then use the Checkpoint Study Plan on page 224.

1. Pipes are for water, veins are for ____.

2. In a group of means ____.

3. The opposite of smooth is ____.

4. To feel silk, use your sense of ____.

5. A jack-o'-lantern is a carved ____.

6. North and south are points on a ____.

7. A thick growth of trees and plants is a ____.

8. An overflow of water is a ____.

9. I cry when I slice an ____.

10. An animal that lives in the jungle is a ____.

11. A nation or state is a ____.

12. To teach is to ____.

13. Another word for marvelous is ____.

14. To crumple is to ____.

15. A joint on your finger is a ____.

16. Twelve is one ____.

17. To decide right and wrong is to ____.

18. The main organ of taste is the ____.

19. Ninety-nine plus one makes one ____.

20. This mystery word looks and sounds like its very old base word, *husbonda*. But the mystery word does not mean what *husbonda* meant. A *husbonda* was a man who lived in a house. Later *husbonda* came to mean farmer. The mystery word that comes from *husbonda* means a married man. Can you guess the mystery word? ____

Use each list word once.

MAD ADS

INSTA-BOAT

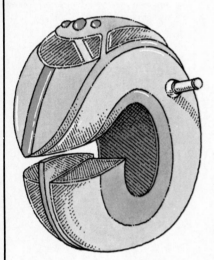

Live near a river? Do you worry about floods? Here's a great way to prepare for next spring's _____. Buy an Insta-Boat. It inflates with a _____ of your finger. Then _____ it up into a ball for easy storage between floods. It comes in one size that is large enough for the whole family: wife, _____, children, and grandparents.

Compass Ring

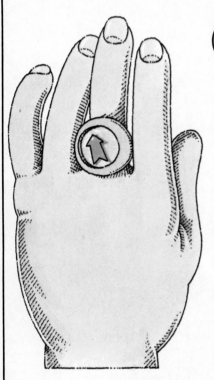

Going for a sail, a trip to another _____, a hike through _____ and rocky country? The _____ ring is a must! You can change the size so that it fits over the largest _____. It always points home. You may not be able to get there, but you will always know which direction it's in! But don't take our word for it, _____ for yourself. (It makes a _____ gift for someone who owns an Insta-Boat.)

COWARD'S BANDAGES

Can't stand the sight of _____? Try Coward's Bandages. As soon as you cut yourself, simply place the bandages over your eyes and stop worrying. When the bleeding stops, remove bandages from the eyes and place them on the wound. Order a _____ (12) now.

A MONKEY'S UNCLE

You can be a monkey's uncle. That's right! Make reservations now to sail through the Amazon waterways. Go sightseeing in a tropical _____. And choose your pet _____ from _____ the thousands you will see. Just sign the adoption papers, pay your _____ dollars, and you are a monkey's uncle! (You also get a set of monkey bars and 500 bananas.)

PUMPIONS

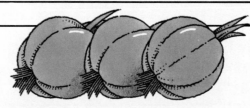

Try this taste treat and give your _____ a surprise. As its name hints, the pumpion is a cross between a _____ and an _____. It's sweet enough for dessert but snappy enough to add zest to any casserole. Send for our colorful, free idea book. It will _____ you in how to prepare such delicious delights as french-fried pumpion rings and homemade pumpion pie.

judge
husband
pumpkin
crush
hundred
jungle
knuckle
instruct
tongue
monkey
onion
dozen
compass
among
wonderful
rough
country
touch
blood
flood

Homographs

Some words in our language are spelled exactly like other words. But they came into our language at different times and from different places. And they have different meanings. Such words are called homographs (*homo* means <u>same</u>, and *graph* means <u>word</u>). Homographs appear as separate entry words in dictionaries, and they are numbered.

---

des·ert[1] | **dĕz′**ərt | *n.* A dry, sandy region.
de·sert[2] | dĭ zûrt′ | *v.* To forsake; abandon: *She did not desert her friends when they needed her.*

★Which entry defines the word <u>desert</u> used in each of these sentences?

1. Thelma left the hot desert and went to live in the jungle. _____

2. Jim had to desert his car to get gas. _____

★Now use these homographs in the sentences below. Write each sentence. Then tell which entry you used.

---

bowl[1] | bōl | *n.* A round dish used to hold things.

bowl[2] | bōl | *v.* To play the game of bowling.

ob·ject[1] | ŏb′jĭkt | *or* | -jĕkt′ | *n.* A thing that has shape and can be touched and seen.

ob·ject[2] | əb jĕkt′ | *v.* To protest, to show disapproval.

---

3. I ____ to having onion in my salad. _____

_____

4. May I have a ____ of berries? _____

_____

5. I like to ____ with my team on Saturdays. _____

_____

6. What is that strange ____ on the table? _____

_____

WORDS AT WORK

Challenge Yourself

blunt   budget   doubly   stomachache

Write what you think each underlined Challenge Word means. Check your Spelling Dictionary to see if you were right. Then write sentences showing that you understand the meaning of each Challenge Word.

1. A pencil point starts out sharp but grows <u>blunt</u> as you write with it.

2. We wrote out a <u>budget</u> for the party so that we would know how much to spend on food and decorations.

3. To finish an hour's work in half an hour, you must work <u>doubly</u> fast.

4. Eating too much food can give you a <u>stomachache</u>.

Write to the Point

Satisfied customers often appear in television commercials. They tell what happened when they used the product and why they were pleased with it. Imagine that you tried one of the "Mad Ads" products. Write a commercial telling why you liked it. Use spelling words from this lesson in your commercial.

Challenge Use one or more of the Challenge Words in your commercial.

Proofreading

Use the proofreading marks to show the errors in the paragraph below. Write the five misspelled words correctly in the blanks.

Do you cry when peel an oniun Just place two No-Cry pills on your tung. No store in the countrie sells them, so order a bottle now. In fact, order a dozan. Each bottle contains a hundred pills. They wonderfull!

◯	word is misspelled
?∧	question mark is missing
∧	word is missing

1. _____

2. _____

3. _____

4. _____

5. _____

Lesson 20 Words with /ô/

Listen for /ô/ in each word.

raw

crawl

lawnmower

straw

dawn

awful

autumn

fault

automobile

daughter

caught

taught

thought

fought

bought

brought

all right

already

wrong

often

1. Which word begins with a letter w that you don't hear?

_____

2. Write the two words that begin with /k/.

_____

3. Which word begins and ends like den? _____

4. Which word begins and ends like laughter and is a compound word? _____

5. Which two words begin and end with vowels?

_____

6. Write two words that begin with the letter f and two that have f in the middle. _____

_____

7. Write the word that ends with /ē/. Circle the letter that spells /ē/. _____

8. Write the two words that end with the letters aw.

_____

9. In which two words is /ô/ spelled a?

_____

10. In which two words is /ô/ spelled o?

_____

11. In which word is /l/ spelled ll? _____

12. Write the word in which you see the letter n but don't hear /n/. _____

13. Write the eight words in which you see the letters gh but don't hear /g/ or /f/ for those letters.

_____   _____

_____   _____

Checkpoint

Write a spelling word for each clue.
Then use the Checkpoint Study Plan on page 224.

1. To move slowly on the hands and knees is to ____.

2. If you make a mistake, it's your ____.

3. If it has been done before, then it has been done ____.

4. Today I buy, yesterday I ____.

5. Today I teach, yesterday I ____.

6. You can drink through a ____.

7. Frequently means ____.

8. I cut the grass with a ____.

9. The time of day when the sun rises is ____.

10. The past tense of fight is ____.

11. After summer comes ____.

12. The opposite of right or correct is ____.

13. Very bad or unpleasant is ____.

14. Today I bring, last week I ____.

15. Father is to son as mother is to ____.

16. The opposite of cooked is ____.

17. O.K. means ____.

18. The past tense of catch is ____.

19. Today I think, last month I ____.

20. Some words have both Greek and Latin roots. This mystery word is such a word. It is made up of two separate words. The first comes from the Greek word for self, *autos*. The second comes from the Latin word for moving, *mobilis*. When we put these words together, we get *automobilis* (self-moving). The mystery word names a means of transportation that runs by itself. Can you guess what it is? ____

CAMP MAIL

Use each list word once.

Dear Mom and Dad,

I know it isn't your _____. Next time, though, I'll read between the lines in any camp ad that says, "GET READY TO LAUNCH INTO AN EXCITING SUMMER!" The only thing we launched was the canoe. Our counselors woke us up at _____ this morning and drove us several miles up river in their _____. The canoe was on top of the car. When we stopped, guess who got to carry the canoe to the water. I _____ that the counselors would help us. Ha!

When the canoe was packed, we all _____ for the best seats. It took awhile to get in, because you can't stand up in a canoe. You must hold the sides with your hands and _____ to your seat. Finally we began the long journey back to camp.

We pulled up to the bank at noon for lunch. The counselors told us we would have to help cook. We cooked the stew while they made fruit salad. Our stew wasn't very good. In fact, it was _____. Some of the meat was still _____. The beans were as dry as _____. But luckily for us, the fruit salad tasted _____.

We got back to camp late this afternoon. The counselors got out their fishing poles and _____ some fish for supper. Then they _____ us how to clean fish. I guess they're not really so bad, after all. And I certainly hope that their fish will taste better than our stew.

Love,

Your _____ Jane

108

Dear Jane,

Your letter was the nicest surprise the mail carrier

_____ us.

I must say, Jane, that I do not think the camp ad gave

us the _____ impression. There wasn't an

automatic guarantee that it was going to be easy right from

the beginning. Being away from home always takes time

to get used to. When _____ comes, you'll

probably miss your summer friends and even the

counselors more than you can imagine.

Our lawn doesn't look the same since you left. Your

long-lost friend, the _____, is always

asking for you. I am sure, though, that is one friend you are

happy to be away from.

By the way, Uncle Todd passed his exams to become a

lawyer. To celebrate, we _____ him a book

by his favorite author. I don't suppose he'll have much time

to read it, however.

It's noon _____ and just about time for

the mail carrier to pick up the mail. I promise to write more

soon. We think of you _____.

                                                    Love,

                                                    Mom

raw
crawl
lawnmower
straw
dawn
awful
autumn
fault
automobile
daughter
caught
taught
thought
fought
bought
brought
all right
already
wrong
often

Apostrophes

Use an apostrophe when writing a contraction. A contraction combines two words into one word by leaving out one or more letters. The apostrophe shows where the letters have been left out.

had not   hadn't

Use an apostrophe to show ownership. Add 's to a singular noun to make it possessive.

Sally's hat   the dog's house

To form the possessive of a plural noun that ends in s, add only an apostrophe.

the boys' bikes

If a plural noun does not end in s, add 's to form the possessive.

the cattle's pen

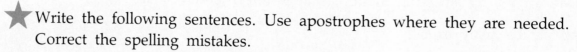

⭐ Write the following sentences. Use apostrophes where they are needed. Correct the spelling mistakes.

1. Mom: Ive brawt you a surprise.

_____

2. Stu: I thawt youd forgotten my birthday.

_____

3. Mom: Youre rong, I remembered.

_____

4. Stu: I cant guess what you bawt me.

_____

5. Mom: Its a little like the Jones automobel.

_____

6. Stu: Dont give me any more afful hints.

_____

7. Mom: Alright, they both have wheels — its a bicycle!

Challenge Yourself

authentic   nautical   fraud   awning

Decide which Challenge Word fits each clue. Check your Spelling Dictionary to see if you were right. Then write sentences showing that you understand the meaning of each Challenge Word.

1. This word could be used to describe all of the following items: an anchor, a sail, and a sailor's cap.

2. Putting the name of a famous artist on a painting by someone else would be an example of this.

3. This is the opposite of fake.

4. This is good to stand under if you're caught in the rain.

Write to the Point

Is there a summer that you remember especially well because of something unusual, exciting, or funny that happened? Write a true story about this incident. Tell how it began, what happened, and how it all came out. Use spelling words from this lesson in your story.

Challenge Use one or more of the Challenge Words in your story.

Proofreading

Use the proofreading marks to show the errors in the paragraph below. Write the five misspelled words correctly in the blanks.

What an awfull mess I was in I was supposed to mow mrs. Hu's lawn each week this summer until she returned in the autum. She taught me how to use her lawn-mower, and I thougt I caught on. When i found out I was wrong, she was allready gone.

◯	word is misspelled
≡	letter should be capitalized
⌄!	exclamation point is missing

1. _____

2. _____

3. _____

4. _____

5. _____

Lesson 21 Words with /o͞o/

Listen for /o͞o/ in each word.

loose

rooster

balloon

shampoo

kangaroo

proof

choose

foolish

raccoon

lose

improve

prove

whose

clue

glue

fruit

juice

truth

shoe

whom

1. Which two words begin with /k/? Circle the letter that spells /k/. _____ _____

2. Write the two words in which you see the letter <u>w</u> but don't hear /w/. _____ _____

3. Which word begins with the letter <u>g</u>? _____

4. Which word begins and ends like <u>front</u>? _____

5. Which word begins and ends with the letter <u>r</u>? _____

6. Write the word that begins with the letters <u>ch</u>. _____

7. Write the word that begins with the letters <u>im</u>. _____

8. Write two words that begin with the letters <u>sh</u> and one that ends with <u>sh</u>. _____ _____ _____

9. Write two words that begin with the letters <u>pr</u> and one that has <u>pr</u> in the middle. _____ _____ _____

10. Which word ends with the letters <u>th</u>? _____

11. Write the three words that end with /z/. _____ _____ _____

12. Write the two words that end with /s/. _____ _____

13. In which word is /l/ spelled <u>ll</u>? _____

14. In which word is /k/ spelled <u>cc</u>? _____

Checkpoint

Write a spelling word for each clue.
Then use the Checkpoint Study Plan on page 224.

1. On a farm you wake up to the call of a ____.

2. On your foot you wear your ____.

3. Yesterday I chose, today I ____.

4. They stick to me like ____.

5. Evidence is part of ____.

6. The opposite of tight is ____.

7. An apple is a kind of ____.

8. To show to be true means to ____.

9. A masked animal is a ____.

10. Another word that sounds like who's is ____.

11. They crossed the Atlantic Ocean in a hot-air ____.

12. Soap for the hair is ____.

13. Yesterday I lost, today I ____.

14. The opposite of a lie is the ____.

15. A hint is a ____.

16. The opposite of wise is ____.

17. To make better means to ____.

18. Squeeze an orange to get ____.

19. We is to us as who is to ____.

20. The people who first settled in Australia are called
Aborigines. The Aborigines have been living in Australia
for 12,000 years. Two hundred years ago some new
people went to live in Australia. They saw plants and
animals there that they had never seen before. Since
they didn't have names for these plants and animals,
they used the Aborigine names. This mystery word
names an Australian animal. It is from the Aborigine
word *kanga*, which means jumper. Can you guess it? ____

113

THE CASE OF THE MISSING SHOE

I was sitting in my office, drinking a glass of orange _____, when the call came from the famous naturalist, Mrs. Annie Mall. Oh, by the way, I'm Pry Vitigh, private eye. I solve mysteries.

I went to Mrs. Mall's zoo and rang the bell. She answered it herself. Right away, I knew something was wrong. She was wearing two socks, but only one _____.

"That's the mystery," she told me. "I took a little nap after lunch, and I took off my shoes. When I woke up, one shoe was gone. Now you can't _____ one shoe. Somebody must have taken it."

I asked Mrs. Mall who she thought was guilty. This is _____ she suspected:

The baboon is a real strong character who could easily walk off with a shoe.

The _____, whose pocket could hide more than you think.

The _____ is a real loud character who is not to be trusted.

The _____, whose mask looked very suspicious.

Mrs. Mall said, "These are the ones that could have done it. But I can't _____ anything."

"Don't worry," I told her. "We'll find out the

_____, and I'll show you _____."

I had to admit it was a tough case. First I searched the house from the basement to the roof, and I couldn't find one single _____. But I did notice some _____ tiles on the roof.

Then I went to see the baboon. He was in the kitchen eating a piece of _____. When I tried to question him, he grabbed my arm so hard that I got a big bruise.

"That was a cruel thing to do," I said. And since I saw no sign of a shoe, I decided to go on to the next suspect.

I went to see the raccoon. She was a smart animal, even though she looked kind of _____ in that silly mask. When I tried to question her, she nipped me on the hand. I didn't _____ to stick around.

I needed to _____ my method of questioning suspects. I decided to go and get Mrs. Mall. After all, she was the one _____ shoe was missing. Let her face the other two suspects with me.

When I got back to the living room, a boy came in the front door. In one hand, he held a long string with a _____ tied to it. In the other hand, he held a paper bag.

"Hi, Mom," the boy said. "I took your shoe to the repair shop. They'll _____ on a new sole this afternoon. I bought some _____ so you can wash your hair, just like you asked me."

Another case was solved.

loose
rooster
balloon
shampoo
kangaroo
proof
choose
foolish
raccoon
lose
improve
prove
whose
clue
glue
fruit
juice
truth
shoe
whom

Pronunciation

A dictionary lists the pronunciation of each entry word. This pronunciation is written in special symbols. The symbols are a guide to the sounds of a word and are called the sound spelling.

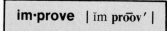

im·prove | ĭm prōōv′ |

Sometimes a word may have more than one acceptable pronunciation. All possible pronunciations are listed after the entry word.

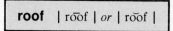

roof | rōōf | *or* | rŏŏf |

To know what sound each of the symbols has, you must refer to the pronunciation key. This key lists all the symbols and gives examples of words that have the sounds of the symbols. The key is usually printed on every other page in a dictionary.

/ă/	pat	/ĭ/	pit	/ŏŏ/	took	/zh/	vision
/ā/	pay	/ī/	pie, by	/ōō/	boot	/ə/	about,
/â/	care	/î/	pier	/ou/	out		item,
/ä/	father	/ŏ/	pot	/th/	thin		edible,
/ĕ/	pet	/ō/	toe	/th/	this		gallop,
/ē/	bee	/ô/	paw, for	/ŭ/	cut		circus
/hw/	whoop	/oi/	noise	/û/	urge	/ər/	butter

★ Write the key words for these symbols:

/ĭ/ _____   /ōō/ _____

★ Write the word that goes with each sound spelling below. Check the answers in the Spelling Dictionary.

truth   balloon   raccoon   juice

1. /ră **koon**′/ _____   2. /jōōs/ _____

3. /bə **loon**′/ _____   4. /trōōth/ _____

★ The words below are followed by two sound spellings. Only one is correct. Look up each word in the Spelling Dictionary and write the correct sound spelling.

5. choose   /chōōs/   /chōōz/   _____

6. whose   /hōōz/   /hwōōz/   _____

7. proof   /prōōf/   /prūf/   _____

8. kangaroo   /kăn găr ōō′/   /kăng′ gə rōō′/   _____

Challenge Yourself

feud   mutual   presume   maroon

Use your Spelling Dictionary to answer these questions. Then write sentences showing that you understand the meaning of each Challenge Word.

1. Would you expect a <u>feud</u> to start between best friends who always say kind words to each other?

2. If you and a friend both like to collect stamps, is stamp-collecting your <u>mutual</u> interest?

3. Would you <u>presume</u> that someone was happy if you saw him or her smile?

4. Would you call the color of a lemon <u>maroon</u>?

Write to the Point

Suppose Mrs. Mall's son had not taken the missing shoe in the detective story. How else might the shoe have disappeared? Imagine that you are the author of the story. Write a new ending for it. Tell what happened to the shoe and how Pry Vitigh solved the mystery. Use spelling words from this lesson in your new ending.

Challenge Use one or more of the Challenge Words in your ending.

Proofreading

Use the proofreading marks to show the errors in the paragraph below. Write the five misspelled words correctly in the blanks.

◯	word is misspelled
/	letter should be lower case
⊙	period is missing

Who had stolen Bushy's fruite? A Rooster named Rudy B. Loud was the one whom the Raccoon suspected Her clew was a feather whoze color matched Rudy's, but how could she proove it had come lose from his tail?

1. _____

2. _____

3. _____

4. _____

5. _____

Lesson 22 Words with /oi/

Listen for /oi/ in each word.

destroy

annoy

enjoy

employ

employment

oyster

loyal

loyalty

voyage

royal

choice

appoint

appointment

moisture

boiler

coin

avoid

voice

noise

broil

1. Which word begins with the letters <u>br</u>?

   _____

2. Which word begins and ends like <u>bother</u>?

   _____

3. Which word begins and ends like <u>ahead</u>?

   _____

4. Which word begins and ends like <u>complain</u>?

   _____

5. Which word begins and ends like <u>real</u>?

   _____

6. Write the two words that end with /s/.

   _____   _____

7. Which word ends with /z/? _____

8. Which three words have the letters <u>st</u> in the middle?

   _____   _____

   _____

9. Which word has /ch/ in the middle? _____

10. Write the two words that contain the /j/ sound.

    _____   _____

11. Write the word in which /n/ is spelled <u>nn</u>.

    _____

12. Three of the list words are base words for other words
    that are also on the list. Write all three pairs.

    _____   _____

    _____   _____

13. Write the three words that have three syllables.

    _____

Checkpoint

Write a spelling word for each clue.
Then use the Checkpoint Study Plan on page 224.

1. To wreck is to ____.

2. Faithful means ____.

3. The opposite of silence is ____.

4. Of a king or queen means ____.

5. Take pleasure means to ____.

6. To keep away from is to ____.

7. If you make a date, you have an ____.

8. To name someone to a position means to ____.

9. A long trip or journey is a ____.

10. If you can go only one way, you have no ____.

11. To make sounds for singing you use your ____.

12. To hire for a job is to ____.

13. Wetness is ____.

14. Faithfulness is ____.

15. To cook close to direct heat is to ____.

16. To bother or irritate is to ____.

17. To make steam heat you need a ____.

18. If you are working, then you have ____.

19. A pearl comes from an ____.

20. This word was first used to describe a tool called a mold or die. This tool was used to make markings on silver and gold money. Later this same word was used to refer to the markings instead of the tool. Finally, it came to be used for the money itself. This word used to be spelled *coigne*. How is it spelled today? ____

Do What You Like

What kind of job would you like to get when you finish school? It's hard to make a _____ about a career. You'll be happiest, though, if you pick something you _____ doing. If you have a _____ collection, you might buy and sell coins as your job. If you like to sing, and you have a good _____, you might want to become a professional singer. Do you like to cook? Look for _____ in a restaurant. Would you like to see other parts of the world? You can take a free ocean _____ if you get someone to _____ you to a ship's crew. Do you like to _____ things? Get a job with a wrecking company. Then you can knock down some old buildings.

Stay away from things you don't like. If animals _____ you, _____ jobs in pet stores. If you don't like lots of _____, don't ask a record store to _____ you. You won't feel any _____ to a job you hate. But you'll find that it's easy to be _____ and true to a job you like. It's more likely you'll be good at it, too.

If you want to ask someone for a job, you must make an

_____ to see that person. As

a chef, your specialty might be _____ stew. A

chef must know when to _____ foods in the

broiler and when to use a double _____.

If you were a maid to a _____ family, you

might ask visitors to wait in the foyer.

A weather forecaster reports the _____

in the air as well as the temperature.

Syllables and Accent Marks

An entry word in a dictionary is divided into syllables. A syllable is a single sound that forms part of a word.

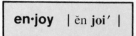

Find each of the words below in the Spelling Dictionary. Write them in syllables, putting a dot between the syllables.

1. oyster _____ 2. loyalty _____

3. avoid _____ 4. voyage _____

The sound spellings in a dictionary tell how to pronounce a word. An accent mark (') is a part of this guide. It tells which syllable in a word is spoken with more stress or force.

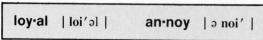

Look at the sound spellings above. Then answer these questions.

5. Which word has the accent on the first syllable? _____

6. Which word has the accent on the second syllable? _____

Write the sound spelling of each word below.

7. destroy _____ 8. royal _____

9. appoint _____ 10. moisture _____

Some words of two or more syllables have two accented syllables. The stronger accent (') is called the primary accent. The weaker accent (') is called the secondary accent.

tin·foil | tĭn′foil′ |

Look at the sound spelling above. Then answer these questions.

11. Which syllable has the primary accent? _____

12. Which syllable has the secondary accent? _____

Challenge Yourself

boisterous   void   exploit   employer

Write what you think each underlined Challenge Word means. Check your Spelling Dictionary to see if you were right. Then write sentences showing that you understand the meaning of each Challenge Word.

1. The class was usually quiet and well-behaved, but today the students were boisterous.

2. We tried to use the torn coupon, but the clerk said it was void.

3. He should exploit his cooking skill by becoming a chef.

4. The people who work for her are glad that she is their employer.

Write to the Point

You have seen adults doing many different jobs, such as teaching, working in stores and libraries, and constructing buildings. Choose a job that you have seen and write a paragraph telling what you would and would not like about this work. Use spelling words from this lesson in your paragraph.

Challenge Use one or more of the Challenge Words in your paragraph.

Proofreading

Use the proofreading marks to show the errors in the paragraph below. Write the five misspelled words correctly in the blanks.

I can't decide which job I'd enjoie.

Each day i seem to have a new choyce.

I'd like to to avoid being a singer,

because my voyce sounds more like

noyze than music! Would someone

employe me to ride horses?

	word is misspelled
	take out word
	letter should be capitalized

1. _____

2. _____

3. _____

4. _____

5. _____

123

Lesson 23 Sports Words

Say each word.

bowling

volleyball

tennis

cycling

swimming

professional

amateur

basketball

competition

football

golf

hockey

skin diving

track

skating

soccer

baseball

champion

skiing

Olympics

1. Which word begins with the letters ch? _____

2. Write the three words that begin with the letters sk. _____ _____ _____

3. Which two words begin with a vowel? Circle the proper noun. _____ _____

4. In which two words do you hear /sh/ but don't see the letters sh? _____ _____

5. Which word begins with a capital? _____

6. In which two words is /k/ spelled ck? _____ _____

7. Which word begins and ends like beginning? _____

8. Which word begins and ends like gulf? _____

9. Which word ends with /ē/? _____

10. Write the word in which the second letter is y. _____

11. Which word has the letters ii? _____

12. Write the word that is made of two separate words. _____

13. Which four words are compounds made with the word ball? _____ _____ _____ _____

14. Write the three words that have these double consonants:

cc _____ mm _____

nn _____

Checkpoint

Write a spelling word for each clue.
Then use the Checkpoint Study Plan on page 224.

1. Riding a bicycle or motorcycle is ____.

2. Running, jumping, and pole-vaulting are events in ____.

3. You can hit a ball with your head in ____.

4. If the ball is pointed at both ends, it's a ____.

5. Playing for pay is done by a ____.

6. Scoring a basket to win is done in ____.

7. An underwater sport is ____.

8. Snowy slopes are good for ____.

9. The final winner is the ____.

10. There are teams on either side of a high net in ____.

11. Try to knock all the pins down when you're ____.

12. Water is for boating, ice is for ____.

13. You say "fore" when you play ____.

14. A home run is a score in ____.

15. The opposite of professional is ____.

16. The backstroke is used when ____.

17. A court sport with a low net is ____.

18. You need a puck to play ____.

19. If teams play to win, they are in ____.

20. Long ago, foot races were held in the Olympian Valley
    in Greece. The races were part of a festival in honor of
    Zeus, the king of the Greek gods. Soon, all the Greek
    states began to take part in these sport festivals.
    Gradually, more events like jumping and wrestling were
    added. Now athletes from many nations get together
    every four years and compete in athletic events. The
    events are named after the old Greek festival. Do you
    know what they're called? ____

Use each list word once.
Identify the sport with which these things are associated.

THE NAME OF THE GAME

Use the remaining words to complete the bulletin board.

Sign up for the Olympic team today!

There will be lots of _____

for medals. Only one _____ can

be chosen in each event.

Remember, _____

athletes, who earn money for their skill in a sport,

are now eligible. Not only _____ athletes

can compete in the _____.

See your gym coach for entry forms.

bowling
volleyball
tennis
skiing
swimming
professional
amateur
basketball
competition
football
golf
hockey
skin diving
track
skating
soccer
baseball
champion
cycling
Olympics

Commas

Use commas in a friendly letter:

- to separate the day from the year in the heading,

    February 4, 199__

- after the person's name in the greeting,

    Dear Bob,

- after the last word in the closing.

    Yours truly,

★ Rewrite the friendly letters below, adding commas to the date, greeting, and closing. Correct the misspelled words in each letter.

April 15 199__

Dear Martha

I am planning a trip to Boston soon. It has been so long since we got together, I thought this would be a good time to do so. What would be a good day? Will it be possible for us to play tenis or gulf during my visit?

Please drop a note or call. I look forward to seeing you!

Your friend
Alicia

May 5 199__

Dear Alicia

I'm so pleased that you're coming to visit. How about the first weekend in June?

We can certainly plan lots of time for sports. As you know, swiming and skatting have always been my favorites. Oh, speaking of sports, you'll be interested to learn that my brother is going to become a profesional baskitball player.

See you soon, fellow amatuer athlete!

Sincerely
Martha

WORDS AT WORK

Challenge Yourself

referee   umpire   rookie   scoreboard

Use your Spelling Dictionary to answer these questions. Then write sentences showing that you understand the meaning of each Challenge Word.

1. At a football game, what can you look at to find out the score?

2. Who makes sure that each team's baseball players follow the rules during a game?

3. Who makes sure that soccer and basketball players follow the rules during a game?

4. What is a nickname that is often given to a new player on a sports team?

Write to the Point

Choose two of the pairs of sports below. For each pair write a sentence or two about how the sports are similar and different. If you wish, you may create other pairs, such as golf/bowling or swimming/track. Use spelling words from this lesson in your comparisons.

tennis/volleyball   baseball/basketball
ice-skating/skiing   swimming/skin diving

Challenge Use one or more of the Challenge Words in your comparisons.

Proofreading

Use the proofreading marks to show the errors in the paragraph below. Write the five misspelled words correctly in the blanks.

◯	word is misspelled
≡	letter should be capitalized
∧	word is missing

Everyone in my family is an amatuer athlete. Dad swims and plays gulf, and mom loves sking. I play basket ball, and my sister leona the star of her trak team. Maybe someday one of us will be in the olympics! Maybe one of us will even become a professional some day!

1. _____

2. _____

3. _____

4. _____

5. _____

Lesson 24 Words in Review

A. compass

flood

rough

judge

B. fault

often

fought

all right

awful

daughter

C. clue

shoe

lose

loose

truth

whom

juice

D. avoid

choice

destroy

★ You will need a piece of paper for these review activities.

1. In Lesson 19 you studied four different ways to spell /ŭ/: **u, o, ou, oo.** Write the words in list A.

_____ _____

_____ _____

2. In Lesson 20 you studied five different ways to spell /ô/: **aw, au, ou, a, o.** Write the words in list B.

_____ _____

_____ _____

★ 3. Look up each review word from lists A and B in the Spelling Dictionary. Divide each word into syllables.

4. In Lesson 21 you studied seven different ways to spell /o͞o/: **oo, o—e, ue, ui, u, oe, o.** Write the words in list C.

_____ _____ _____

_____ _____ _____

_____

5. In Lesson 22 you studied two different ways to spell /oi/: **oy, oi .** Write the words in list D.

_____ _____

★ 6. Use each review word from lists C and D in a sentence.

Your teacher may give you a test. Answer these questions when you have finished.

7. Did you spell all the words correctly? _____

8. Did you leave out a letter? _____

9. Did you write the wrong letter? _____

10. Did you miss the spelling of a vowel sound? _____

130

Writer's Workshop

A Description

When you write a description, you picture something in your mind and then use words to help your reader see or imagine the same thing. A description can do more than tell what something looks like. It can also tell how something sounds, feels, smells, or tastes. To appeal to readers' senses, writers choose the most vivid details of the thing they are describing and use words that describe those details as closely as possible. Here is Mark's description of the ocean.

The Ocean

The ocean was huge. It stretched as far as I could see. White gulls soared above it in the blue sky. The water was green and shining like glass, and the waves rolled and sparkled in the sun. They rumbled and roared as they crashed against the rocks. When the waves reached the shore, they slapped and splashed against the sand, bursting into white foam. Walking into the water, I felt the slippery seaweed and the rough pebbles under my feet. Little waves smacked gently against my legs. The icy water cooled me, and I breathed in its fishy scent. When I licked my lips, I tasted salt water.

To write his description, Mark followed the steps in the writing process. He used a senses web as a **Prewriting** activity. The web helped Mark think of words and phrases that describe the ocean. Once he had completed his web, he decided which details to use in his description. Part of Mark's senses web is shown here. Study what Mark did.

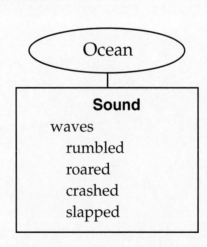

Ocean

Sound
waves
  rumbled
  roared
  crashed
  slapped

Get ready to write your own description. Choose an object or a place that is very familiar to you and that you would enjoy describing. After you have decided what to write about, make a senses web. Then follow the other steps in the writing process—**Writing, Revising, Proofreading,** and **Publishing.**

Lesson 25 Words with /ô/

Listen for /ô/ in each word.

adore

shore

before

wore

score

tore

export

perform

fortunate

orchard

import

important

quarrel

reward

warn

toward

court

course

roar

board

1. Which word begins with the letters <u>sh</u>?

   _____

2. Write the five words that begin with a vowel.

   _____ _____

   _____ _____

   _____

3. Which two words begin with /k/? Circle the letter that spells /k/. _____ _____

4. Which word begins with /sk/? Circle the letters that spell /sk/. _____

5. Which word begins with /kw/? Circle the letters that spell /kw/. _____

6. Which three words have the same spelling of /ô/ as <u>qu</u>arrel? _____ _____

   _____

7. Which two words have the same spelling of /ô/ as <u>soar</u>?

   _____ _____

8. Which word begins with the letters <u>per</u>?

   _____

9. Which word begins and ends like <u>believe</u>?

   _____

10. Which word begins and ends like <u>telephone</u>?

    _____

11. Which word begins with the letter <u>f</u>? _____

12. Which word is pronounced exactly like <u>war</u>?

    _____

13. Write the word in which /r/ is spelled <u>rr</u>.

    _____

132

Checkpoint

Write a spelling word for each clue.
Then use the Checkpoint Study Plan on page 224.

1. The opposite of after is ____.

2. A loud yell is a ____.

3. The opposite of hate is ____.

4. Another word for ripped is ____.

5. The route taken or the path followed is the ____.

6. The winner is the one with the highest ____.

7. If you act in a play, then you ____.

8. A river has a bank, a sea has a ____.

9. Today I wear, last week I ____.

10. The opposite of unlucky is ____.

11. Tennis is played on a ____.

12. In the direction of means ____.

13. If you find my lost cat, I'll give you a ____.

14. These apples come from an ____.

15. An argument is a ____.

16. A piece of wood is a ____.

17. Something really needed is something ____.

18. To alert to danger is to ____.

19. Sometimes two words that have the same base word are antonyms. This is because they contain prefixes that have opposite meanings. Both mystery words have the base word *portare*. *Portare* meant carry in Latin. The first mystery word begins with the Latin prefix *im*. *Im* meant into. *Importare* meant to carry in. Can you guess this mystery word? ____

20. The other mystery word begins with the Latin prefix *ex*. *Ex* meant away from. *Exportare* meant to carry out. Can you guess this word? ____

Use each list word once.

The Daily Herald

SCIENTIST'S NEW DISCOVERY

Mr. Ivor Gott, who works for the Sigh Ents Company, has discovered a formula that improves the memory.

"With this pill," explained Mr. Gott, "you can remember just about anything."

Mr. Gott says he got the idea for his formula while looking at the ocean. "I was walking along the _____. I just _____ the sea. I forget exactly when it was. I forget how I worked it out, but it's written in my notes somewhere. Or maybe I _____ that page out."

Ms. Selma Gradey, President of the Sigh Ents Company, said, "We couldn't be more pleased with Mr. Gott's idea. For years, our major business has been to _____ toothpicks from other countries. Then we _____ them to other places. But now we'll be famous."

Can the formula do any harm? Mr. Gott told us, "We did lots of tests, but I forget what the results were."

FLEAS FLEE FLUE'S FLEA CIRCUS

Ten performing fleas escaped from Flue's Fabulous Flea Circus last night. "The fleas were just about ready to _____ the most _____ part of their act. That's the part where they jump off a tiny diving _____," Mr. Flue said. "Just _____ they began, a dog came into the hall. Before I knew it, my fleas were rushing _____ the dog. That was the last time I saw them."

When the fleas landed on it, the dog made a noise between a howl and a _____. Then the dog raced out of the room. It was last seen near the apple _____ on the Edgeware farm. No one seems to know the dog, even though it _____ a collar. Mr. Flue is offering a $25 _____ for the return of his fleas.

"Those fleas are very unusual," he explained. "They were brought here by an explorer. I was _____ to get them. Of _____, I'll organize a search party, but I fear the worst. I may have to find a new source of income."

SPORTS

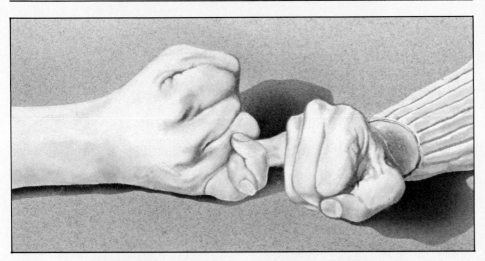

LOWE HIGH WINS TITLE

Lowe High School won the city pinky wrestling championship, but it was a rough match. The match was held on Lowe High's basketball _____. It was attended by several noisy fans. During the match, an argument broke out. The referee had to _____ the fans not to _____.The final _____ was tied, 1-1, but Lowe's rival decided to let Lowe have the title, so that its team could go home.

adore
shore
before
wore
score
tore
export
perform
fortunate
orchard
import
important
quarrel
reward
warn
toward
court
course
roar
board

Multiple Spellings

A dictionary is a good place to look for correct spellings of words. Some words have two acceptable spellings. The more common spelling is listed first.

ax or **axe** |ăks| *n.*, *pl.* **ax·es** |ăk'sĭz|. A chopping or cutting tool consisting of a head with a sharp blade, mounted on a long handle.

light-year |līt'yīr'| *n.* Also **light year.** A measure of distance equal to the distance light travels through empty space in a year; about 5.878 trillion (5.878 × 10^{12}) miles.

★ In the sentences below, one or two of the words in parentheses are misspelled. Write each sentence with the more common spelling of the word in parentheses. If the word has another acceptable spelling in the parentheses, write the other spelling after the sentence. Check your choices in the Spelling Dictionary.

1. Joan likes to wash the dishes (befor, bifore, before) she watches her favorite television program. _____

2. Michael will (perform, prefrom, purform) at the piano recital. _____

3. The young reporter wrote such a good story that he got his first (byline, by line, by-line). _____

4. Ray is sorry that he had such a bad (quarel, quarrel, quarrle) with his sister. _____

5. Davida wants to mow the lawn, but the (lawnmower, lawn mower, lawn-mower) is broken. _____

6. We could finish building our tree house if we had just one more (bored, board, bord). _____

WORDS AT WORK

Challenge Yourself

pore   furor   resourceful   distort

Write what you think each underlined Challenge Word means. Check your Spelling Dictionary to see if you were right. Then write sentences showing that you understand the meaning of each Challenge Word.

1. You sweat through the <u>pores</u> in your skin.

2. The crowd was in a <u>furor</u> because their favorite band never showed up for the concert.

3. A <u>resourceful</u> student uses library books to find and check facts.

4. A mirror that is bent or cracked can <u>distort</u> your image.

Write to the Point

Imagine you are a reporter for <u>The Daily Herald</u>. Write another funny news article like the ones you read on pages 134 and 135. Choose any subject that you might find in a real newspaper, such as sports, weather, science, and important events. Then have some fun with it. Use spelling words from this lesson in your news article.

Challenge Use one or more of the Challenge Words in your article.

Proofreading

Use the proofreading marks to show the errors in the paragraph below. Write the five misspelled words correctly in the blanks.

◯	word is misspelled
⊙	period is missing
/	letter should be lower case

The Newspaper said that Dr. G.Y. Nott made an importent Discovery He found that people who woar funny hats usually didn't kwarrel with each other Of coarse, this makes me feel fortunat. I adore funny hats!

1. _____

2. _____

3. _____

4. _____

5. _____

Lesson 26 Words with /û/

Listen for /û/ in each word.

certain

service

perfect

permit

perfume

personal

dirty

thirteen

firm

skirt

third

earn

early

learning

heard

pearl

purpose

furnish

hurt

furniture

1. Write the two words that begin with the letters th.

   _____ _____

2. Which word begins with a vowel and ends with a consonant? _____

3. Which three words begin with the letter f? First write the word that has one syllable. Then write the word that has two syllables. Write the word that has three syllables last. _____ _____

   _____

4. Which word begins with /s/ but isn't spelled with the letter s? _____

5. Which word begins and ends like hard? _____

6. Which word begins and ends with /s/? _____

7. Which two words begin with the letter p and end with the letter l? _____ _____

8. Which two words begin with the letter p and end with the letter e? _____ _____

9. Which two words begin with the letter p and end with the letter t? _____ _____

10. Write the other two words that end with the letter t.

    _____ _____

11. Which word ends with ing? _____

12. Which two words end with /ē/? Circle the letter that spells /ē/. _____ _____

13. Write the word that ends with the letters sh.

    _____

Checkpoint

Write a spelling word for each clue.
Then use the Checkpoint Study Plan on page 224.

1. Something often worn with a blouse is a ____.

2. Another word for allow is ____.

3. The opposite of clean is ____.

4. Another word for sure is ____.

5. Two is to second as three is to ____.

6. The act of helping or assisting others is ____.

7. Another word for solid or hard is ____.

8. To fill a room with chairs, tables, and shelves is to ____.

9. Something without any mistakes or flaws is ____.

10. An apple is a kind of fruit, a chair is a piece of ____.

11. To be given money for working is to ____ a living.

12. It wasn't an accident, it was on ____.

13. Another word for a pleasing scent is ____.

14. Twelve comes before ____.

15. A kind of jewel is a ____.

16. The opposite of late is ____.

17. My diary is private and ____.

18. If you listened, you ____ the bell.

19. Education and instruction are part of ____.

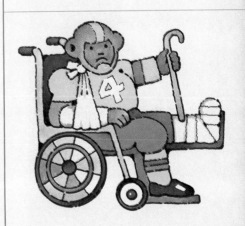

20. This word comes from an old German word, *hurten*. *Hurten* meant to butt like a ram. The French borrowed this word. In Old French it meant to strike or knock. Then the English took the word. In Old English it meant to strike. Today its meaning has changed. It does not mean to strike or hit. But it tells what sometimes happens as a result of being struck or hit. Today, it means a wound or injury. Can you guess the word?____

139

Use each list word once.

A Pearl of a Problem

Every time our family tells "remember when" stories, the story of Mom's missing ring is _____ to come up. That afternoon Mom was getting ready to roast a chicken and bake a pumpkin pie. She put an apron on over her new _____, took off her beautiful _____ ring, and laid it on the kitchen table. Just then the doorbell rang, and our neighbor came in. She likes to _____ extra money selling _____ and soap to her friends.

When the neighbor left, Mom started supper. I _____ someone at the front door. It was the delivery man with a new piece of _____ that Mom and Dad had bought. I showed him where to put it and went upstairs to write in my _____ diary. I have a _____ rule: I don't _____ anyone to read my diary but me!

A little while later my brother Jake came home with some friends from the school band. They began practicing. One boy was so bad that I began to count his mistakes. He made _____ mistakes in one song. My ears began to _____. I complained to Mom, but she said, "They're only _____, dear. And if you're finished with your diary, you can help in the kitchen."

140

It was after I started washing the _____ dishes that Mom noticed her ring was gone. We looked on the table, on the floor, in the sink, and everywhere. Mom was really upset. Dad had given her the ring for their anniversary. She kept saying, "I'm sure no one took it on _____. Someone must be playing a joke."

We had dinner _____ that night. I dished out the chicken and dressing. Jake laughed and said, "Now that's what I call _____."

Then we all tried to solve the mystery. But no one could _____ any clues. We couldn't believe that one of the people there that day took the ring.

We finished dinner, and Mom brought in dessert. The pumpkin pie was _____. I had eaten all my lima beans to make sure that I'd be allowed a big slice. Mom gave the first piece to me and the second to my brother. She gave the _____ piece to Dad. We all started eating. Then Dad yelled, "Ouch!" He put his hand to his mouth and out came the pearl ring. We all cheered. And Dad got another piece of pie.

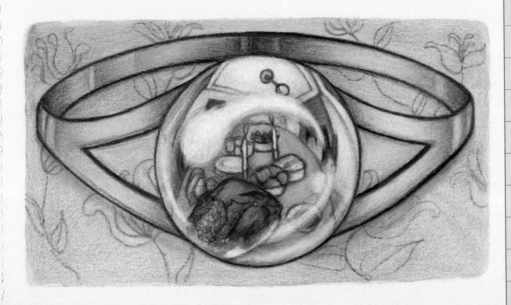

141

certain
service
perfect
permit
perfume
personal
dirty
thirteen
firm
skirt
third
earn
early
learning
heard
pearl
purpose
furnish
hurt
furniture

Adjectives

An adjective describes a noun or pronoun by telling what kind, how many, or which one.

> A *colorful* bird was singing in the *old* tree.
> A *big, fat* cat scared it away.

⭐ Write each sentence below, correcting each misspelled word. Then underline the adjectives.

1. I'm sertain today will be a beautiful, cool day.

2. I herd there is a fantastic movie downtown.

3. The earyl bird catches the worm.

4. My perpus is to get a good grade on my report.

5. We made new ferniture for the tree house.

6. I'd like to fernish my dark room with large, bright posters.

7. I hert my foot when I dropped the heavy suitcase.

8. Jennifer wants a perl necklace for her birthday.

9. That is the purfect costume for the wicked king in the play.

10. Karen wore a wool skert.

Challenge Yourself

conserve   absurd   earthenware   virtual

Use your Spelling Dictionary to answer these questions. Then write sentences showing that you understand the meaning of each Challenge Word.

1. Do taking short showers and turning off the water while you brush your teeth help to <u>conserve</u> our water?

2. Would it be <u>absurd</u> to ride a bicycle while wearing ice skates or flippers on your feet?

3. Are cars and airplanes made out of <u>earthenware</u>?

4. Is a <u>virtual</u> fact a completely true fact?

Write to the Point

Do your family members like to retell any "remember when" stories about something funny or interesting that happened in the family? Put one of these stories into writing. Try to show your reader what made the story worth remembering. Use spelling words from this lesson in your story.

Challenge Use one or more of the Challenge Words in your story.

Proofreading

Use the proofreading marks to show the errors in the paragraph below. Write the five misspelled words correctly in the blanks.

◯	word is misspelled
≡	letter should be capitalized
⋀	exclamation point is missing

When Kate was thurteen, she did extra chores around the house to earn money. Her perpose was to buy grandma Rita a surtain kind of pirfume. The day she bought it, her baby brother spilled the whole bottle on her skurt. Good grief What a stink

1. _____

2. _____

3. _____

4. _____

5. _____

Lesson 27 Words with /â/ and /ä/

Listen for /â/ or /ä/ in each word.

aware

prepare

fare

stare

carefully

bare

declare

compare

square

share

discharge

harvest

alarm

farther

marbles

apartment

charge

starve

margin

depart

1. Which word begins with the letters ch?

_____

2. Which word begins with the letters sh?

_____

3. Write the two words that begin with the letter f.

_____ _____

4. Write the three words that begin with the letter d.

_____

_____

_____

5. Which three words begin with a vowel? Circle the word that has a suffix. _____

_____ _____

6. Write two words that begin with the letters st and one that ends with st. _____

_____ _____

7. Which word begins with /skw/? _____

8. Write the two words that begin with /k/.

_____ _____

9. Which word begins with the letters pre?

_____

10. Which word is pronounced exactly like bear?

11. Which word is pronounced exactly like fair?

_____

12. Write the three words in which you hear /j/ but don't see the letter j.

_____ _____

13. Which word ends with /z/? _____

Checkpoint

Write a spelling word for each clue.
Then use the Checkpoint Study Plan on page 224.

1. The opposite of arrive is ＿＿.

2. With great care means ＿＿.

3. A shape with four equal sides is a ＿＿.

4. To warn people, sound the ＿＿.

5. To let go or fire is to ＿＿.

6. The price of a bus ride is the ＿＿.

7. I live in a house, she lives in an ＿＿.

8. To get ready is to ＿＿.

9. To show how things are alike is to ＿＿.

10. The person who doesn't eat will ＿＿.

11. If you know about something then you are ＿＿ of it.

12. Little glass balls are ＿＿.

13. To or at a greater distance is ＿＿.

14. In the winter most trees are ＿＿.

15. What was the ＿＿ for fixing the bicycle?

16. A portion or a part of is a ＿＿.

17. The border of a page is the ＿＿.

18. To announce is to ＿＿.

19. To look steadily for a long time is to ＿＿.

20. Have you ever heard of a harrow? A harrow is a farm tool. It is used to break up lumps of earth. The harrow shares a common word history with our mystery word. They both come from the Viking word *harfr*. The German word for autumn, *herbst*, is also related to *harfr*. What do a harrow and autumn have in common with our mystery word? The mystery word names the act of gathering crops. A harrow is used to plow. Autumn is the time when crops are gathered. Can you guess the mystery word? ＿＿

145

Use each list word once.

THE BROADWAY LIMITED

"All aboard for the Broadway Limited to Chicago!"
Every day at 2:45 P.M., the conductor in New York's
Penn Station gives the final call. The train to Chicago is
about to leave.

You've paid your _____. You check your baggage
_____ to make sure you haven't
forgotten anything. Then you get on board, and you
_____ yourself for the 18-hour trip ahead.
You unpack the snacks you've brought so you won't
_____ before dinner. You've even brought
enough to _____ with the other passengers. And
you set your _____ clock so you can wake up
early tomorrow morning. The conductor comes by and
punches holes in the _____ of your ticket. As
she moves on, she asks some children not to play with their
_____ in the aisle. Then you settle back in
your seat without a care in the world. (There's an extra
_____ for a bed, so you've taken a coach seat.)

As you _____ from New York, you ride
in a tunnel under the Hudson River. When you come out in
New Jersey, you can see New York's offices and the tall
_____ buildings. As the train rolls
_____ away from New York, factories give

way to hills and woods. In the winter, the trees will look cold and _____. At first you _____ at the scenery and _____ the different areas of New Jersey and Pennsylvania. You become _____ of hills and flatlands, farms and cities. In some cities, the train stops to take on and _____ passengers and freight.

As you go farther west into Ohio, you see lots of farms. Each field looks like a _____ in a giant patchwork quilt. If it's _____ time, you can watch as big machines cut the crops.

By this time, it's dark, and soon you fall asleep as the train speeds west through Ohio and Indiana. You wake up early, and you hear the conductor _____ that the next stop is Gary, Indiana. Soon you can see the big steel-manufacturing town. By this time, you're almost in Chicago. And at 9:00 A.M. you arrive. You've traveled more than 700 miles in 18 hours, and you've seen a big piece of the United States.

aware
prepare
fare
stare
carefully
bare
declare
compare
square
share
discharge
harvest
alarm
farther
marbles
apartment
charge
starve
margin
depart

Capitals

Follow all the rules for capitalizing when you write a friendly letter. In addition, follow these rules for the heading, greeting, and closing.

HEADING: Capitalize the month of the year.
GREETING: Capitalize dear and the person's name.
CLOSING: Capitalize the first word of the closing.

Greeting

Heading

April 5, 199____

Dear Sean,

   How would you like to go on vacation with me? Mother said I could ask you to come along on our Florida trip.
   Give the idea some thought and call me next week.

Your pal,

Closing

Paul

⭐ Rewrite the friendly letter below, filling the blanks with these spelling words. Put capital letters where necessary.

carefully   apartment   charge   square   aware
starve   compare   bare   share   declare

september 14, 199____

dear cathy,

   i was never _____ of how expensive _____ living can be! my cupboards are so _____, i am sure to _____ before the week is done. perhaps i should _____ myself poor and return home. i'll have to consider my choices _____.

   my best bet is to find someone to help _____ my rent. i could _____ her half of the monthly expenses. and, if i can find a roommate whose cooking doesn't _____ with mine, i'm sure to get a _____ meal!

   write soon.

your big sister,

jeannie

WORDS AT WORK

Challenge Yourself

bearable   precarious   pecan   sparse

Write what you think each underlined Challenge Word means. Check your Spelling Dictionary to see if you were right. Then write sentences showing that you understand the meaning of each Challenge Word.

1. The aspirin didn't stop the pain, but it made it more <u>bearable</u>.

2. Standing at the top of the wobbly ladder, he was in a <u>precarious</u> position.

3. A <u>pecan</u> looks something like a walnut but with a smooth shell.

4. The grass that used to cover the yard like a thick carpet now grows in <u>sparse</u> patches.

Write to the Point

Think about a trip you have taken and write a description of the different sights you saw along the way. You may describe things you saw on a short trip, such as a bus ride to school or to someone's house. Or you might describe sights you saw on a longer trip to another city, state, or country. Use spelling words from this lesson in your description.

Challenge Use one or more of the Challenge Words in your description.

Proofreading

Use the proofreading marks to show the errors in the paragraph below. Write the five misspelled words correctly in the blanks.

⬭	word is misspelled
⟋	take out word
?ᨆ	question mark is missing

Have you have been to the desert
The farthur we traveled, the more awair
I became of its beauty. It is bear of trees,
but nothing can compair to it. I took
some pictures to share with with you.
Sunday we deppart for home.

1. _____

2. _____

3. _____

4. _____

5. _____

Lesson 28 Compound Words

Say each word.

hallway

strawberry

thunderstorm

birthday

cheeseburger

nightmare

upset

cartwheel

flashlight

notebook

chalkboard

grasshopper

suitcase

uproar

homework

blueberry

sawdust

breakfast

weekend

sailboat

1. Write the three words that begin with the letter b.

_____ _____

_____

2. Write the four words that begin with the letter s.

_____ _____

_____ _____

3. Which word begins with the letters th?

_____

4. Write the two words that begin with the letters ch.

_____ _____

5. Write one word that begins with /k/ and two that end with /k/. Circle the letters that spell /k/.

_____ _____

_____

6. Which word begins with the letter w? _____

7. Which two words begin with the letter n?

_____ _____

8. Which word begins and ends like flight? _____

9. Which two words end with the ay spelling of /ā/?

_____ _____

10. In which two words do you hear /o͞o/? Circle the letters that spell /o͞o/. _____ _____

11. Which word has two pairs of double consonants?

_____

12. Write the two compound words made with each of these words: berry, up.

_____ _____

150

Checkpoint

Write a spelling word for each clue.
Then use the Checkpoint Study Plan on page 224.

1. A bad dream is a ____.

2. To flip over on your hands is to do a ____.

3. To overturn or tip over is to ____.

4. Saturday and Sunday make up the ____.

5. Pack your clothes into your ____.

6. Noisy excitement and confusion make an ____.

7. A kind of insect is a ____.

8. Heavy rain with thunder and lightning is a ____.

9. In class you need a pencil and a ____.

10. When you celebrate your age, it is your ____.

11. The morning meal is ____.

12. From sawed wood comes ____.

13. Pink ice cream may be ____.

14. A boat moved by wind is a ____.

15. Schoolwork done at home is ____.

16. A corridor is a ____.

17. A fruit that's blue is a ____.

18. A slate is a ____.

19. A hamburger with melted cheese is a ____.

20. The English use different words from Americans for some things. For instance, what we call the hood of a car, the English call a bonnet. What we call an elevator, the English call a lift. The English word <u>torch</u> names a small electric light that we call by a very different name. This name is a compound with the word <u>light</u>. Can you guess it? ____

STORMY WEATHER

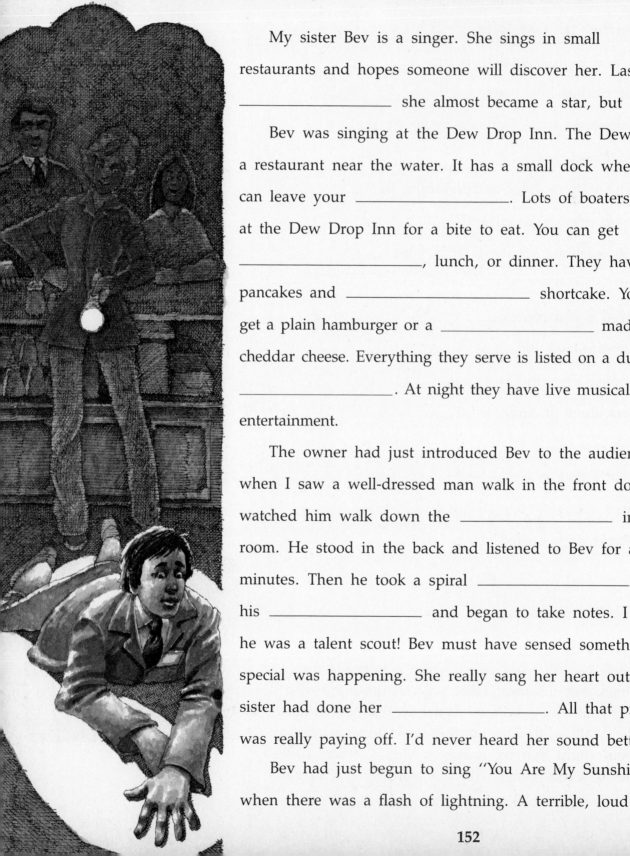

My sister Bev is a singer. She sings in small restaurants and hopes someone will discover her. Last _____ she almost became a star, but . . .

Bev was singing at the Dew Drop Inn. The Dew Drop is a restaurant near the water. It has a small dock where you can leave your _____. Lots of boaters stop at the Dew Drop Inn for a bite to eat. You can get _____, lunch, or dinner. They have great pancakes and _____ shortcake. You can get a plain hamburger or a _____ made with cheddar cheese. Everything they serve is listed on a dusty _____. At night they have live musical entertainment.

The owner had just introduced Bev to the audience when I saw a well-dressed man walk in the front door. I watched him walk down the _____ into the room. He stood in the back and listened to Bev for a few minutes. Then he took a spiral _____ out of his _____ and began to take notes. I realized he was a talent scout! Bev must have sensed something special was happening. She really sang her heart out. My sister had done her _____. All that practicing was really paying off. I'd never heard her sound better.

Bev had just begun to sing "You Are My Sunshine" when there was a flash of lightning. A terrible, loud

152

_____ was under way. Within a few seconds the lights went out. Bev just kept singing, "You are my sunshine, my only sunshine . . ." Everyone was laughing. There was quite an _____. The talent scout tried to move closer to the stage to hear Bev. In the dark, he bumped into a chair and slipped in the _____ that covered the floor. Someone had just lit a _____ and you could see the man's long legs go out from under him. He looked like a _____ doing a _____. The man was still on the floor when the lights went on. The audience couldn't stop laughing.

I went over to Bev to tell her about the scout (Bev had wisely stopped singing by this time). She ran over to help the scout and to try to talk to him. The man said, "This has been a _____. I want to forget this place, forget you, and forget every song with the word 'sunshine.'" He was out the door before Bev could reply.

As you can imagine, Bev was very _____. But my sister's a trooper. The next night she was back on stage, even though she had changed her act. Her best number was "Stormy Weather"!

hallway
strawberry
thunderstorm
birthday
cheeseburger
nightmare
upset
cartwheel
flashlight
notebook
chalkboard
grasshopper
suitcase
uproar
homework
blueberry
sawdust
breakfast
weekend
sailboat

Finding Correct Spellings

Sometimes a dictionary is used to find the meaning of a word or the proper pronunciation. Other times, it is used to check on the spelling of a word.

> **sail·boat** | sāl′bōt′ | *n.* A boat that travels by wind blowing against its sails.

saleboat? sialboat? sailboat?

⭐ Kent wants to write a letter to a friend. He is not sure how to spell some words, so he has written three choices for them. Write the sentences with the correct spelling. Check your answers in the Spelling Dictionary, and write the page number for each word.

1. For a (berthday, burthday, birthday) present, I was given a trip.

2. When I found out, I could have turned a (kartwhel, cartwheel, cart wheel).

3. I was to go away for the (weakend, wekend, weekend) with my friends.

4. I can't say that anyone was (upset, upsit, up set) with the idea!

5. As a matter of fact, the prospect of no (hoamwork, homework, homeworc) didn't worry me at all!

6. Once I packed my (suitcase, sootcase, sootkase), I couldn't wait.

7. First Dad insisted that I have (brakefast, brecfast, breakfast).

8. I finished my (blewberry, blueberry, bluberry) muffin and was on my way at last!

WORDS AT WORK

Challenge Yourself

sweatshirt   tablespoon

roommate   handmade

Use your Spelling Dictionary to answer these questions. Then write sentences showing that you understand the meaning of each Challenge Word.

1. What is one kind of measuring tool that you can find in most people's kitchen?

2. What piece of clothing might keep you warm on a chilly day?

3. What word might describe a sweater knitted by a person at home?

4. What person might you share a room with?

Write to the Point

A restaurant review is an article that tells what the writer likes and dislikes about a restaurant. Write your own review of a real or an imaginary restaurant. Tell what you liked and disliked about the food and how it was served. Use spelling words from this lesson in your review.

Challenge Use one or more of the Challenge Words in your review.

Proofreading

Use the proofreading marks to show the errors in the paragraph below. Write the five misspelled words correctly in the blanks.

The day I turned ten, Mom took me out brekkfast at the Dew Drop Inn. What a nightmair! The bluberry pancakes were as dry as saudust, and the strawbury jam tasted like glue. Then all the waiters came out and sang "Happy birthday" me.

word is misspelled	⬭
letter should be capitalized	≡
word is missing	∧

1. _____

2. _____

3. _____

4. _____

5. _____

Lesson 29 Space Words

Say each word.

revolution

celestial

solar

astronomy

comet

motion

galaxy

axis

meteors

universe

light-year

rotation

eclipse

telescope

asteroids

satellite

lunar

shuttle

constellation

orbit

1. Write the two words that begin with the letter <u>m</u>.

   _____ _____

2. Which word begins with /sh/? _____

3. Which three words begin with /s/? _____

   _____ _____

4. Which three words begin and end with a vowel?

   _____ _____

   _____

5. Which three words begin with a vowel and end with a

   consonant? _____ _____

   _____

6. In which words do you hear /o͞o/? Circle the letter that

   spells /o͞o/. _____ _____

7. Which word begins and ends like <u>comfort</u>?

   _____

8. Which word begins and ends like <u>telephone</u>?

   _____

9. Which two words begin and end like <u>relaxation</u>?

   _____ _____

10. Which word has a hyphen? _____

11. Write the words in which a double consonant spells

    one sound.

    ll _____ ll _____

    tt _____

12. Which two words end with /ē/? Circle the letter that

    spells /ē/. _____ _____

13. Write the word in which the letters <u>ti</u> spell /ch/, not /sh/.

    _____

156

Checkpoint

Write a spelling word for each clue.
Then use the Checkpoint Study Plan on page 224.

1. Look at the stars through a ____.

2. A kind of spacecraft is a space ____.

3. Light or heat from the sun is ____ heat.

4. If the moon blocks the sun, there is an ____.

5. To rotate once means to make a ____.

6. A measurement of distance in space is a ____.

7. The Big Dipper is a ____.

8. All matter and space make up the ____.

9. Solid fragments from space are ____.

10. To revolve around the sun once means to make a ____.

11. The path of a planet around the sun is its ____.

12. Of the moon is the meaning of ____.

13. Something related to the sky is ____.

14. Another word for movement is ____.

15. The study of heavenly bodies is ____.

16. A heavenly body with a long tail is a ____.

17. A large collection of stars is a ____.

18. The earth turns on its ____.

19. The moon is the earth's ____.

20. This word names any of the many small planets between Mars and Jupiter. These small planets look like stars. Their name comes from the Greek words *astēr* and *eīdos*. *Astēr* meant star. *Eīdos* meant form. When these two words were put together they looked like this: *asteroeidēs*. *Asteroeidēs* meant star-like. Can you guess what these planets are called? ____

157

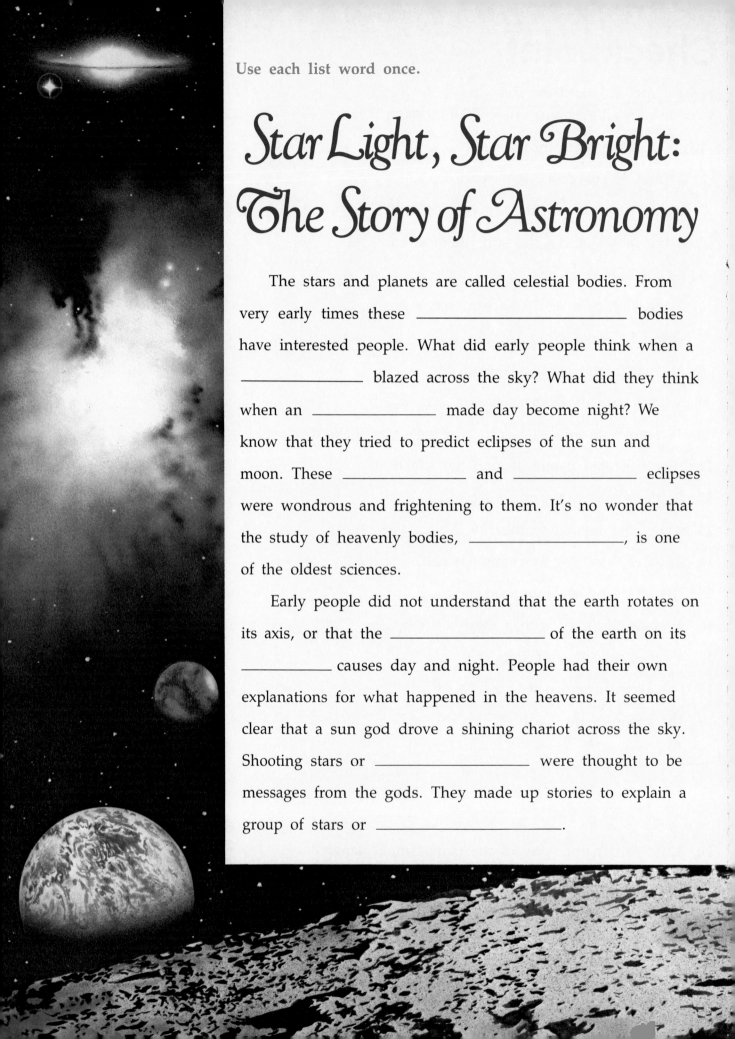

Star Light, Star Bright: The Story of Astronomy

The stars and planets are called celestial bodies. From very early times these _____ bodies have interested people. What did early people think when a _____ blazed across the sky? What did they think when an _____ made day become night? We know that they tried to predict eclipses of the sun and moon. These _____ and _____ eclipses were wondrous and frightening to them. It's no wonder that the study of heavenly bodies, _____, is one of the oldest sciences.

Early people did not understand that the earth rotates on its axis, or that the _____ of the earth on its _____ causes day and night. People had their own explanations for what happened in the heavens. It seemed clear that a sun god drove a shining chariot across the sky. Shooting stars or _____ were thought to be messages from the gods. They made up stories to explain a group of stars or _____.

Early Greeks, however, had some surprisingly correct ideas about the heavens. Two men stand out. Thales is the man we call the father of astronomy. He observed that the moon moved in an _____ around the earth. He thought that the whole universe was always in _____. Pythagoras is another Greek who knew much about the stars. He believed that the earth was not the center of the _____. We know now that the earth revolves around the sun. But thousands of years ago, the idea of the _____ of the earth around the sun caused many fights!

Most people continued to believe that the sun and stars moved around the earth until the _____ proved that idea wrong. With the telescope, people such as Galileo and Copernicus were able to prove Pythagoras was right! The moon was the only _____ that circled the earth.

Technology improved our knowledge. New tools made it possible for scientists to gather new facts. They were able to watch the many _____ between Mars and Jupiter. When astronomers realized the huge distances between stars, a _____ became a way to measure space.

We are already used to having people on the moon. The day when you can hop on an intergalactic space _____ and visit another _____ may not be far away.

revolution
celestial
solar
astronomy
comet
motion
galaxy
axis
meteors
universe
light-year
rotation
eclipse
telescope
asteroids
satellite
lunar
shuttle
constellation
orbit

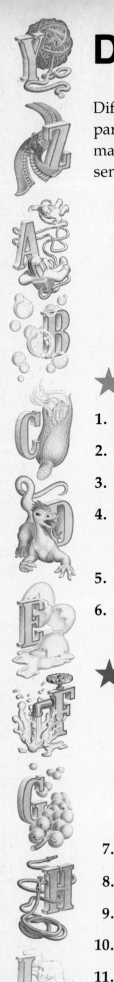

Dictionaries

Different dictionaries show entry words and definitions in different ways. The part of speech may be listed before or after the definition. The sound spelling may be set off in parentheses ( ) or in slashes: / / or │ │. Sometimes example sentences are given. Sometimes a picture helps illustrate the meaning.

A.

eclipse The disappearance of the sun or moon behind another heavenly body.

e•clipse (ĭ klĭps′) *n., plural* **eclipses.**

B.

eclipse
Total eclipse of the sun.

e•clipse │ĭ klĭps′│ *n.* **1. a.** The blocking by another celestial body of part or all of the light that reaches an observer from a given celestial body. **b.** The time during which such a blocking occurs. **2.** A decline; downfall: *His fame has suffered an eclipse.* —*v.* **e•clipsed, e•clips•ing. 1.** To block the light of: *as one of a pair of binary stars eclipses the other.* **2.** To obscure or overshadow the importance, fame, or reputation of; reduce in importance by comparison: *This news eclipses everything. Columbus was destined to eclipse his fellow navigators completely.* [SEE PICTURE]

★ Study these two dictionary entries. Then answer the questions.

1. Is the entry word the same for each of the entries? _____

2. What is the entry word? _____

3. Which entry contains example sentences? _____

4. Where is the part of speech shown in example A? _____

   in example B? _____

5. Which entry has a picture? _____

6. Which entry has the longer definition? _____

★ Put these words in alphabetical order. Then look up each word in two different dictionaries and make notes about the differences you find.

solar   **galaxy**   **axis**   **comet**   **lunar**

Word	Dictionary Notes
7. _____	_____
8. _____	_____
9. _____	_____
10. _____	_____
11. _____	_____

160

Challenge Yourself

hemisphere   cosmos   velocity   aurora

Decide which Challenge Word fits each clue. Check your Spelling Dictionary to see if you were right. Then write sentences showing that you understand the meaning of each Challenge Word.

1. These lights are a beautiful sight to see in the night sky.

2. Everything in the universe is a part of this.

3. This is what each half of the earth is called.

4. How long it takes you to get somewhere depends on the distance you are traveling and this.

Write to the Point

Write an explanation like the ancient Greeks did for an event or thing in nature, such as "Why the Sun Sets" or "Why There Are Stars in the Sky." Make up a creative explanation. Use spelling words from this lesson in your explanation.

Challenge Use one or more of the Challenge Words in your explanation.

Proofreading

Use the proofreading marks to show the errors in the paragraph below. Write the five misspelled words correctly in the blanks.

⬯	word is misspelled
⊙	period is missing
≡	letter should be capitalized

As her small ship easily left the orbet of Mars, the captain looked through her telascope to view the distant galaxy. This new univers was many light-years away, and captain Yee feared that the shuttel might crash into astoroids on the way there

1. _____

2. _____

3. _____

4. _____

5. _____

Lesson 30 Words in Review

A. quarrel

roar

tore

perform

course

important

B. service

furniture

firm

certain

perfect

pearl

C. prepare

carefully

declare

compare

D. marbles

apartment

starve

margin

★ You will need a piece of paper for these review activities.

1. In Lesson 25 you studied four different ways to spell /ô/: **o, a, ou, oa.** Write the words in list A.

_____ _____ _____

_____ _____ _____

2. In Lesson 26 you studied four different ways to spell /û/: **e, i, ea, u.** Write the words in list B.

_____ _____ _____

_____ _____ _____

★ **3.** Use each review word from lists A and B in a sentence.

4. In Lesson 27 you studied one way to spell /â/: **a.** Write the words in list C.

_____ _____

_____ _____

5. In Lesson 27 you also studied one way to spell /ä/: **a.** Write the words in list D.

_____ _____

_____ _____

★ **6.** Look up each review word from lists C and D in the Spelling Dictionary. Write the sound spelling of each.

Your teacher may give you a test. Answer these questions when you have finished.

7. Did you spell all the words correctly? _____

8. Did you leave out a letter? _____

9. Did you write the wrong letter? _____

10. Did you miss the spelling of a vowel sound? _____

An Explanation

An explanation gives readers information. It might tell how to do something, why something happens, or what something is made of. Here is the beginning of Anna's explanation of the different kinds of roller-skates people wear. Note that she gives interesting facts about what roller-skates are made of and what they look like.

Kinds of Roller-Skates

Roller-skating is an exciting activity. It can be done indoors or outdoors, just for fun, or in races. Roller-skates used outdoors have metal wheels. They last longer on the rough surface of sidewalks and roads. Indoor skaters use skates with wooden or plastic wheels. These wheels do not scratch the wooden floors at the rinks.

Most roller skates have four wheels. The wheels form a rectangle on the boot or a straight line down the middle of the boot. Wheels in a rectangle are more stable. Wheels in a straight line go faster. Racers use skates with five wheels.

To write her explanation, Anna followed the steps in the writing process. She first used a list as a **Prewriting** activity. The list helped her think of all the facts she wanted to include about roller-skating. This graphic organizer also helped her to remember her ideas once she was ready to begin writing. Part of Anna's list is shown here. Study what Anna did.

Kinds of Roller-Skates

ones used outdoors
   metal wheels

ones used indoors
   wooden wheels
   plastic wheels

ones with wheels set in rectangle
in-line skates

Get ready to write your own explanation. You might explain how to play a favorite sport or game. Or you might give facts about your hobby or another activity. Just make sure that your explanation is clear and complete. After you have decided what to write about, make a list to note all the facts and details you will include. Then follow the other steps in the writing process—**Writing, Revising, Proofreading,** and **Publishing.**

Lesson 31 Words with /ə/

Listen for /ə/ in each word.

against

canoe

again

banana

approve

ocean

perhaps

government

dangerous

beautiful

qualify

cousin

comfort

mosquito

memory

season

surprise

citrus

chorus

industry

1. Which word begins with the letter p? _____

2. Which word begins with the letter a and ends with the letter n? _____

3. Write the word that ends with o. _____

4. Which three words begin with /s/? Circle the letter that spells /s/. _____

_____

5. Which word begins with /kw/? Circle the letters that spell /kw/. _____

6. Which four words begin with /k/? Circle the letters that spell /k/. _____ _____

_____ _____

7. In which word does a double consonant spell one sound?

_____

8. In which word do you hear /j/ but don't see the letter j?

_____

9. Which word has the same vowel letter repeated three times? _____

10. Which word ends with the letters st? _____

11. Which three words end with the letter y? Circle the words in which the y is pronounced /ē/.

_____

_____

12. Write the two words that have the suffixes ment and ful.

_____ _____

13. In which word do you hear /sh/ but don't see the letters sh? _____

Checkpoint

Write a spelling word for each clue.
Then use the Checkpoint Study Plan on page 224.

1. A yellow fruit with easy-to-peel skin is a ___.

2. The opposite of ugly is ___.

3. Once more means ___.

4. Another word for maybe is ___.

5. One type of flying insect is a ___.

6. The opposite of safe is ___.

7. To make someone feel better is to give ___.

8. The water that covers 72 percent of the earth is the ___.

9. The President is the head of our ___.

10. Your aunt's child is your ___.

11. If you are not for something, you are ___ it.

12. Another word for business is ___.

13. A group of singers may be a ___.

14. Past events are stored in your ___.

15. July is a month, summer is a ___.

16. To consider right or good is to ___.

17. Something unexpected is a ___.

18. Trees that grow oranges or limes are ___.

19. To meet certain conditions is to ___.

20. When Christopher Columbus first came to the Americas, he landed in the West Indies. He met a group of Indians and took one of their boats back to Europe. People in Europe called the boat by its Indian name. This name is our mystery word. Can you name the boat? ___

Oranges and Alligators

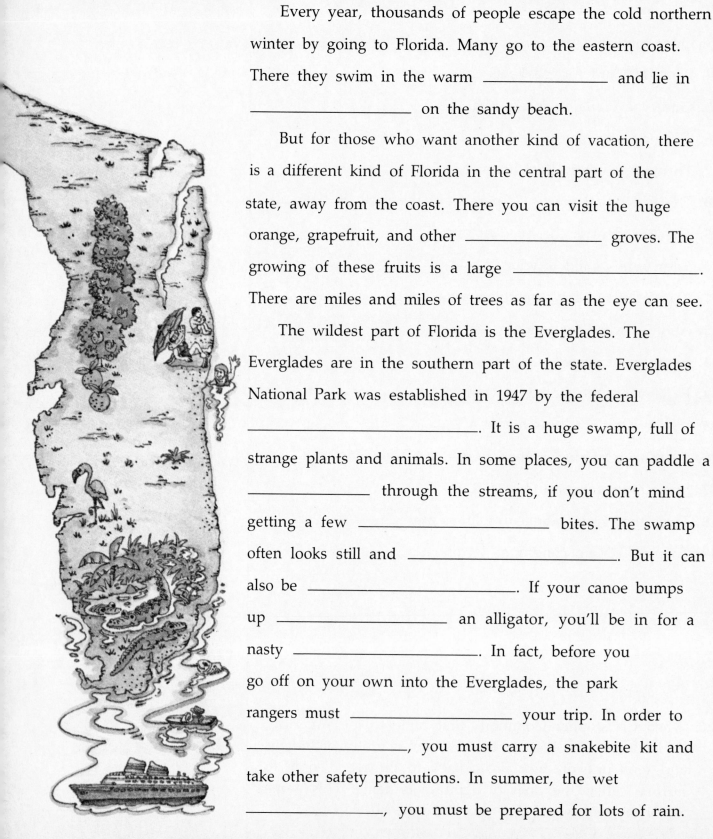

Every year, thousands of people escape the cold northern winter by going to Florida. Many go to the eastern coast. There they swim in the warm _____ and lie in _____ on the sandy beach.

But for those who want another kind of vacation, there is a different kind of Florida in the central part of the state, away from the coast. There you can visit the huge orange, grapefruit, and other _____ groves. The growing of these fruits is a large _____. There are miles and miles of trees as far as the eye can see.

The wildest part of Florida is the Everglades. The Everglades are in the southern part of the state. Everglades National Park was established in 1947 by the federal _____. It is a huge swamp, full of strange plants and animals. In some places, you can paddle a _____ through the streams, if you don't mind getting a few _____ bites. The swamp often looks still and _____. But it can also be _____. If your canoe bumps up _____ an alligator, you'll be in for a nasty _____. In fact, before you go off on your own into the Everglades, the park rangers must _____ your trip. In order to _____, you must carry a snakebite kit and take other safety precautions. In summer, the wet _____, you must be prepared for lots of rain.

166

However, many people love the Everglades, and they come back again and _____ to explore this area.

- My aunt, my uncle, and my _____ Herman took me to Everglades National Park.

- Because I have a good _____, I can remember every detail of that trip to Florida.

- Herman and I turned on the car radio and sang the _____ of every song we knew.

- Once, when we stopped for lunch, I ordered a _____ split. It tasted so good, I ordered another. Wow, did I have an upset stomach!

- Maybe I should have ordered just one. Or _____ I shouldn't have had even one.

167

against
canoe
again
banana
approve
ocean
perhaps
government
dangerous
beautiful
qualify
cousin
comfort
mosquito
memory
season
surprise
citrus
chorus
industry

Capitals

The first word, the last word, and all other important words in a title are capitalized. Small words, such as <u>a</u>, <u>the</u>, <u>in</u>, <u>to</u>, and <u>of</u> are not capitalized when they are in the middle of a title. This is true for titles of books, stories, songs, movies, and television programs.

<u>*Butch Cassidy and the Sundance Kid*</u>
<u>*Newsweek*</u>
<u>*A Night to Remember*</u>

★ Write the following titles. Correct the spelling error in each title.

1. a seasun of song
   _____

2. ocaen life
   _____

3. the memery bank
   _____

4. the most dangerus game
   _____

5. house beautifull
   _____

6. indutry and the u.s. goverment
   _____

7. men agianst the sea
   _____

8. my cusin, my friend
   _____

9. play it agaen, sam
   _____

10. the bananna cookbook
    _____

Challenge Yourself

tyrant	omen	ultimate	random

Write what you think each underlined Challenge Word means. Check your Spelling Dictionary to see if you were right. Then write sentences showing that you understand the meaning of each Challenge Word.

1. We hoped the king would be just, but he turned out to be a tyrant.

2. Some people think finding a four-leaf clover is a good omen.

3. I have read ten pages, but my ultimate goal is to finish the book.

4. You can plan the colors of your design or simply choose random colors.

Write to the Point

If a friend of yours is visiting the area where you live for the first time, what would you want him or her to see? Write a short tourists' guide to your community or city. Describe some of the interesting or beautiful sights. Use spelling words from this lesson in your guide.

Challenge Use one or more of the Challenge Words in your guide.

Proofreading

Use the proofreading marks to show the errors in the paragraph below. Write the five misspelled words correctly in the blanks.

Maine is a beautyful state in any seasen, but perhaps the best time to visit is october. the ocian crashes agenst the shore, and the brilliant colors of the trees will please and suprize you. What an awesome sight

	word is misspelled
≡	letter should be capitalized
⋀	exclamation point is missing

1. _____

2. _____

3. _____

4. _____

5. _____

Lesson 32 Words with /ə/

Listen for /ə/ in each word.

example

couple

pickles

double

tremble

puzzle

sample

whistle

tumble

simple

trouble

wrinkle

nickel

barrel

musical

animal

natural

final

general

signal

1. Write the three words that begin with the letter s.

   _____ _____

   _____

2. Which word begins with the letter f? _____

3. Which word begins and ends like metal?

   _____

4. Write the two words that begin with a vowel.

   _____ _____

5. In which word do you hear /j/ but don't see the letter j?

   _____

6. Write the word in which you see the letter w but don't hear /w/. _____

7. Write the three words that begin with the letter t.

   _____ _____

   _____

8. Write the two words in which you see the letter t but don't hear /t/. _____ _____

9. Write the two words in which /k/ is spelled ck.

   _____ _____

10. In which word is /z/ spelled zz? _____

11. In which word is /r/ spelled rr? _____

12. Write the three words in which /ŭ/ is spelled ou.

    _____ _____

    _____

13. Which two words end with the letters el?

    _____ _____

14. Write the three words in which you hear /z/ but don't see the letter z. _____ _____

    _____

170

Checkpoint

Write a spelling word for each clue.
Then use the Checkpoint Study Plan on page 224.

1. The clues fit together like pieces of a ____.

2. Difficulty is another word for ____.

3. Another word for easy is ____.

4. To shake is to ____.

5. A sample or model is an ____.

6. The last one is ____.

7. A fern is a plant, a cat is an ____.

8. Two people together make a ____.

9. Nation is to national as music is to ____.

10. A sound or small instrument used for a signal is a ____.

11. When cucumbers are treated, they become ____.

12. Start the race when I give the ____.

13. The opposite of specific is ____.

14. To fall or roll over is to ____.

15. A kind of large container is a ____.

16. The opposite of man-made is ____.

17. Five pennies equal one ____.

18. It's a new product, so take a free ____.

19. If it's twice as much, it's ____.

20. The origin of this mystery word is uncertain. It may
    have come from the Old English word *wringan*. *Wringan*
    meant to twist. When cloth is twisted, it becomes
    creased. The mystery word means an unwanted crease.
    Can you guess the mystery word? ____

The Goose Bay

THE CASE OF THE PILFERED PICKLES

Someone blew the _____ on Shifty Louie today. It solved a _____ that has been bothering the police for weeks.

Shifty Louie had been causing _____ by stealing pickles. Pickle supplies across the country were dropping sharply. Just the name of Shifty Louie made grocery store owners _____.

Upon hearing of his capture, Mr. Del E. Catessen, owner and manager of the _____ store in Goose Bay, was most relieved.

"I was down to the last pickle in my pickle _____," Mr. Catessen said. "His capture means one less _____ on my forehead."

"What would a _____ like us have done?" asked Mrs. Catessen. "Pickles cost a _____

apiece! We can't afford to have people taking a _____ from our barrel whenever they want.

Captain John Darm, of the Goose Bay Police, was the principal person in the plan to catch the thief.

"As Chief of Police, it was only _____ for me to try to end this crime wave. I wanted to make an _____ of Shifty Louie."

When asked how he managed to trap the thief, Captain Darm said, "It was _____! My first move was to _____ the number of officers working on the case. Then I put five police dogs on Louie's trail. We call them our Pooch Patrol."

Captain Darm went on to explain the Pooch Patrol and how the police use it. He explained that Mutt, who caught Shifty Louie, is the kind of dog the

Gazette

police use every day. This noble _____ will even go on stakeouts. He is trained to wait without a sound until he is given a _____. Then he will make his move, corner the thief, and wait for help to arrive.

Shortly after 9:00 A.M. this morning, a citizen reported seeing "a funny-looking character who smelled like a delicatessen." In minutes Mutt, following the smell of dill _____, sniffed Louie out on the far side of town. The dog chased him through the city streets. People saw pickle after pickle _____ out of Louie's pockets as he ran. Mutt finally cornered Louie in an alley. And soon after, neighbors heard the _____ sound of sirens speeding to the scene.

Later that day at the police station, Shifty Louie's _____ statement was: "I am not a common thief! I prefer to be called a pickle-pocket!"

173

example
couple
pickles
double
tremble
puzzle
sample
whistle
tumble
simple
trouble
wrinkle
nickel
barrel
musical
animal
natural
final
general
signal

Adverbs

An adverb is the part of speech that tells how, when, or where the action in a sentence takes place.

Jane skates gracefully.
Her brother dances beautifully.

Write the sentences below, and underline the adverbs.

1. The circus parade marches noisily past the general store.

2. We tremble quietly with excitement.

3. The leader blows a whistle loudly.

4. Each animal steps quickly into place.

5. The animals form a double line and march obediently behind the leader.

6. A couple of people busily sell souvenirs.

7. A clown happily jumps out of a barrel.

8. Acrobats tumble energetically on the streets.

9. Suddenly, the signal is given.

10. The parade makes a final turn on Main Street and disappears slowly from sight.

Challenge Yourself

spaniel   vocal   pedestal   agile

Use your Spelling Dictionary to answer these questions. Then write sentences showing that you understand the meaning of each Challenge Word.

1. Would you keep your spaniel on your bookshelf?

2. When you give a speech, are you making a vocal presentation to your audience?

3. Is a pedestal something that might be found at the base of a statue in a museum or a garden?

4. Would it help to be agile if you were training to become a dancer or a gymnast?

Write to the Point

Write a funny story about a mystery involving food. For instance, you might write about "The Case of the Disappearing Doughnuts" or "The Missing Pizza Puzzle." Try to keep your readers guessing until the mystery is solved. Use spelling words from this lesson in your mystery.

Challenge Use one or more of the Challenge Words in your mystery.

Proofreading

Use the proofreading marks to show the errors in the paragraph below. Write the five misspelled words correctly in the blanks.

The Goose Bay police rushed to the generel store on bank street. What was the trubble at the store A couple of things had been stolen—for example, a dog wistle and a jigsaw puzzel. Clearly this would be no simpal crime for the police detectives to solve.

⬯	word is misspelled
≡	letter should be capitalized
?︵	question mark is missing

1. _____

2. _____

3. _____

4. _____

5. _____

Lesson 33 Words with /ər/

Listen for /ər/ in each word.

rather

another

toaster

member

teacher

discover

character

master

whether

gather

answer

silver

center

similar

cellar

sugar

polar

calendar

humor

actor

1. Which word begins with the letters <u>wh</u>? _____

2. Which word begins with /sh/? _____

3. Write the other two words that begin with the letter <u>s</u>.

   _____   _____

4. Which two words begin with the letter <u>c</u> that is
   pronounced /s/?

   _____   _____

5. Which two words begin with /k/? Circle the letters that
   spell /k/. _____   _____

6. Which three words begin with a vowel?

   _____   _____

   _____

7. Which word begins and ends like <u>daughter</u>?

   _____

8. Which word begins with the letter <u>p</u>? _____

9. Write the two words that begin and end like <u>meter</u>.

   _____   _____

10. Write the two words that begin and end like <u>timber</u>.

    _____   _____

11. Which two words have the same spelling of /ər/ as
    <u>director</u>? _____

12. Write the word in which you see the letter <u>w</u> but don't
    hear /w/. _____

13. Write the four words that contain the letters <u>th</u>.

    _____   _____

    _____   _____

Checkpoint

Write a spelling word for each clue.
Then use the Checkpoint Study Plan on page 224.

1. Alike but not the same is ＿＿.

2. An animal's owner is its ＿＿.

3. A large, white animal from the north is a ＿＿ bear.

4. A storage space beneath a house is a ＿＿.

5. Coins made of ＿＿ are valuable.

6. The middle part is the ＿＿.

7. The opposite of question is ＿＿.

8. A person in a book is a ＿＿.

9. If you would prefer, then you would ＿＿.

10. A sweetener is ＿＿.

11. If you can laugh at yourself, you have a sense of ＿＿.

12. She joined, so she is now a ＿＿.

13. If you don't like this one, then try ＿＿.

14. A person with a part in a play is an ＿＿.

15. An instructor is a ＿＿.

16. You can heat English muffins in a ＿＿.

17. The opposite of scatter is ＿＿.

18. Another word for if is ＿＿.

19. To find is to ＿＿.

20. The Latin word for months was *calendae*. Roman merchants called their monthly account books *calendārium*. The mystery word comes from *calendārium*. It names our system of dividing the year into twelve months. Can you find the word? ＿＿

An Interview with Jamie Knight

Many people consider Jamie Knight to be the greatest movie _____ alive today. However, not everybody knows that Jamie has held many different jobs. Here, Jamie tells My Magazine (MM) about his career.

MM: Jamie, when did you _____ that you wanted to be an actor?

JK: When I saw my first play. I knew right away that I'd _____ be in the _____ of the stage than be a _____ of the audience.

MM: What was your first acting job?

JK: Well, that's a hard question to _____. When I was nine, my friends and I put on a play in the neighborhood. We held it downstairs in the _____ of my parents' house. There were lots of acts. I was the _____ of ceremonies.

But my first real acting job was in a TV commercial. I was a piece of bread popping out of a _____.

MM: I _____ that you don't like doing commercials very much.

JK: It pays well, but I found myself doing one after _____. In commercials, I played a bowl of _____ and a _____ bear, among other things. My _____ in acting school taught me to keep a sense of

_____. But I used to wonder

_____ I'd ever get a real acting job.

MM: What is your favorite _____

to play on stage?

JK: Captain Hook in <u>Peter Pan</u> is my favorite role. I love

playing a pirate. I've had many _____

roles since. Having chests of gold and

_____ and roaring to scare people is

great fun.

MM: What are you doing next, Jamie?

JK: Let me look at my _____ for

next month. Oh yes! I'm opening in a new play in San

Francisco. In this play, I have several roles. It will be

interesting.

MM: It sounds unusual; that's for certain. Thank you,

Jamie, for giving us your time.

JK: The pleasure was mine.

rather
another
toaster
member
teacher
discover
character
master
whether
gather
answer
silver
center
similar
cellar
sugar
polar
calendar
humor
actor

Idioms

An idiom is a phrase that may not be understood from the meanings of its separate words. Idioms are usually listed at the end of the entry for the main word in the idiom.

You make my blood boil when
you say things like that!

> **blood** | blŭd | *n.* **1.** The red liquid that is pumped through the body by the heart.
> **2.** Family relationship: *My cousin and I are related by blood.*
>   *Idioms.* **make one's blood boil.** To anger. **make one's blood run cold.** To frighten.

⭐ Write the sentences below. Unscramble the spelling word in each sentence. Then underline each idiom.

1. John won't sanwre me because he's feeling down in the dumps.

2. He's probably snowed under with homework from his math heactre.

3. Perhaps he has his hands full trying to become a bermem of the drama club.

4. It is out of chtrraace for me to go poking my nose into his business.

5. We should put on our thinking caps to codsienr how to help him.

6. Let's tell some jokes to rhoum him and keep him on his toes.

Challenge Yourself

badger   muscular   tutor   razor

Decide which Challenge Word fits each clue. Check your Spelling Dictionary to see if you were right. Then write sentences showing that you understand the meaning of each Challenge Word.

1. This might describe the legs of someone who climbs mountains.

2. If you are having difficulty with math or English, this person might be able to help you.

3. Many men use this every morning to remove hair from their face.

4. It has short legs and long claws for digging.

Write to the Point

Interview one of your classmates about his or her activities, plans, likes, and dislikes. Write your questions ahead of time, using spelling words from this lesson. Take notes as the answers are given. Then write a final draft of the interview, like the one on pages 178 and 179.

Challenge Use one or more of the Challenge Words in your questions.

Proofreading

Use the proofreading marks to show the errors in the paragraph below. Write the five misspelled words correctly in the blanks.

◯	word is misspelled
∧	word is missing
/	letter should be lower case

At first I didn't know weather to be

an acter a dancer. I finally decided I

would rathur dance, even though ballet

is hard to mastor. My mother found me

a good Teacher, and I became a membur

a ballet company.

1. _____

2. _____

3. _____

4. _____

5. _____

Lesson 34 Words with ion

Say each word.

nation

action

vacation

election

instruction

direction

invention

selection

collection

information

inspection

mention

pollution

transportation

population

station

fraction

location

section

education

1. Write the four words that begin with the letters <u>in</u>.

_____   _____

_____   _____

2. Write the three words that begin with the letter <u>s</u>.

_____   _____

_____

3. Write the word that begins with /k/. _____

4. Which word begins with the letter <u>d</u>?

_____

5. Which word begins with the letter <u>m</u>?

_____

6. Which two words begin with the letter <u>e</u>?

_____   _____

7. Which two words begin with the letter <u>p</u>?

_____   _____

8. In which three words is /ā/ the first vowel sound?

_____   _____

_____

9. In which word is /ō/ the first vowel sound?

_____

10. In which three words is /ă/ the first vowel sound?

_____   _____

_____

11. In which word do you hear /j/ but don't see the letter <u>j</u>?

_____

12. Write the two words in which /l/ is spelled <u>ll</u>.

_____   _____

Checkpoint

Write a spelling word for each clue.
Then use the Checkpoint Study Plan on page 224.

1. To talk about briefly is to ____.

2. They waited for the train to pull into the ____.

3. Another word for news is ____.

4. All of the people in an area make up the ____.

5. Director is to direction as inventor is to ____.

6. An instruction for doing something is a ____.

7. A rest from work is a ____.

8. Smog is a type of air ____.

9. Checking out or looking things over is an ____.

10. Trains, cars, and skateboards are forms of ____.

11. The process of doing something is ____.

12. The process of learning is ____.

13. Something that is taught is ____.

14. Another word for country is ____.

15. Part of a whole unit is a ____.

16. Another word for place is ____.

17. A part or a division of an area is a ____.

18. These three mystery words all come from the Latin verb *legere*. *Legere* meant to gather. It was used in many words. Three of these words were *colligere*, *eligere*, and *sēligere*. *Colligere* meant to gather together. Can you guess the mystery word that comes from *collectus*, a past tense form of *colligere*? ____

19. *Eligere* meant to choose. Can you guess the mystery word that comes from *electus*, a past tense form of *eligere*? ____

20. *Sēligere* meant to choose from a number. Guess the word that comes from *selectus*, a past tense form of *sēligere*. ____

183

Use each list word once.

Public Service Announcements

1. It's time to start planning your next _____.

Why not take a trip across the _____?

There are many means of _____

To get to just about any _____.

If you need more _____,

Write to U.S. Travel Destinations

In care of this TV _____.

★★★

2. Isn't it time you furthered your _____

about the dangers of _____?

Pollution upsets the animal _____

in our wild areas. Isn't it time for each of us to take

_____? We can start in a new

_____ before it's too late for the

manatees, the prairie chickens, and the last hundred

foxes living in one small _____ of Texas.

   If you would like to help, please take up a

_____ in your neighborhood or

school club. You can help correct this sad situation.

★★★

3. It's _____ time again. Have you

signed up to vote?

4. Starting your own business? Our book tells how to set up a business. Each _____ is clear and easy to follow. Do you plan to run an office? Or do you want to set up a factory for making clothes? This free book can help you. Write for <u>The Business Manager's Guide</u>. When you order our book, just _____ this TV station, and we'll send you a gift that will aid in the _____ of your office furniture.

★★★

5. Don't be fooled by a salesclerk's gift for fast talk. Be careful when he or she presents you with the latest new _____ to cut your work to a _____ of its time.

All merchandise is inspected by our company. After _____, it is rated. Simply call us or write for our free book, <u>Better Merchandise Rating</u>.

Colons

Use a colon between the hour and the minutes in expressions of time.

I leave the house at 7:15 every morning.

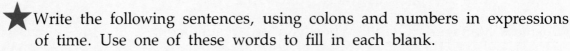Write the following sentences, using colons and numbers in expressions of time. Use one of these words to fill in each blank.

station　　**vacation**

1. The train left the ——— in Boston at two thirty and arrived in New York at six forty-five.

2. We are leaving for our summer ——— promptly at nine in the morning.

Use a colon after a word that introduces a series or a list.

Be sure to pack everything you'll need: blankets, warm clothing, boots, and food.

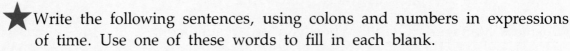Write each sentence below, putting a colon after the word that introduces the list.

3. Three topics will be covered on our test pollution, transportation, and why populations move.

4. There have been many important inventions the wheel, the gasoline engine, the telephone, and pizza.

5. There are three candidates running for election Mayor Hibbs, Mrs. Gold, and Mr. Santos.

WORDS AT WORK

Challenge Yourself

consternation	pension
friction	audition

Decide which Challenge Word fits each clue. Check your Spelling Dictionary to see if you were right. Then write sentences showing that you understand the meaning of each Challenge Word.

1. You might feel this emotion if your rowboat began to leak in the middle of the lake.

2. This wears down the heels of your shoes.

3. This might help someone pay the rent after retiring from a job.

4. You must do well at this if you want a part in a play.

Write to the Point

Write an announcement for an event at your school. Choose a real event or make up one. It could be a meeting, a show, a festival, a sports event, or anything you wish. Give all the information students will need, and tell them why they should attend. Use spelling words from this lesson in your announcement.

Challenge Use one or more of the Challenge Words in your announcement.

Proofreading

Use the proofreading marks to show the errors in the paragraph below. Write the five misspelled words correctly in the blanks.

⬭	word is misspelled
⊙	period is missing
≡	letter should be capitalized

Tonight at City Hall on Oak Road, mayor Bond will discuss the acttion we must take to stop polution in our city and to provide better educasion for the entire popullation   She will also mension the new train station.

1. _____

2. _____

3. _____

4. _____

5. _____

Lesson 35 Homophones

Say each word.

threw

through

right

write

hole

whole

road

rode

plain

plane

waist

waste

its

it's

to

too

two

their

there

they're

1. Write the five words that begin with the letters <u>th</u>.

   _____   _____

   _____   _____

   _____

2. Which word ends with the letters <u>ane</u>? _____

3. Which word ends with the letters <u>oad</u>? _____

4. Which three words begin with the letter <u>w</u> and end with the letter <u>e</u>? _____

   _____   _____

5. Write the two words that have an apostrophe.

   _____   _____

6. Which word is spelled the same as another word on the list but doesn't have an apostrophe? _____

7. Write the shortest word on the list. _____

8. In which four words do you see the letter <u>w</u> but don't hear /w/? _____

   _____   _____

9. In which word is /o͞o/ spelled <u>oo</u>? _____

10. Which word has the same spelling of /o͞o/ as <u>blew</u>?

   _____

11. In which two words is /ā/ spelled <u>ai</u>?

   _____   _____

12. In which three words is /ō/ spelled <u>o-e</u>?

   _____   _____

   _____

13. Which word has the same spelling of /ī/ as <u>might</u>?

   _____

Checkpoint

Write a spelling word for each clue.
Then use the Checkpoint Study Plan on page 224.

1. The opposite of wrong is ____.

2. A highway is a kind of ____.

3. If you're finished, then you're ____.

4. Another word for also is ____.

5. A piece of pie is part of the ____.

6. The opposite of fancy is ____.

7. One and one make ____.

8. A belt goes around your ____.

9. Today I ride, last week I ____.

10. We flew over your house in a jet ____.

11. With a brush you paint, with a pencil you ____.

12. If you want to say it is, say ____.

13. Another word for tossed is ____.

14. You can use a shovel to dig a ____.

15. If you want to say they are, say ____.

16. He asked me to give this package ____ you.

17. The way to say belonging to it is ____.

18. It's not here. It's over ____.

19. The way to say belonging to them is ____.

20. The English word <u>vast</u> means very large. It comes from the Latin word *vastus.* In addition to meaning very large, *vastus* meant destroyed. From this second meaning of *vastus* comes another English word. This word as a verb means to destroy. As a noun it means something that has been destroyed. Can you guess this word? ____

Use each list word once.

Important People

Jody loosened the seat belt around her _____. The experience of flying was completely new to her. She tried to act as if she rode planes as often as school buses.

Across the aisle _____ men were studying important-looking papers. Were they Representatives on their way to the Capitol building to vote on some law? The woman sitting next to her was trying to _____ something. Jody wondered what it was. She knew it was rude to look _____ much. But she was curious.

All week at school Jody had been Ms. Big Shot, the winner of the All-State Social Studies prize. Her prize was a trip to Washington, D.C., the capital of the country. Now as she _____ through the skies, she didn't feel like such a big shot. Everyone else on the _____ seemed so important and serious.

She looked _____ the window. She saw tiny cars on the _____ below. The buildings were tiny squares. Is that the way the _____ world looks to birds, she wondered.

Jody glanced here and _____ around the plane. Then she _____ a glance at what the woman next to her was writing. Written across the top of the page was SENATOR CLAUDIA GREEN!

190

"Wow!" said Jody out loud. "I mean wow!"

The woman looked up and smiled. "That's just what I'd like to say in this speech I'm writing. Would you like to know what _____ about? It's about our country's energy problems. By the way, my name is Claudia Green."

"I'm Dody Javis. I mean Jody Davis." Poor Jody was so embarrassed she could have crawled into a _____.

"I'm pleased to meet you, Jody," said the Senator. "I'm concerned about what will happen if this country doesn't use _____ natural resources better."

"I know," said Jody. "All the kids at school are trying not to _____ things like paper and electricity. If parents really thought about _____ kids, maybe they wouldn't drive their cars so much. What's going to be left when we grow up?"

"That's as _____ as can be, Jody. I'd like to put what you just said in my speech. Is that all _____ with you?"

"Wow! The kids at school are never going _____ believe I got to talk to a real senator! And _____ never going to believe something I said got into a speech."

"Well, how about some proof?" asked the Senator. She took out a card with her name on it. On the back she wrote, "Thanks for the help with my speech, Jody."

"Thank you, Senator," said Jody. "Thanks a lot!"

"We'll be landing in ten minutes," announced the flight attendant. "Please fasten your seat belts."

Jody touched the card in her pocket. Maybe she wasn't so unimportant after all!

191

threw
through
right
write
hole
whole
road
rode
plain
plane
waist
waste
its
it's
to
too
two
their
there
they're

Homophones

Words that sound alike but have different spellings and meanings are called homophones (*homo* means <u>same</u>, and *phone* means <u>sound</u>).

> *They rode on the new road.*

Some dictionaries list homophones at the end of an entry.

road |rōd| *n.* **1.** An open way for the passage of vehicles, persons, and animals. **2.** Any path or course; *the road to enlightenment.* **3.** A railroad. **4. roads.** An offshore anchorage area for ships; a roadstead: *ships lying in the roads.* **—modifier:** *road signs.* ¶*These sound alike* **road, rode.**

rode |rōd|. Past tense of **ride.** ¶*These sound alike* **rode, road.**

★ Look up <u>plain</u> and <u>plane</u> in the Spelling Dictionary. Write the sound spelling and first definition for each.

1. plain _____

_____

2. plane _____

_____

★ Write each sentence below, using the correct word in the blank.

3. We flew to San Diego in a jet ____.

_____

4. My uncle likes ____ food with no rich sauces.

_____

★ Use the Spelling Dictionary to answer the questions about these homophones:

its   it's   waist   waste   write   right

5. Which word is the contraction of "it is"? _____

6. Which word names a part of the body? _____

7. Which word means "belongs to it"? _____

8. Which word means the opposite of left? _____

9. Which word means "to use carelessly"? _____

10. Which word names something you do with a pencil? _____

WORDS AT WORK

Challenge Yourself

alter   altar   chili   chilly

Decide which Challenge Word fits each clue. Check your Spelling Dictionary to see if you were right. Then write sentences showing that you understand the meaning of each Challenge Word.

1. You may find this in a church or temple.

2. If you like spicy food, you might enjoy this dish.

3. This describes the kind of weather that makes you want to put on a sweater.

4. You do this to pants or a skirt when you put in a hem to make the pants or skirt shorter.

Write to the Point

Have you ever wanted to tell people about an issue you care about? Write a short speech about something that is important to you. You could write about honesty, animal rights, recycling, or whatever you wish. Include reasons and examples that will help your audience see your point of view. Use spelling words from this lesson in your speech.

Challenge Use one or more of the Challenge Words in your speech.

Proofreading

Use the proofreading marks to show the errors in the paragraph below. Write the five misspelled words correctly in the blanks.

In there new book called <u>It's Not Too late</u>, the authors right that the future of the hole world depends on on our stopping the waist of natural resources. They say their is still time to save it our planet.

> ⬭ word is misspelled
> ≡ letter should be capitalized
> ⸜ take out word

1. _____

2. _____

3. _____

4. _____

5. _____

Lesson 36 Words in Review

A. memory

ocean

beautiful

surprise

against

dangerous

B. nickel

final

example

whistle

general

C. character

whether

similar

calendar

humor

D. direction

invention

collection

education

★ You will need a piece of paper for these review activities.

1. In Lesson 31 you studied five different ways to spell /ə/: **a, e, i, o, u.** Write the words in list A.

_____ _____

_____ _____

2. In Lesson 32 you studied two different ways to spell /ə/: **e, a.** Write the words in list B.

_____ _____

_____ _____

★ 3. Look up each review word from lists A and B in the Spelling Dictionary. Write the first definition of each word.

4. In Lesson 33 you studied three different ways to spell /ər/: **er, ar, or.** Write the words in list C.

_____ _____

_____ _____

5. In Lesson 34 you studied words with **ion.** Write the words in list D.

_____ _____

_____ _____

★ 6. Use each review word from lists C and D in a sentence.

Your teacher may give you a test. Answer these questions when you have finished.

7. Did you spell all the words correctly? _____

8. Did you leave out a letter? _____

9. Did you write the wrong letter? _____

10. Did you miss the spelling of a vowel sound? _____

Writer's Workshop

A Persuasive Letter

If you have a strong opinion that you want someone to share, you can try to convince the person by writing a persuasive letter. When you write your letter, it is important to state your opinion clearly and to let the reader know exactly what you would like for him or her to do. Your letter will be most convincing if you back up your opinion with solid reasons and give your reader all the important information he or she needs to know. Here is part of James's letter. In it he tries to persuade the school principal to have a covered bench installed at his bus stop.

> Dear Dr. Bronstein,
>
> I feel that a covered bench should be built at the corner of Marshall Avenue and Broad Street. Right now we students don't have anywhere to sit while we wait for the bus. Many students sit on the curb. Sitting that close to the road is dangerous. When it rains, we get wet waiting for the bus. A covered bench set about ten feet back from the road would keep us safe and dry.
>
> My mom and dad say that a covered bench like we need would not be very expensive. Our school could even ask parents to give money toward the bench.

To write his persuasive letter, James followed the steps in the writing process. He began with a cluster map as a **Prewriting** activity. On his cluster map he first wrote his opinion. Then he added reasons to support his opinion. The cluster map also helped James organize his ideas. Part of his cluster map is shown here. Study what James did.

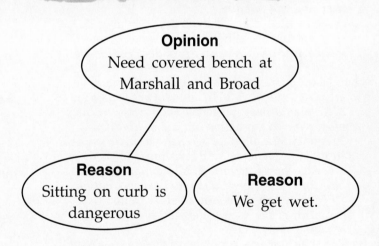

Opinion
Need covered bench at Marshall and Broad

Reason
Sitting on curb is dangerous

Reason
We get wet.

Get ready to write your own persuasive letter. You can write to a friend, a teacher, the mayor, or anyone else you wish. After you have decided what to write about, jot down your opinion and reasons in a cluster map. Then follow the other steps in the writing process—**Writing, Revising, Proofreading,** and **Publishing.**

SPELLING
Dic·tion·ar·y

absurd | alone

A

ab·surd | əb **sûrd′** | *or* | **-zûrd′** | *adj.* Silly; foolish: *It is absurd to wear a heavy coat when it is very hot outside.*

a·byss | ə **bĭs′** | *n., pl.* **a·byss·es.** A hole or space so deep that it cannot be measured: *If you looked into an abyss, you probably could not see the bottom.*

act | ăkt | *v.* **1.** To do something: *A lifeguard must act quickly.* **2.** To behave: *act your age.* **3.** To play a part; perform: *Sean acted in the play.* —*n.* **1.** An action: *an act of kindness.* **2.** A part of a play: *Let's rehearse the third act.*

ac·tion | ăk′ shən | *n.* **1.** Something that is done; a deed: *a brave action.* **2.** Motion; activity: *At half time, the cheerleaders jumped into action.*
   Idiom. **take action.** To start to do something: *The mayor decided to take action to settle the strike.*

ac·tor | ăk′ tər | *n.* A person who acts in a play, in a movie, on television, or on radio.

ac·tress | ăk′ trĭs | *n., pl.* **ac·tress·es.** A girl or woman who acts in a play, a movie, on television, or on radio.

ad·dress | ə **drĕs′** | *n.* **1.** | *also* ăd′ rĕs′ | The place where someone lives, works, or gets mail. **2.** | *also* ăd′ rĕs′ | The information on the outside of an envelope that tells where the envelope is being sent. **3.** A formal speech. —*v.* **1.** To write the street, city, state, and zip code on an envelope or package: *address an envelope.* **2.** To make a speech to: *address a crowd.*

a·dore | ə **dôr′** | *or* | ə **dōr′** | *v.* **a·dored, a·dor·ing.** **1.** To worship. **2.** *Informal.* To like very much.

a·gain | ə **gĕn′** | *adv.* Once more; another time.

a·gainst | ə **gĕnst′** | *prep.* **1.** In an opposite direction: *We sailed against the wind.* **2.** In contact with: *The rake is leaning against the fence.* **3.** In opposition to: *Our team will compete against yours and win!*

ag·ile | ăj′ əl | *or* | ăj′ īl′ | *adj.* Able to move easily and quickly; nimble: *The agile deer leaped over the fence and disappeared into the trees.*

a·gree | ə **grē′** | *v.* **a·greed, a·gree·ing.** **1.** To have the same opinion. **2.** To say "yes"; consent: *She agreed to run for president.* **3.** To be the same: *Their stories about the accident do not agree.*

ail·ment | āl′ mənt | *n.* A sickness or disease: *The doctor said that the ailment was not serious.*

a·larm | ə **lärm′** | *n.* **1.** Sudden fear caused by a feeling of danger: *The animals ran away in alarm.* **2.** A warning that danger is near: *It was only a false alarm.* **3.** A warning signal, such as a bell: *fire alarm.* —*v.* to frighten.

all right | ôl′ rīt′ | *adj.* **1.** Acceptable; satisfactory: *The pizza was all right, but I've tasted better.* **2.** Correct: *His answers are all right.* —*adv.* **1.** Healthy; safe: *I feel all right.* **2.** Yes: *All right, we'll go with you.*

a·lone | ə **lōn′** | *adj.* Not near other people or things: *Sometimes I enjoy being alone.*
   Idioms. **leave alone or let alone.** To not bother or interrupt. **let well enough alone.**

To be satisfied with things as they are and not try to change them.

al·read·y | ôl **rĕd′** ē | *adv.* By this time: *We are already 30 minutes late!*

al·tar | **ôl′** tər | *n.* A table or raised place that is used in religious services: *The altar was in the front of the temple. These sound alike* **altar, alter.**

al·ter | **ôl′** tər | *v.* To make or become different; change: *Mother had to alter my dress because I grew two inches taller. These sound alike* **alter, altar.**

am·a·teur | **ăm′** ə choŏr′ | *or* | -chər | *or* | -tyoŏr′ | *n.* **1.** A person who does something for pleasure, not for money. **2.** A person who does something in an unskilled way.

a·mong | ə **mŭng′** | *prep.* **1.** In the company of: *a party among friends.* **2.** With a portion for each of: *We divided the clay among the class.* **3.** With or between one another: *Let's not argue among ourselves.*

an·gry | **ăng′** grē | *adj.* **an·gri·er, an·gri·est.** **1.** Feeling or showing anger: *an angry look; angry at him.* **2.** Stormy: *angry clouds in the sky.* **3.** Inflamed: *an angry cut on her knee.*

an·i·mal | **ăn′** ə məl | *n.* **1.** A living thing that isn't a plant. **2.** Any animal other than a human being.

an·noy | ə **noi′** | *v.* To make angry; bother.

an·oth·er | ə **nŭ***th***′** ər | *adj.* **1.** Different: *Let's try another road.* **2.** One more: *May I have another glass of milk? —pron.* One of a group: *one problem after another.*

an·swer | **ăn′** sər | *or* | **än′**- | *n.* **1.** Something said or written in reply: *I received an answer to my letter.* **2.** The solution to a problem: *Did you get the answer to this math problem? —v.* To speak or write in reply to something: *Sarah likes to answer the telephone.*

a·part·ment | ə **pärt′** mənt | *n.* A room or group of rooms to live in, usually found in large buildings.

a·pol·o·gy | ə **pŏl′** ə jē | *n., pl.* **a·pol·o·gies.** A statement that one is sorry for being rude, doing something wrong, or making a mistake: *Juan gave his apologies to both the host and hostess of the party for being an hour late.*

ap·point | ə **point′** | *v.* **1.** To select for an office or position: *Jason will appoint a chairman.* **2.** To decide on; set: *We will appoint a time for the meeting.*

ap·point·ment | ə **point′** mənt | *n.* **1.** The act of naming someone for an office or position. **2.** An arrangement to meet someone at a certain time and place: *My appointment with the dentist is right after school.*

ap·prove | ə **prōōv′** | *v.* **ap·proved, ap·prov·ing.** **1.** To think or speak well of something: *My parents don't approve of my riding my bike on that busy street.* **2.** To agree or consent to something: *The mayor approved the new city budget.*

A·pril | **ā′** prəl | *n.* The fourth month of the year. April has 30 days.

a·rith·me·tic | ə **rĭth′** mə tĭk | *n.* The science of adding, subtracting, multiplying, and dividing numbers.

ar·row | **ăr′** ō | *n.* **1.** A thin stick, with a point at one end and feathers at the other, made to be shot from a bow. **2.** Anything shaped like an arrow, such as a road sign.

a·sleep | ə **slēp′** | *adj.* **1.** Sleeping: *Were you asleep when I called?* **2.** Numb: *My foot was asleep because I crossed my legs. —adv.* Into sleep: *She always falls asleep in a car.*

as·ter·oid | **ăs′** tə roid′ | *n., pl.* **as·ter·oids.** Any of the thousands of small objects that revolve around the sun. Most are between Mars and Jupiter.

as·tron·o·my | ə **strŏn′** ə mē | *n.* The science that deals with the sun, moon, stars, planets, and other heavenly bodies.

ath·lete | **ăth′** lēt′ | *n., pl.* **ath·letes.** A person who is trained to take active part in sports.

au·di·tion | ô **dĭsh′** ən | *n.* A short performance that shows the ability of an actor, speaker, singer, or other performer: *The audition for the play is tonight. —v.* To try out in an audition: *I plan to audition for the main part in the play.*

Au·gust | **ô′** gəst | *n.* The eighth month of the year. August has 31 days.

aunt | ănt | *or* | änt | *n.* **1.** The sister of one's mother or father. **2.** The wife of one's uncle.

au·ro·ra | ə **rôr′** ə | *n.* Shining bands of flashing light sometimes seen in the night sky.

au·then·tic | ô **thĕn′** tĭk | *adj.* **1.** Real; genuine: *Eduardo has an authentic autograph of a famous baseball player.* **2.** True: *The witness's story of the accident is authentic.*

au·to·mo·bile | ô′ tə mə **bēl′** | *or* | -**mō′** bēl′ | *or* | **ô′** tə mə bēl′ | *n.* A vehicle made to carry passengers; a car.

au·tumn | ô′ təm | *n.* The season of the year between summer and winter; fall.

a·void | ə **void′** | *v.* To keep away from: *You should avoid ice cream and cake when you're on a diet.*

a·ware | ə **wâr′** | *adj.* Knowing; realizing: *Be aware of the dangers along the hiking trail.*

aw·ful | ô′ fəl | *adj.* **1.** Causing fear; terrible: *the awful silence in the empty house.* **2.** *Informal.* Very bad: *an awful movie.* **3.** *Informal.* Very large; great: *an awful lot of dishes to wash.*

a·while | ə **hwīl′** | *or* | ə **wīl′** | *adv.* For a short time: *We studied awhile before supper.*

awn·ing | ô′ nĭng | *n.* A cover that is like a roof over a window or door: *The awning kept the sun off the porch.*

ax·is | ăk′ sĭs | *n., pl.* **ax·es** | ăk′ sēz′ |. A straight line around which an object turns or rotates. The axis of the earth runs from the North Pole to the South Pole.

B

badg·er | băj′ ər | *n.* An animal with thick grayish fur, short legs, and long claws: *Badgers live in holes that they burrow in the ground.*

bak·er·y | bā′ kə rē | *n., pl.* **bak·er·ies.** A place where bread, pies, cookies, cakes, etc. are baked or sold.

bal·loon | bə **loon′** | *n.* **1.** A large bag filled with hot air or a gas that is lighter than air, used to lift heavy loads into the air. **2.** A child's toy made of brightly colored rubber that can be blown up by mouth. —*v.* To swell out like a balloon: *The sails ballooned in the wind as we raced through the water.*

ba·nan·a | bə **năn′** ə | *n.* A slightly curved fruit with yellow or reddish skin that peels easily: *Bananas grow in clusters.*

bare | bâr | *adj.* **bar·er, bar·est. 1.** Without covering or clothing: *bare feet.* **2.** Empty: *bare walls.* **3.** Just enough: *the bare necessities of life.*

bar·rel | băr′ əl | *n.* A large wooden container with round, flat ends of equal size and sides that bulge out slightly.

base·ball | bās′ bôl′ | *n.* **1.** A game between two teams of nine players each, played with a ball and bat. Baseball is played on a field with four bases that form a diamond pattern. Players score runs by touching all the bases. **2.** The ball used in this game.

bas·ket·ball | băs′ kĭt bôl′ | *or* | bä′ skĭt- | *n.* **1.** A game played with a large ball by two teams of five players each. The game is played on a rectangular court with a raised basket at each end. Players score by throwing the ball through the basket at the other team's end of the court. **2.** The large, round ball used in this game.

bear·a·ble | bâr′ ə bəl | *adj.* Able to be put up with: *The hot day was bearable because the air conditioner kept us cool.*

beau·ti·ful | byoo′ tə fəl | *adj.* Pleasing to hear or see: *beautiful music; a beautiful smile; beautiful weather.*

be·fore | bĭ **fôr′** | *or* | -**fōr′** | *adv.* Earlier; already: *I've read this book before.* —*prep.* Earlier than: *We finished before noon.* —*conj.* Sooner than the time when: *The soup started to boil before I finished making my sandwich.*

be·lieve | bĭ **lēv′** | *v.* **be·lieved, be·liev·ing. 1.** To think that something is true or real. **2.** To think; suppose: *I believe she went home.* *Idiom.* **make believe.** To pretend.

bench | bĕnch | *n., pl.* **bench·es. 1.** A long seat: *park bench.* **2.** A heavy work table: *the carpenter's bench.* **3.** The seat for judges in a court of law. —*v.* To take a player out of a game: *The referee benched the player for bad conduct.*

be·neath | bĭ **nēth′** | *prep.* Below; under; underneath.

birth·day | bûrth′ dā′ | *n.* **1.** The day on which a person was born. **2.** The anniversary of that day.

blind | blīnd | *adj.* **blind·er, blind·est. 1.** Not able to see: *a blind person.* **2.** Hidden: *a blind driveway.* **3.** Without reason or good sense: *a blind guess.* —*n.* Something that shuts out light or blocks sight, such as a window shade. —*v.* **1.** To take away sight: *The sun can blind you.* **2.** To take away reason: *Fright blinded him.*

bliss | blĭs | *n.* Great happiness; joy: *I think it is bliss to see my favorite baseball player hit a home run.*

blood | blŭd | *n.* **1.** The red liquid that is pumped through the body by the heart. **2.** Family relationship: *My cousin and I are related by blood.* *Idioms.* **make one's blood boil.** To anger. **make one's blood run cold.** To frighten.

blue·ber·ry | bloo′ bĕr′ ē | *n., pl.* **-ber·ries.** A small, round, dark blue, sweet berry that grows on a shrub.

blunt | blŭnt | *adj.* Having a dull point or edge; not sharp: *Even though a stick may have a blunt point, it hurts if you are poked with it.*

Blvd. Abbreviation of **Boulevard** | bōol′ ə värd′ |. A wide street usually lined with trees.

board | bôrd | *or* | bōrd | *n.* **1.** A flat, thin piece of lumber. **2.** A flat piece of hard material used for a special purpose: *a diving board; a game board.* **3.** A group of people who manage something: *a school board.* —*v.* **1.** To cover with boards. **2.** To get on a plane, train, ship, or bus.
  Idiom. **on board.** Aboard.

boast | bōst | *v.* **1.** To brag. **2.** To take pride in owning: *This city boasts lovely lakes and parks.* —*n.* Bragging statement: *Don't believe all his boasts that he is the best player on the team.*

boil·er | **boi′** lər | *n.* **1.** A large tank for heating water and turning it into steam. **2.** A pot or kettle used for boiling liquids.

bois·ter·ous | **boi′** stər əs | *or* | **boi′** strəs | *adj.* Noisy and not having discipline; unruly: *The speaker asked the boisterous audience to be quiet.*

bor·row | **bŏr′** ō | *or* | **bôr′** ō | *v.* **1.** To take something from someone with the understanding that it must be given back: *borrow a pencil; borrow a library book.* **2.** To adopt: *The English language borrowed many words from other languages.*
  Idiom. **borrow trouble.** To take on trouble unnecessarily.

both·er | **bŏ***th***′** ər | *v.* **1.** To trouble; disturb; annoy: *Don't bother me while I'm reading.* **2.** To take the trouble; to be concerned: *Don't bother waiting for me.* —*n.* Something or someone that is annoying: *Washing dishes is a bother.*

bot·tom | **bŏt′** əm | *n.* **1.** The lowest part: *the bottom of the well.* **2.** The under or lower part: *The bottom of the boat was covered with barnacles.* **3.** The ground under water: *The bottom is muddy here.* **4.** The basis; heart: *get to the bottom of the problem.*
  Idiom. **from top to bottom.** Thoroughly: *The detective searched the house from top to bottom.*

bought Look up **buy.**

bowl¹ |bōl | *n.* **1.** A round dish used to hold things. **2.** Something shaped like a bowl.

bowl² | bōl | *v.* **1.** To play the game of bowling:

Carol likes to bowl after school. **2.** To roll a ball in the game of bowling: *Who bowls first?*

bowl·ing | **bō′** lĭng | *n.* A game played by rolling a heavy ball down a wooden alley to knock over ten wooden pins at the opposite end.

brain | brān | *n.* **1.** The large mass of nerve tissue inside the skull of a person or animal. **2. brains.** Intelligence: *The pioneers had brains as well as courage.*
  Idiom. **rack one's brains.** To try hard to solve something.

branch | brănch | *or* | bränch | *n., pl.* **branch·es.** **1.** A part of a tree or shrub that grows out from the trunk. **2.** Any part that grows out of a main part: *a branch of the river.* —*v.* To divide into branches: *Turn left where the road branches.*

break | brāk | *v.* **broke** | brōk|, **bro·ken** | **brō′** kən |, **break·ing.** **1.** To make something come apart by force; smash. **2.** To harm; damage. **3.** To fail to obey; break the law. **4.** To change: *break an Olympic record.* **5.** To fill with sorrow: *break a heart.* —*n.* **1.** A gap; opening: *a break in the fence.* **2.** A beginning: *the break of day.* **3.** A sudden change: *a break in the weather.*

break·fast | **brĕk′** fəst | *n.* The first meal of the day. —*v.* To eat breakfast.

breath | brĕth | *n.* The air inhaled into and exhaled from the lungs.
  Idioms. **hold one's breath.** To wait anxiously or excitedly. **out of breath.** Breathing hard; panting. **save one's breath.** To refrain from useless talking: *Save your breath—he won't go.* **take one's breath away.** To excite or surprise greatly. **under one's breath.** In a whisper.

breathe | brēth | *v.* **breathed, breath·ing.** **1.** To inhale and exhale. **2.** To stop for a rest: *The athlete needed a minute to breathe.* **3.** To say quietly; whisper: *I won't breathe a word about the surprise party.*

bridge¹ | brĭj | *n.* **1.** Something built over a river, road, or other obstacle so that people can get across. **2.** The top part of a person's nose. —*v.* **bridged, bridg·ing.** To build a bridge over.

bridge² | brĭj | *n.* A card game for four people.

bring | brĭng | *v.* **brought** | brôt |, **bring·ing.** **1.** To carry along or escort: *Bring your sister to our party.* **2.** To cause to happen: *April showers bring May flowers.* **3.** To recall: *bring back happy memories.*

broad·cast | **brôd′** kăst′ | *or* | -kăst′ | *v.*
broad·cast *or* **broad·cast·ed, broad·cast·ing.**
1. To send out news, music, etc. by radio or
television. **2.** To make known: *broadcast
gossip.* —*n.* A radio or television program: *We
listen to the news broadcast at noon.*

broil | broil | *v.* **1.** To cook directly over or under
heat: *Dad likes to broil steak.* **2.** To be very
hot: *We broiled in the hot sunlight.*

brooch | brōch | *or* | brōōch | *n., pl.* **brooch·es.**
A large pin worn for decoration: *The woman
wore a diamond brooch on her dress.*

brought Look up **bring.**

budg·et | **bŭj′** ĭt | *n.* A plan for using the money
that one receives: *We have a budget so that
we won't spend more money than we earn.*
—*v.* **budg·et·ed, budg·et·ing.** To make a plan
in advance for spending money: *I budget my
allowance so that I can save a little each week.*

build | bĭld | *v.* **built** | bĭlt |, **build·ing. 1.** To
make by putting parts together. **2.** To make
gradually: *She wanted to build a good
business.* —*n.* A person's physical make-up:
The athlete had a good build.

built Look up **build.**

busi·ness | **bĭz′** nĭs | *n., pl.* **busi·ness·es.**
1. What one does to earn a living; occupation:
Her family is in the jewelry business.
2. A factory or store: *They sold their business
when they retired.* **3.** Concern, affair: *none of
your business.*

bus·y | **bĭz′** ē | *adj.* **bus·i·er, bus·i·est. 1.** Active:
We are busy getting ready for a vacation.
2. Full of activity: *a busy day.* **3.** In use: *The
phone is busy.*—*v.* **bus·ied, bus·y·ing, bus·ies.**
To make busy: *busy yourself with homework.*

buy | bī | *v.* **bought** | bôt|, **bought, buy·ing.** To
purchase. —*n.* A bargain: *This jacket was a
good buy.*

by-line, also **by·line** | **bī′** lĭn′ | *n.* A line at the
beginning of a newspaper or magazine article
giving the name of the writer.

C

cal·en·dar | **kăl′** ən dər | *n.* **1.** A chart that shows
the days, weeks, and months of the year.
2. A schedule; a list of things to be done

arranged in order: *the school calendar.*

calf[1] | kăf | *or* |kăf | *n., pl.* **calves** | kăvs | *or*
| kävz |. **1.** A young cow or bull. **2.** A young
whale, elephant, or seal. **3.** Leather made
from the hide of a calf; calfskin.

calf[2] | kăf | *or* |kăf | *n., pl.* **calves** | kăvs | *or*
| kävz |. The fleshy back of the human leg
below the knee.

cam·er·a | **kăm′** ər ə | *or* | **kăm′** rə | *n.* **1.** A machine
for taking photographs or motion pictures. **2.** The
part of a television system that changes an image
into electronic signals.

can·did | **kăn′** dĭd | *adj.* Honest; frank; open:
*Because the mayor wanted everyone to know
all the facts, she gave candid answers at the
town meeting.*

ca·noe | kə **nōō′** | *n.* A light, narrow boat with
pointed ends that is moved with a paddle. —*v.*
ca·noed, ca·noe·ing. To paddle or go in a
canoe.

can·o·py | **kăn′** ə pē | *n., pl.* **can·o·pies.**
1. A covering made of cloth or other material
hung over a bed, throne, or entrance: *The
canopy over the bed was made of white cloth.*
2. A covering that is similar but found
somewhere else: *In the rain forest, a canopy
of leaves from the taller trees shades the
smaller plants.*

care·ful | **kâr′** fəl | *adj.* **1.** Watchful; cautious:
Be careful crossing busy streets. **2.** Done with
care: *careful handling of the expensive
equipment.*

cart·wheel | **kärt′** hwēl′ | *or* | -wēl′ | *n.* **1.** The
wheel of a cart. **2.** A sideways handspring.

cas·sette | kə **sĕt′** | *or* | kă- | *n.* **1.** A small case
that holds magnetic tape for use in a tape
recorder. **2.** A case that holds a roll of film for
a camera.

catch | kăch | *v.* **caught** | kôt |, **catch·ing.**
1. To get hold of something that is moving.
2. To be in time for: *catch a train.* **3.** To
become infected: *catch a cold.* —*n.* **1.** The act
of grabbing a ball: *The baseball player made a
great catch.* **2.** The amount of something you
have caught: *a catch of five trout.* **3.** A game
in which a ball is thrown back and forth.
Idiom. **catch one's breath.** To rest.

caught Look up **catch.**

ce·les·tial | sə **lĕs′** chəl | *adj.* **1.** Related to the
sky: *The moon and stars are celestial bodies.*
2. Heavenly; divine.

cel·lar | **sĕl′** ər | *n.* An underground storage room.

cen·ter | **sĕn′** tər | *n.* The middle point of a
circle or a ball. **2.** The middle of anything: *the
center of the table.* **3.** A center of activity: *a
shopping center.*

cen·tu·ry | **sĕn′** chə rē | *n., pl.* **cen·tu·ries.**
A period of 100 years.

cer·tain | **sûr′** tn | *adj.* **1.** Positive; sure: *I'm
certain this is the right road.* **2.** Some: *Certain
animals hibernate in winter.*

chalk·board | **chôk′** bôrd′ | *or* | -bōrd′ | *n.*

A hard surface used for writing on with chalk; a blackboard.

cham·pi·on | **chăm'** pē ən | *n.* A person or animal that wins first place in a contest.

chap·ter | **chăp'** tər | *n.* **1.** A main division of a book. **2.** A small division of a club.

char·ac·ter | **kăr'** ĭk tər | *n.* **1.** All the qualities that make a person or thing what it is. **2.** A person in a book, play, or story. **3.** *Informal.* A person who is different or funny.

charge | chärj | *v.* **charged, charg·ing. 1.** To ask as a price. **2.** To delay payment: *We charged our new rug.* **3.** To attack: *charge the fort.* **4.** To give electricity to: *charge a flashlight battery.* —*n.* **1.** The price asked: *the charge for delivery.* **2.** Responsibility; supervision: *take charge of someone or something.* **3.** An amount of electricity.

check·er | **chĕk'** ər | *n.* **1. a. checkers** (*used with a singular verb*). A game played on a checkerboard by two players. **b.** One of the flat, round pieces used in this game. **2.** One square in a pattern of squares. **3.** An employee who checks out purchases in a self-service store.

cheese·burg·er | **chēz'** bûr' gər | *n.* A hamburger sandwich with melted cheese on the meat.

chick·en | **chĭk'** ən | *or* | -ĭn | *n.* **1.** A hen or rooster. **2.** The meat of this bird. —*adj. Slang.* Afraid.

chil·i | **chĭl'** ē | *n., pl.* **chil·ies. 1.** The pod of a red pepper that is often dried and ground to make a spicy seasoning. **2.** A spicy food made of chili powder, beef, tomatoes, and sometimes beans. *These sound alike* **chili, chilly.**

chill·y | **chĭl'** ē | *adj.* **chill·i·er, chill·i·est. 1.** Cold enough to be somewhat uncomfortable: *Fall days are often chilly.* **2.** Unfriendly: *I was upset by the chilly greeting my friend gave me after our vacation. These sound alike* **chilly, chili.**

chim·ney | **chĭm'** nē | *n., pl.* **chim·neys.** An upright, hollow structure connected to a furnace, fireplace, or stove to carry away smoke.

choice | chois | *n.* **1.** The act of choosing: *make a choice between two things.* **2.** Someone or something that is chosen: *Your choices for a*

job *are many.* —*adj.* **choic·er, choic·est.** Very good; excellent: *choice fruit.*

choose | chooz | *v.* **chose** | chōz |, **cho·sen** | **chō'** zən|, **choos·ing. 1.** To pick out: *choose a dessert.* **2.** To decide: *Do as you choose.*

cho·rus | **kôr'** əs | *or* | **kŏr'**- | *n., pl.* **cho·rus·es. 1.** A group of people who sing together. **2.** The part of a song that is repeated after each verse.

chose Look up **choose.**

cit·rus | **sĭt'** rəs | *adj.* Belonging to orange, lemon, lime, or grapefruit trees. —*n., pl.* **cit·rus·es** or **cit·rus.** One of these trees.

climb | klīm | *v.* To go up or move up. —*n.* **1.** The act of climbing: *the climb up the mountain.* **2.** A place to be climbed: *The rocky path is a difficult climb.*

clos·et | **klŏz'** ĭt | *n.* A small room or cabinet used for hanging or storing things.

cloth·ing | **klō'** thĭng | *n.* Coverings worn on the body.

clue | kloo | *n.* Something that helps solve a mystery.

coach | kōch | *n.* **1.** A large carriage pulled by horses. **2.** A train car for passengers. **3.** A low-priced seat on a bus, train, or plane. **4.** A trainer: *a basketball coach; a voice coach.*

coast | kōst | *n.* The edge of land along the sea. —*v.* To move without power or effort: *coast down a hill.*

code | kōd | *n.* **1.** A set of signals that stand for letters and numerals: *Morse Code.* **2.** Secret writing: *The spy wrote the message in code.* **3.** A set of rules or laws: *a traffic code.* —*v.* **cod·ed, cod·ing.** To put into code.

coin | koin | *n.* A piece of metal issued by a government for use as money. —*v.* **1.** To make coins. **2.** To invent: *coin a phrase.*

col·lar | **kŏl'** ər | *n.* Something that is worn around the neck: *lace collar; dog collar.* —*v. Informal.* To capture: *collar a thief.*

col·lec·tion | kə **lĕk'** shən | *n.* **1.** A group of things gathered and kept together: *stamp collection.* **2.** Money that is gathered: *We took up a collection to buy him a gift.*

col·um·nist | **kŏl'** əm nĭst | *or* | -ə mĭst | *n.* One who writes a newspaper or magazine column.

com·et | **kŏm'** ĭt | *n.* A heavenly body with a bright head and a long tail. Comets travel around the sun.

com·fort | **kŭm'** fərt | *v.* To ease someone's sorrow. —*n.* **1.** A condition of ease: *They live in comfort.* **2.** A person or thing that gives relief: *He is a comfort to his mother.*

com·ma | kŏm′ ə | *n.* A punctuation mark (,) that separates parts of a sentence, parts of an address, and dates.

com·mer·cial | kə mûr′ shəl | *adj.* Relating to or engaged in business: *a commercial product.* —*n.* A radio or television advertisement.

com·mit | kə mĭt′ | *v.* **com·mit·ted, com·mit·ting.** To do, carry out, or be guilty of: *commit a crime.*

com·mon | kŏm′ ən | *adj.* **com·mon·er, com·mon·est. 1.** Shared by all: *common knowledge; common property.* **2.** Occurring often; usual: *Rain is common along the coast.* **3.** Average; ordinary: *common housefly.*
    Idiom. **in common.** Jointly: *interests in common.*

com·pa·ny | kŭm′ pə nē | *n., pl.* **com·pa·nies. 1.** One or more guests. **2.** Companionship. **3.** A business firm. **4.** A group of actors.

com·pare | kəm pâr′ | *v.* **com·pared, com·par·ing.** To show how things are alike or different: *Let's compare our answers.*

com·pass | kŭm′ pəs | *or* | kŏm′- | *n.* **1.** An instrument used to show direction north, south, east, or west. **2.** An instrument used for drawing circles.

com·pel | kəm pĕl′ | *v.* **com·pelled, com·pel·ling.** To force or make someone do something: *A big snowstorm might compel schools to close early.*

com·pete | kəm pēt′ | *v.* **com·pet·ed, com·pet·ing.** To try hard against others to win something: *compete in a race; compete in business.*

com·pe·ti·tion | kŏm′ pĭ tĭsh′ ən | *n.* **1.** A contest: *a diving competition.* **2.** The person or persons one competes with: *Is the competition any good?*

com·plain | kəm plān′ | *v.* To say that something is wrong: *complain about a headache.*

com·plete | kəm plēt′ | *adj.* **1.** Whole: *a complete set of the encyclopedia.* **2.** Finished; ended: *My report is complete.* **3.** Fully equipped: *a new car complete with power steering.* —*v.* **com·plet·ed, com·plet·ing.** To finish.

con·cept | kŏn′ sĕpt′ | *n.* A general idea, notion, or understanding: *The concept of equal rights for all is important in the United States.*

con·demn | kən dĕm′ | *v.* **1.** To strongly disapprove of: *I condemn cheating on a test.* **2.** To find someone guilty and give the punishment: *The judge condemned the robber to five years in prison.* **3.** To say something is unsafe: *The inspector may condemn the run-down apartment building.*

con·serve | kən sûrv′ | *v.* **con·served, con·serv·ing.** To keep from loss, waste, or harm by using carefully: *Our class learned how to conserve the earth's natural resources.*

con·stel·la·tion | kŏn′ stə lā′ shən | *n.* A group of stars, such as the Big Dipper.

con·ster·na·tion | kŏn′ stər nā′ shən | *n.* Great fear, shock, or loss of courage: *Even though there was consternation when the fire alarm sounded, everyone got out safely.*

con·tain·er | kən tā′ nər | *n.* A box, jar, or can used to hold something.

con·trol | kən trōl′ | *v.* **con·trolled, con·trol·ling.** To have power over: *control a country; control a car.* —*n.* **1.** Authority or power: *the athlete's control over his body.* **2. controls.** Instruments for operating a machine.

cop·per | kŏp′ ər | *n.* **1.** A reddish-brown metal. **2.** Small coin. —*adj.* Reddish brown.

cos·met·ic | kŏz mĕt′ ĭk | *n., pl.* **cos·met·ics.** A preparation, such as powder, lipstick, or skin cream, used to make the face or body more beautiful.

cos·mos | kŏz′ məs | *or* | kŏz′ mōs′ | *n.* The universe thought of as an orderly and harmonious system.

cot·tage | kŏt′ ĭj | *n.* **1.** A small house. **2.** A summer house at the beach.

coun·try | kŭn′ trē | *n., pl.* **coun·tries. 1.** A nation or state: *Mexico is a country.* **2.** The land outside of towns and cities: *Farms are in the country.*

cou·ple | kŭp′ əl | *n.* **1.** Two things of the same kind; a pair. **2.** A man and a woman who are engaged, married, or partners in a dance. **3.** *Informal.* A few: *a couple of months.* —*v.* **cou·pled, cou·pling.** To join together.

course | kôrs | *or* | kōrs | *n.* **1.** Onward motion; progress: *the course of history.* **2.** Direction; path: *the course of a river.* **3.** Lessons and classes in a subject. **4.** A piece of land laid out for a sport: *golf course.*
    Idiom. **of course.** Naturally; certainly.

court | kôrt | *or* | kōrt | *n.* **1.** An open place enclosed by buildings or walls. **2.** A place marked for a game: *tennis court.* **3.** A place for holding legal trials. —*v.* **1.** To seek the favor of. **2.** To try to win in marriage.

cous·in | kŭz′ ən | *n.* The daughter or son of an aunt or uncle.

crack | krăk | *v.* To break with a sharp, snapping sound. —*n.* **1.** A sharp, snapping sound. **2.** A long, narrow opening; a narrow space.

crash | krăsh | *v.* **1.** To fall against or bump into noisily. **2.** To collide. —*n., pl.* **crash·es. 1.** A loud noise like that made by things falling and breaking. **2.** A violent collision.

crawl | krôl | *v.* **1.** To move slowly on hands and knees or by dragging the body along the ground. **2.** To move very slowly: *The cars crawled up the crowded street.* —*n.* **1.** A slow movement. **2.** A swimming stroke.

crush | krŭsh | *v.* **1.** To press together so as to crumple or injure; squash. **2.** To break into small pieces: *crush ice.* —*n.* A dense crowd: *a crush of people.*

cy·cling | sī′ klĭng | *n.* The sport of riding a bicycle or motorcycle.

D

dam·age | dăm′ ĭj | *n.* Injury or harm. —*v.* To injure; harm; hurt.

dan·ger·ous | dān′ jər əs | *adj.* Unsafe; risky; likely to do harm.

daugh·ter | dô′ tər | *n.* A female child; a girl or woman, when thought of in relation to her parents.

dawn | dôn | *n.* The coming of daylight in the morning. —*v.* **1.** To begin to grow light in the morning. **2.** To begin to appear or develop: *A new age dawned.*

De·cem·ber | dĭ sĕm′ bər | *n.* The 12th month of the year. December has 31 days.

de·cide | dĭ sīd′ | *v.* **de·cid·ed, de·cid·ing.** To make up one's mind; come to a conclusion.

de·clare | dĭ klâr′ | *v.* **de·clared, de·clar·ing. 1.** To make known; announce: *The company declared a new policy.* **2.** To take a stand: *He declared himself in favor of building a new school.*

ded·i·ca·tion | dĕd′ ĭ kā′ shən | *n.* The fact of giving oneself completely to something; devotion: *She shows her dedication to the violin by practicing two hours every day.*

de·feat | dĭ fēt′ | *v.* To overcome; beat; win a victory over. —*n.* An overthrow.

de·gree | dĭ grē′ | *n., pl.* **de·grees. 1.** A unit of measuring temperature. **2.** A unit used in measuring angles: *a 90-degree angle.* **3.** A title given by a college or university. **4.** Amount, extent: *a high degree of skill.*

de·lay | dĭ lā′ | *v.* To put off until later. —*n.* The act of putting off; a wait.

de·liv·er·y | dĭ lĭv′ ə rē | *n., pl.* **de·liv·er·ies. 1.** Distribution; handing over: *mail delivery.* **2.** Manner of speaking: *Her forceful delivery made us listen to her speech.*

de·part | dĭ pärt′ | *v.* **1.** To go away; leave: *The bus departs in five minutes.* **2.** To change: *The builders departed from the original plan for the house.*

depth | dĕpth | *n.* **1.** The distance from the top to the bottom: *the depth of the lake.* **2.** Deepness of thought, tone, color, etc.

des·ert[1] | dĕz′ ərt | *n.* A dry, sandy region.

de·sert[2] | dĭ zûrt′ | *v.* To forsake; abandon: *She did not desert her friends when they needed her.*

de·stroy | dĭ stroi′ | *v.* To ruin; make useless; lay waste.

dif·fer·ent | dĭf′ ər ənt | *or* | dĭf′ rənt | *adj.* **1.** Not alike: *Our paintings are different.* **2.** Separate; distinct; not the same: *We saw him at three different times today.* **3.** Unusual: *a different way of dressing.*

di·rec·tion | dĭ rĕk′ shən | *or* | dī- | *n.* **1.** Management; guidance. **2.** The point toward which a person or thing faces, points, or moves. **3. directions.** Orders; instructions: *Read the directions before you begin the test.*

di·rec·tor | dĭ rĕk′ tər | *or* | dī- | *n.* A person who directs or manages something.

dirt·y | dûr′ tē | *adj.* **dirt·i·er, dirt·i·est. 1.** Not clean: *dirty clothes.* **2.** Unfair: *a dirty trick.*

dis·charge | dĭs chärj′ | *v.* **dis·charged, dis·charg·ing. 1.** To let go; release. **2.** To remove; unload: *discharge cargo.*

dis·close | dĭ sklōz′ | *v.* **dis·closed, dis·clos·ing.** To reveal or make known: *The teacher will disclose the answer to the puzzle later.*

dis·cov·er | dĭ skŭv′ ər | *v.* **1.** To find out: *They discovered they were late.* **2.** To make known for the first time: *The explorer discovered the source of the river.*

dis·cuss | dĭ skŭs′ | *v.* To talk over thoughtfully; consider.

dis·ease | dĭ **zēz′** | *n.* Sickness; illness.

dis·lodge | dĭs **lŏj′** | *v.* **dis·lodged, dis·lodg·ing.**
To move out of a place or position: *It is hard to dislodge the big rock from the soil.*

dis·tort | dĭ **stôrt′** | *v.* **1.** To twist or bend out of the usual shape: *When I look in the lake, the ripples of the water distort my face.* **2.** To change the facts so that what one says is partly false: *Don't distort what really happened.*

di·vide | dĭ **vīd′** | *v.* **di·vid·ed, di·vid·ing.**
1. To separate; keep apart. **2.** To share.

dol·lar | **dŏl′** ər | *n.* **1.** The unit of money in the United States and some other countries. **2.** A paper note or silver coin equal to 100 cents.

dou·ble | **dŭb′** əl | *adj.* **1.** Twice as much. **2.** In pairs: *double doors.* —*v.* **dou·bled, dou·bling.** **1.** To make twice as great. **2.** To fold over: *double the blanket.*

dou·bly | **dŭb′** lē | *adv.* In twice the amount or degree: *I wanted to win the bicycle race, so I pedaled doubly fast.*

dough | dō | *n.* A thick mixture of flour, water or milk, and other ingredients for baking into bread, cake, etc.

doz·en | **dŭz′** ən | *n.* A group of twelve.

E

ear·ly | **ûr′** lē | *adj.* **ear·li·er, ear·li·est.** **1.** Near the beginning: *the early evening.* **2.** Before the usual time: *The early bird catches the worm.* —*adv.* **1.** At or near the beginning of: *early in the morning.* **2.** Before the usual time: *to arrive early.*

earn | ûrn | *v.* **1.** To receive as payment in return for work: *earn $10 a week.* **2.** To gain through effort: *He earned good grades.* **3.** To deserve: *earn gratitude.*

ear·phone | **îr′** fōn′ | *n., pl.* **ear·phones.** A telephone, radio, TV, or stereo receiver that is held to the ear by a band over the head.

earth·en·ware | **ûr′** thən wâr′ | *n.* Pots, bowls, dishes, vases, and other like objects made from clay and baked at a low temperature.

ea·sel | **ē′** zəl | *n.* A tall stand or frame used to support, hold, or display things such as artists' paintings, chalkboards, or signs: *The artist put the canvas on the easel and began to paint.*

ech·o | **ĕk′** ō | *n., pl.* **ech·oes.** A repetition of sound, caused by the throwing back of sound waves. —*v.* To give back or repeat sound.

e·clipse | ĭ **klĭps′** | *n.* **1.** A complete or partial darkening of the sun caused by passage of the moon between it and the earth. **2.** A darkening of the moon by the earth's shadow. —*v.* **e·clipsed, e·clips·ing.** To overshadow: *Her performance eclipsed all the others.*

ed·i·to·ri·al | ĕd′ ĭ **tôr′** ē əl | *or* | -**tōr′-** | *n.* An article in a newspaper or magazine or a comment on a radio or TV station that gives the opinions of the editor, owner, or publisher.

ed·u·ca·tion | ĕj′ ŏŏ **kā′** shən | *n.*
1. Training, schooling: *public school education.* **2.** Knowledge and skill.

el·bow | **ĕl′** bō | *n.* The joint in the arm between wrist and shoulder. —*v.* To nudge, jostle, or push: *elbow through the crowd.*

e·lec·tion | ĭ **lĕk′** shən | *n.* A choosing or selecting by vote.

el·e·phant | **ĕl′** ə fənt | *n.* A very large Asian or African animal with a thick, wrinkled hide, stout legs, long tusks, and a long, flexible trunk.

else | ĕls | *adj.* **1.** Besides; in addition. **2.** Instead. **3.** Otherwise.

em·ploy | ĕm **ploi′** | *v.* **1.** To hire; give work to. **2.** To make use of: *Employ your study time to good advantage.*

em·ploy·er | ĕm **ploi′** ər | *n.* A person or business that hires people to work for pay: *The employer gave everyone who worked for the company a raise.*

em·ploy·ment | ĕm **ploi′** mənt | *n.* **1.** Work; occupation; job. **2.** The act of putting to use: *The employment of harsh measures was necessary to save the city.*

emp·ty | **ĕmp′** tē | *adj.* **1.** Containing nothing. **2.** Without meaning: *empty promises.* —*v.* **emp·tied, emp·ty·ing, emp·ties.** To remove the contents of.

en·deav·or | ĕn **dĕv′** ər | *n.* A serious attempt; effort: *My endeavor to learn to swim paid off when I was able to swim in the ocean on our vacation.* —*v.* To seriously try; attempt: *Let's endeavor to get better grades.*

en·er·gy | **ĕn′** ər jē | *n., pl.* **en·er·gies.** **1.** The ability to do work. **2.** Force; strength.

en·joy | ĕn **joi′** | *v.* **1.** To take pleasure in: *enjoy the parade.* **2.** To have or benefit by: *enjoy good health.*

e·nough | ĭ **nŭf′** | *adj.* As much or as many as necessary or desirable: *There is enough paint for everyone in the art class.* —*n.* A sufficient amount: *We have had enough to eat.* —*adv.* Fully; quite: *I felt well enough to go to school.*

e·quip·ment | ĭ **kwĭp′** mənt | n. The things needed for a particular purpose: *garden equipment.*

es·cape | ĭ **skāp′** | v. **es·caped, es·cap·ing. 1.** To break loose; get free; get away: *escape from jail.* **2.** To avoid: *escape a storm.* —n. **1.** The act of escaping. **2.** A means of escape: *the fire escape.*

eve·ning | **ēv′** nĭng | n. The time between sunset and bedtime; early night.

ex·am·ple | ĭg **zăm′** pəl | *or* | -**zăm′**- | n. **1.** Sample. **2.** Someone or something that is a model. **3.** A warning: *Let this be an example.*
   Idioms. **for example.** Serving as a model.
set an example. To be a model worthy of imitation.

ex·cel·lent | **ĕk′** sə lənt | adj. Extremely good; unusually high in quality.

ex·cept | ĭk **sĕpt′** | prep. Outside of; apart from: *everyone except me.* —conj. Only: *I could finish reading my book except I'd rather play the piano.*

ex·er·cise | **ĕk′** sər sīz′ | n., pl. **ex·er·cis·es.** Physical or mental activity that improves the body or mind. —v. **ex·er·cised, ex·er·cis·ing. 1.** To put into action: *exercise care.* **2.** To do exercise: *exercise your muscles.*

ex·ile | **ĕg′** zīl′ | *or* | **ĕk′** sīl′ | n. An enforced living away from one's country, often as punishment: *The spy's exile meant that he couldn't visit his native land.* —v. **ex·iled, ex·il·ing.** To send away from one's native land as punishment.

ex·pect | ĭk **spĕkt′** | v. **1.** To look forward to something that will probably happen. **2.** To wait for or feel sure of the arrival of: *I was expecting you.* **3.** To require: *You are expected to do a good job.*

ex·pert | **ĕk′** spûrt′ | n. A person who has special skill or knowledge. —adj. | ĭk **spûrt′** | *or* | **ĕk′** spûrt′ |. **1.** Having special skill or knowledge: *an expert swimmer.* **2.** Given by an expert: *expert advice.*

ex·plain | ĭk **splān′** | v. **1.** To make plain or clear; tell the meaning of: *explain directions.* **2.** To give the reason for: *explain your mistake.*

ex·ploit | **ĕk′** sploit′ | v. To make the best use of: *Maria wants to exploit her ability to get along with animals by becoming an animal trainer.* —n. A daring act: *The exciting book was about the exploits of the hero.*

ex·port | ĭk **spôrt′** | *or* | -**spōrt′** | *or* | **ĕk′** spôrt′ | *or* | -spōrt′ | v. To send or carry out goods to another country for sale or trade. —n. **1.** The act of exporting. **2.** Goods sold and sent to another country.

ex·tra | **ĕk′** strə | adj. More than what is usual or expected: *earn extra cash.* —adv. Especially: *an extra good dinner.* —n. Often **extras.** Something additional: *a car with all the extras.*

fac·to·ry | **făk′** tə rē | n., pl. **fac·to·ries.** A building or group of buildings where things are made.

fan·cy | **făn′** sē | adj. **fan·ci·er, fan·ci·est.** Not plain; elaborate: *fancy clothes.* —n., pl. **fan·cies. 1.** Imagination. **2.** A whim: *a sudden fancy for ice cream.* —v. **fan·cied, fan·cy·ing, fan·cies. 1.** To imagine. **2.** To like.

fare | fâr | n. The cost of a ride on a plane, bus, train, taxi, etc.

far·ther | **fär′** thər | adv. To a greater distance: *She hiked farther than I did.* —adj. More distant: *He lives a mile farther down the road.*

fault | fôlt | n. **1.** Blame; responsibility: *It was my fault.* **2.** A weakness; shortcoming. **3.** A mistake.

Feb·ru·ar·y | **fĕb′** rōō ĕr′ ē | *or* | **fĕb′** yōō- | n. The second month of the year. February has 28 days except in leap years, when it has 29 days.

fe·male | **fē′** māl′ | adj. Having to do with women or girls; a female voice. —n. **1.** A girl or woman. **2.** A female animal.

feud | fyōōd | n. A very long, unpleasant quarrel between two people, families, groups, or countries: *The feud lasted so long that people forgot why they were angry at each other.* —v. **feud·ed, feud·ing.** To carry on a long, bitter quarrel: *Let's not feud with each other.*

fight | fīt| v. **fought** | fôt|, **fight·ing.** To take part in a struggle or battle: *Doctors fight disease.* —n. **1.** A struggle; battle. **2.** A quarrel.

film | fĭlm | n. **1.** A thin strip or roll prepared for taking photographs. **2.** A motion picture; movie. —v. To make a movie of.

fi·nal | **fī′** nəl | adj. **1.** Coming at the end; last: *the final act of a play.* **2.** Settling the matter; deciding: *the final words on the subject.* —n. Often **finals.** The last game or last examination.

firm¹ | fûrm | adj. **firm·er, firm·est. 1.** Solid; not easily moved. **2.** Not changing: *a firm belief.* **3.** Steady: *a firm voice.*

firm² | fûrm | n. A group of persons who have joined in a business: *a law firm.*

flash·light | **flăsh′** līt′ | n. A small portable electric light.

float | flōt | v. **1.** To be held up by liquid or air. **2.** To move or drift freely. —n. **1.** Something that floats: *a float on a fishline.* **2.** An exhibit on a platform with wheels, used in a parade. **3.** A soft drink made with ice cream floating in it.

flood | flŭd | n. **1.** A great flow of water over land that is usually dry. **2.** A great outpouring: *a flood of tears; a flood of letters.* —v. **1.** To cover with water. **2.** To supply in large quantity.

fol·low | fŏl′ ō | v. **1.** To come after; go after: *follow me.* **2.** To go along: *follow this road.* **3.** To accept as a guide; obey: *follow the rules; follow directions.*

fool·ish | fōo′ lĭsh | adj. Without sense; unwise; silly; ridiculous.

foot·ball | fŏot′ bôl′ | n. **1.** A game played by two teams of 11 players each on a long field with a goal at either end. The object is to carry the ball across the opponent's goal line or kick it over his goal. **2.** The oval leather ball used in this game.

for·tu·nate | fôr′ chə nĭt | adj. Favored; lucky.

fought Look up **fight.**

frac·tion | frăk′ shən | n. **1.** A part of a fragment. **2.** A ratio: *¹/₂; ³/₄.*

fraud | frôd | n. An intentional trick or deception of someone in order to gain an unfair advantage or to cheat: *It is fraud to copy a video game and sell it as an original.*

fray | frā | v. **frayed, fray·ing.** To wear away and separate into loose threads, especially along the edge: *My favorite shirt began to fray at the collar.*

freeze | frēz | v. **froze** | frōz |, **froz·en** | frō′ zən |, **freez·ing. 1.** To change into ice. **2.** To make or become hard or solid with cold: *freeze meat in the refrigerator.* **3.** To become very cold: *I froze in that wind.* **4.** To become motionless: *freeze in terror.* —n. A frost; a condition of extreme coldness: *a sudden freeze.*

fric·tion | frĭk′ shən | n. The rubbing of one thing or surface against another: *The friction of the tires and the road causes tires to wear out.*

Fri·day | frī′ dē | or | -dā′ | n. The sixth day of the week.

friend·ly | frĕnd′ lē | adj. **friend·li·er, friend·li·est. 1.** Like a friend; kind: *a friendly person.* **2.** Not hostile: *a friendly game.*

front-page | frŭnt′ pāj′ | adj. Printed on or important enough to be printed on the first page of the newspaper: *a front-page headline.*

fruit | frōot | n., pl. **fruit** or **fruits.** The part of a plant that contains the seeds.

fur·nish | fûr′ nĭsh | v. **1.** To equip with furniture: *furnish a house.* **2.** To supply; provide: *furnish cookies for the party.*

fur·ni·ture | fûr′ nə chər | n. Articles, usually movable, to make a room fit for living or working, such as tables, desks, chairs, beds, etc.

fu·ror | fyŏor′ ôr′ | or | -ər | n. An outburst or noisy commotion; uproar: *The closing of the popular zoo caused a furor in the town.*

G

gal·ax·y | găl′ ək sē | n., pl. **gal·ax·ies. 1.** A large group of stars, dust, and gas. **2. the Galaxy.** The Milky Way; the galaxy that contains our sun and solar system.

gar·bage | gär′ bĭj | n. **1.** Scraps of food that are thrown away. **2.** Trash.

gath·er | găth′ ər | v. **1.** To bring together; collect: *We gathered around the scoutmaster.* **2.** To conclude: *I gather you are excited about your new bike.* **3.** To pull cloth together with a thread: *gather a skirt.* —n. a small fold made by gathering cloth.

gen·er·al | jĕn′ ər əl | adj. **1.** For everyone; for the whole: *a general meeting.* **2.** Common to most; widespread: *general interest in sports.* **3.** Not detailed: *Give us a general idea of how your invention works.* —n. A high-ranking officer in the Army, Air Force, or Marine Corps.

  ***Idiom.* in general.** Usually; for the most part.

gen·tle | jĕn′ tl | adj. **gen·tler, gen·tlest. 1.** Mild: *a gentle hug.* **2.** Tame: *a gentle donkey.* **3.** Soft; low: *gentle lapping of the waves.* **4.** Gradual; not steep: *gentle slope of the hill.*

glue | glōo | n. A substance used to stick things together. —v. **glued, glu·ing. 1.** To fasten together with glue. **2.** To hold firmly: *My eyes were glued to the clock.*

golf | gŏlf | or | gôlf | n. A game played outdoors over a large course. The course has 9 or 18 holes into which a player must try to hit a ball with a club. —v. To play this game.

gov·ern·ment | gŭv′ ərn mənt | n. **1.** The group of people who rule a country, state, city, etc.: *We elect our government.* **2.** A way of ruling: *a democratic government.*

grass·hop·per | grăs′ hŏp′ ər | or | grăs′- | n. A winged insect with strong back legs for jumping.

greet | grēt | *v.* **1.** To welcome politely: *greet the guests.* **2.** To receive; to respond to: *Her arrival was greeted with joy.*

grind | grīnd | *v.* **ground** | ground |, **grind·ing. 1.** To crush into fine pieces: *grind wheat into flour.* **2.** To sharpen or smooth: *grind a knife.* **3.** To grate: *grind your teeth.*

groan | grōn | *v.* To make a deep, sad or annoyed sound. —*n.* A moan. *These sound alike* **groan, grown.**

grow | grō | *v.* **grew** | grōō |, **grown** | grōn |, **grow·ing. 1.** To become bigger. **2.** To exist: *Moss grows in the shade.* **3.** To raise; produce: *grow vegetables.* **4.** To become: *grow cold.*

grown Look up **grow.** *These sound alike* **grown, groan.**

guide | gīd | *n.* Someone or something that shows the way or directs: *a museum guide.* —*v.* **guid·ed, guid·ing.** To direct; show the way; lead.

guilt·y | gĭl′ tē | *adj.* **guilt·i·er, guilt·i·est. 1.** Having done wrong; deserving blame or punishment: *guilty of a crime.* **2.** Feeling that one has done wrong: *a guilty conscience.*

gui·tar | gĭ tär′ | *n.* A musical instrument that has a long neck and a large sound box. Its six strings are played with the fingers or a pick.

H

half | hăf | *or* | häf | *n., pl.* **halves** | hăvz | *or* | hävz |. **1.** One of two equal parts. **2.** One of two equal periods of time in certain games: *the first half of the football game.*

Idioms. **in half.** Into two equal parts. **not half bad.** Good.

hall·way | hôl′ wā′ | *n.* Corridor; passageway; hall.

hand·made | hănd′ mād′ | *adj.* Made by hand rather than by a machine: *a handmade kite.*

har·vest | här′ vĭst | *n.* **1.** The act of gathering in a crop: *Farmers expect an early harvest this year.* **2.** The crop that is gathered: *We store our harvest in large barns.* —*v.* To gather a crop.

head·line | hĕd′ līn′ | *n.* Words printed in large, heavy type at the top of a newspaper or magazine article telling what the article is about.

health·y | hĕl′ thē | *adj.* **health·i·er, health·i·est. 1.** Having good health: *a healthy body.* **2.** Giving good health: *healthy exercise.*

hear | hîr | *v.* **heard** | hûrd |, **hear·ing. 1.** To receive sound through one's ears: *hear music.* **2.** To listen to with care: *hear both sides of the argument.*

heard Look up **hear.**

hem·i·sphere | hĕm′ ĭ sfîr′ | *n., pl.* **hem·i·spheres.** One half of the earth's surface as divided by either the equator or a meridian. The equator divides the Northern and Southern Hemispheres, and a meridian divides the Eastern and Western Hemispheres.

he·ro | hîr′ ō | *n., pl.* **he·roes. 1.** A person admired for courage or special achievements. **2.** The main character in a story, play, movie, etc. **3.** A large sandwich served on a long roll.

hob·by | hŏb′ ē | *n., pl.* **hob·bies.** An interesting activity that a person does for his or her own pleasure.

hock·ey | hŏk′ ē | *n.* **1.** Also **ice hockey.** A game played on ice by two teams of six players each. The players wear skates and use sticks to try to hit a puck into the other team's goal. **2.** Also **field hockey.** A similar game played on a field with a ball and eleven players on a team.

hole | hōl | *n.* **1.** An opening: *hole in the ground; hole in a sock.* **2.** An animal's burrow: *a fox hole.* **3.** A hollow on a golf course into which a ball must be hit. *These sound alike* **hole, whole.**

hol·i·day | hŏl′ ĭ dā′ | *n.* A day when people don't work, such as Thanksgiving or a vacation.

home·work | hōm′ wûrk′ | *n.* School work assigned to be done outside the classroom.

hon·est | ŏn′ ĭst | *adj.* Truthful; fair; sincere.

hon·or | ŏn′ ər | *n.* **1.** A mark of distinction: *Winning the award was a great honor for her.* **2.** A sense of what is right; reputation; good name: *He is a man of honor.* —*v.* **1.** To show special respect to. **2.** To accept as payment.

Idiom. **on one's honor.** As a solemn promise.

hos·pi·tal | hŏs′ pĭ təl | *or* | -pĭt′ l | *n.* A place where sick or injured people are cared for.

ho·tel | hō tĕl′ | *n.* A public house where rooms and food are provided for pay.

hu·mor | hyōō′ mər | *n.* **1.** The quality of being funny: *Clowns provide humor at the circus.* **2.** The ability to enjoy something funny: *a sense of humor.* **3.** State of mind; mood: *in a bad humor.* —*v.* To give in to someone's wishes: *humor a fussy child.*

hun·dred | hŭn′ drĭd | *n.* The number 100; ten times ten.

hurt | hûrt | *v.* **hurt, hurt·ing. 1.** To cause pain to; injure: *hurt your foot.* **2.** To feel pain: *My eyes hurt after a day at the beach.* **3.** To have a bad effect on; harm: *hurt one's chances.* —*n.* An injury; pain.

hus·band | hŭz′ bənd | *n.* A married man.

I

i·de·a | ī dē′ ə | *n.* **1.** A thought or belief. **2.** The point or purpose of something: *The idea of this invention is to do away with homework.*

i·den·ti·cal | ī děn′ tĭ kəl | *adj.* **1.** Exactly alike: *My sister and I wore identical blouses.* **2.** The very same: *Natasha recited the identical poem yesterday and today.*

im·port | ĭm **pôrt′** | *or* | -**pōrt′** | *or* | **ĭm′** pôrt′ | *or* | -pōrt′ |. *v.* To bring in something from another country for sale, trade, or use. —*n.* | **ĭm′** pôrt′ | *or* | -pōrt′ |. Something imported from another country.

im·por·tant | ĭm′ **pôr′** tnt | *adj.* Having value; significant.

im·prove | ĭm **proov′** | *v.* **im·proved, im·prov·ing.** To make or become better: *improve your golf swing.*

in·crease | ĭn **krēs′** | *v.* **in·creased, in·creas·ing.** To make or become greater or larger. —*n.* |**ĭn′** krēs′ |. The amount by which something is increased: *an increase of 25 percent.*

in·dus·try | **ĭn′** də strē | *n., pl.* **in·dus·tries. 1.** Manufacturing, business, and trade: *a center of industry; the steel industry.* **2.** Hard work; steady effort: *It takes a lot of industry to become a doctor.*

in·for·ma·tion | ĭn′ fər **mā′** shən | *n.* **1.** Facts or knowledge about a subject. **2.** A service that gives facts: *Call information for his phone number.*

in·sect | **ĭn′** sěkt′ | *n.* Any of a group of small animals without backbones, having wings, six legs, and a body divided into three parts.

in·sist | ĭn **sĭst′** | *v.* To make a firm demand; take a strong stand.

in·spec·tion | ĭn **spěk′** shən | *n.* **1.** The act of examining. **2.** An official examination: *daily inspection of the soldiers.*

in·stead | ĭn **stěd′** | *adv.* In place of someone or something.

> *Idiom.* **instead of.** Rather than: *I went home instead of going to the library.*

in·struct | ĭn **strŭkt′** | *v.* **1.** To teach. **2.** To give orders to: *The crossing guard instructed us to remain on the sidewalk.*

in·struc·tion | ĭn **strŭk′** shən | *n.* **1.** Lessons: *music instruction.* **2. instructions.** Directions; orders.

in·tend | ĭn **těnd′** | *v.* **1.** To have in mind; plan: *to intend to go somewhere.* **2.** To mean for a particular use or person: *The surprise was intended for you.*

in·vent | ĭn **věnt′** | *v.* **1.** To think up and make for the first time: *invent a new machine.* **2.** To make up: *invent excuses.*

in·ven·tion | ĭn **věn′** shən | *n.* **1.** Something invented: *a new invention.* **2.** The act of inventing: *the invention of the wheel.* **3.** A false statement: *His story is only an invention.*

in·vite | ĭn **vīt′** | *v.* **in·vit·ed, in·vit·ing. 1.** To ask someone to go somewhere or to do something: *invite to a party.* **2.** To ask for politely: *invite questions.*

is·land | **ī′** lənd | *n.* **1.** A body of land that is surrounded by water. An island is smaller than a continent. **2.** Something that is different or separated from things around it: *There is a traffic island in the middle of the street.*

its | ĭts | *pron.* The possessive of **it:** *The bird flapped its wings. These sound alike* **its, it's.**

it's | ĭts |. The contraction for "it is" and "it has." *These sound alike* **it's, its.**

J

jab·ber | **jăb′** ər | *v.* To talk in a fast, silly, or mixed-up way; chatter: *Sometimes very young children seem to jabber to themselves.*

Jan·u·ar·y | **jăn′** yoo ěr′ ē | *n.* The first month of the year. January has 31 days.

jave·lin | **jăv′** lĭn | *or* | **jăv′** ə- | *n.* A long, thin, light spear that is thrown for distance in an athletic track and field event: *It requires good balance to throw the javelin a long way.*

jos·tle | **jŏs′** əl | *v.* **jos·tled, jos·tling.** To bump, shove, and push against one another: *I was jostled by the big crowd as I entered the stadium.*

jot | jŏt | *v.* **jot·ted, jot·ting.** To write quickly or briefly: *Please jot down your telephone number, so I can call you later.*

jour·nal·ism | **jûr′** nə lĭz′ əm | *n.* The gathering, reporting, writing, and publishing of news in newspapers or magazines or on television or radio.

judge | jŭj | *n.* **1.** A public official who decides cases in a law court. **2.** A person who decides the winner in a contest. **3.** A person who can decide the value of something. —*v.* **judged, judg·ing. 1.** To hear and decide a case in a law court. **2.** To decide: *judge a contest.* **3.** To form an opinion: *Judge this book for yourself.*

juice | joos | *n.* **1.** The liquid in fruit, vegetables, and meats. **2.** *Slang.* Electricity.

Ju·ly | joo **lī′** | *n.* The seventh month of the year. July has 31 days.

June | joon | *n.* The sixth month of the year. June has 30 days.

jun·gle | jŭng′ gəl | *n.* **1.** Land with a thick growth of trees and plants in the tropics. **2.** A confused mass of objects.

Ju·pi·ter | jōō′ pĭ tər | *n.* **1.** The largest planet in our solar system and the fifth closest to the sun. **2.** In ancient Roman mythology, the ruler of the gods.

K

kan·ga·roo | kăng′ gə rōō′ | *n.* An animal from Australia and New Guinea that has short forelegs, long and powerful hind legs for leaping, and a long tail. The female carries her young in a pouch in front of her body.

kitch·en | kĭch′ ən | *n.* A room where food is prepared.

knife | nīf | *n., pl.* **knives** | nīvz |. A thin blade used for cutting or spreading.

know | nō | *v.* **knew** | nōō | *or* | nyōō |, **known** | nōn |, **know·ing.** **1.** To understand: *know the answers.* **2.** To be acquainted with: *I know her well.* **3.** To have skill in: *know how to ride a bike.*
Idiom. **in the know.** Having inside information.

known Look up **know.**

knuck·le | nŭk′ əl | *n.* A joint of a finger.

L

land·slide | lănd′ slīd′ | *n.* The sliding of rocks and soil down a steep slope: *Sometimes an earthquake may cause a landslide down the mountainside.*

laugh·ter | lăf′ tər | *or* | läf′- | *n.* The act of making sounds to express happiness, amusement, or scorn.

lawn·mow·er | lôn′ mō′ ər | *n.* Also **lawn mower.** A machine with revolving blades for cutting grass.

learn·ing | lûr′ nĭng | *n.* Knowledge gained by study.

length | lĕngkth | *or* | lĕngth | *n.* **1.** How long something is from one end to another; its measured distance. **2.** How long something lasts from beginning to end: *the length of your visit.*

lib·er·ty | lĭb′ ər tē | *n., pl.* **lib·er·ties.** **1.** The state of being able to speak and act freely. **2.** Political freedom.

li·brar·y | lī′ brĕr′ ē | *n., pl.* **li·brar·ies.** **1.** A building where books, magazines, and reference material are collected. **2.** Any collection of books: *a library in the living room.*

light-year | līt′ yîr′ | *n.* Also **light year.** A measure of distance equal to the distance that light travels in one year through space.

loathe | lōth | *v.* **loathed, loath·ing.** To dislike very much; hate: *Readers may loathe the cruel actions of some of the characters in the book.*

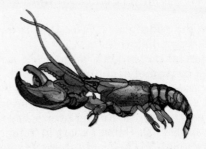

lob·ster | lŏb′ stər | *n.* **1.** A large, hard shellfish with five pairs of legs having large claws on the front pair. **2.** The meat of this shellfish, used as food.

lo·ca·tion | lō kā′ shən | *n.* A place where something is positioned: *the location of the restaurant.*

loose | lōōs | *adj.* **loos·er, loos·est.** **1.** Not fastened or firmly attached: *a loose cap.* **2.** Not closed in; free: *The dog was loose.* **3.** Not tightly fitted: *a loose pair of jeans.*

lose | lōōz | *v.* **lost** | lôst | *or* | lŏst |, **los·ing.** **1.** To be without: *Don't lose the keys.* **2.** To be unable to keep: *to lose your temper.* **3.** To fail to win: *I won't lose this race.* **4.** To waste: *I'll lose an hour in this traffic.*

loy·al | loi′ əl | *adj.* True and faithful.

loy·al·ty | loi′ əl tē | *n.* The act of being true and faithful; faithfulness.

lu·nar | lōō′ nər | *adj.* Having to do with the moon.

lyr·ics | lĭr′ ĭks | *pl. n.* The words of a song: *The lyrics of the song came from a poem.*

M

mag·ic | măj′ ĭk | *n.* Mysterious effects produced by tricks, usually as entertainment. —*adj.* Having magic power; done by magic: *a magic wand.*

mag·net | măg′ nĭt | *n.* **1.** A piece of metal or ore that draws iron toward it. **2.** Anything that attracts.

male | māl | *adj.* Having to do with men or boys: *a male voice.* —*n.* **1.** A man or a boy. **2.** A male animal.

mar·ble | mär′ bəl | *n.* **1.** A smooth, hard stone that is streaked or colored, often used in buildings. **2.** A small ball made of hard substance such as glass. **3. marbles.** A children's game played with small balls.

March | märch | *n.* The third month of the year. March has 31 days.

mar·gin | **mär′** jĭn | *n.* **1.** An edge or rim: *Water lilies grew along the margin of the pond.* **2.** A border around print or writing on a page: *Don't write in the margin of the book.* **3.** An extra amount beyond what is needed: *She gave herself a margin of ten minutes to catch the plane.*

ma·roon | mə **rōōn′** | *n.* A color that is dark brownish purplish red.

mas·ter | **măs′** tər | *or* | **mä′** stər | *n.* **1.** A person who has control of something: *the dog's master; the ship's master.* **2.** A person who has a great skill or ability: *a master of foreign languages.* —*adj.* **1.** Ruling over others: *the master switch.* **2.** Being expert at something: *master artist.* **3.** The original: *the master list.* —*v.* **1.** To bring under control: *to master your angry feelings.* **2.** To become skilled: *to master your spelling words.*

mast·head | **măst′** hĕd′ | *or* | **mäst′-** | *n.* **1.** The top of a ship's mast. **2.** The section in a newspaper or magazine that gives its name, owner, chief editors, address, and other information about the publication.

May | mā | *n.* The fifth month of the year. May has 31 days.

mea·ger | **mē′** gər | *adj.* Hardly enough; very little: *The meager amount of water did not satisfy my thirst.*

meas·ure | **mĕzh′** ər | *n.* **1.** A device for finding length, size, time, etc., such as a foot ruler, a pint cup, a pound weight. **2.** A basis of judgment or comparison: *Deeds are a better measure than words.* —*v.* **meas·ured, meas·ur·ing.** **1.** To find the length, size, contents, weight, or length of time of anything in standard units: *Let's measure these plants.* **2.** To be of a certain size, weight: *I measure five feet tall.*

med·dle | **mĕd′** l | *v.* **med·dled, med·dling.** To interfere in the business of other people:
Sometimes it is hard not to meddle in the affairs of others.

mem·ber | **mĕm′** bər | *n.* **1.** A part of the body. **2.** A person or thing belonging to a group, society, etc.: *a club member; a class member.*

Me·mo·ri·al Day | mə **môr′** ē əl dā | *n.* A holiday in the United States that honors members of the armed forces who have died in wars. The official date is May 30, but it is observed on the last Monday in May.

mem·o·ry | **mĕm′** ə rē | *n., pl.* **mem·o·ries.** **1.** The power of recalling something learned: *I have a poor memory for names.* **2.** A person or thing remembered: *Our old house is only a memory.*

men·tion | **mĕn′** shən | *v.* To speak or write about: *Don't mention our plans.* —*n.* A statement or reference: *You are worthy of mention.*

mer·ry | **mĕr′** ē | *adj.* **mer·ri·er, mer·ri·est.** Happy and cheerful; full of good spirits; jolly: *a merry twinkle in his eye.*

mes·sage | **mĕs′** ĭj | *n.* **1.** Any news or information sent from one person to another. **2.** A written statement or speech. **3.** The main subject or meaning of something: *After reading my note, did you understand my message?*

met·al | **mĕt′** l | *n.* **1.** A chemical element that is shiny when pure or polished and is a good conductor of electricity or heat. Gold, silver, copper, tin, iron, and aluminum are metals. **2.** An alloy made by mixing two or more metals.

me·te·or | **mē′** tē ər | *or* | -ôr′ | *n., pl.* **me·te·ors.** A shooting star; a piece of matter that falls toward the earth at great speed from outer space. Meteors burn with a bright glow when they hit the air around the earth and usually burn up before they reach the ground.

met·ric | **mĕt′** rĭk | *adj.* Anything involving the system of weights and measures based on the meter for length and the gram for weight.

mi·cro·scope | **mī′** krə skōp′ | *n.* An instrument which, by an arrangement of lenses, makes tiny things look large enough to be seen and studied.

mild | mīld | *adj.* **mild·er, mild·est.** **1.** Gentle; kind; calm: *a mild person.* **2.** Not extreme, harsh, or severe: *a mild winter.*

mois·ture | **mois′** chər | *n.* **1.** Dampness; slight wetness: *There is still moisture in the ground from the spring rains.* **2.** Water vapor in the air or condensed on a surface: *Beads of moisture formed on the outside of the pitcher.*

Mon·day | **mŭn′** dē | *or* | -dā′ | *n.* The second day of the week.

mon·key | **mŭng′** kē | *n., pl.* **mon·keys.** An animal that has hands with thumbs and usually has a long tail; not a gorilla, chimp, or other large ape. —*v.* **mon·keyed, mon·key·ing, mon·keys.** To play carelessly: *Do not monkey with that knife.*

mos·qui·to | mə **skē′** tō | *n., pl.* **mos·qui·toes** or **mos·qui·tos.** A slender, long-legged, blood-sucking insect with wings, the bite of which may cause swelling and itching. Some kinds carry yellow fever or malaria germs.

mo·tion | **mō′** shən | *n.* **1.** An action or movement; a changing from one place or position to another: *The motion of a boat on a rough sea makes some people ill.* **2.** Gesture: *He made a motion for silence.* **3.** A formal suggestion or proposal made at a meeting: *The secretary made a motion to select a program committee.* —*v.* To make a gesture or movement to express meaning; to signal: *He motioned to me to be quiet.*

mus·cu·lar | **mŭs′** kyə lər | *adj.* **1.** Having muscles that are strong and well-developed: *a muscular body.* **2.** Relating to or having to do with muscle.

mu·si·cal | **myoo′** zĭ kəl | *adj.* **1.** Having to do with music: *a musical instrument; a musical play.* **2.** Pleasing to the ear; melodious: *the musical song of a bird.* —*n.* A light, amusing play with songs and dances: *a musical comedy.*

mu·si·cian | myoo **zĭsh′** ən | *n.* A person skilled in music, especially one whose profession is playing music.

mu·tu·al | **myoo′** choo əl | *adj.* **1.** Shared; held in common: *My friend and I have a mutual love of shopping.* **2.** Given and received equal in equal amounts: *Our friendship is mutual.*

mys·te·ry | **mĭs′** tə rē | *n., pl.* **mys·te·ries.** **1.** Something that is secret, strange, or unexplained: *The name of the thief is a mystery.* **2.** A story dealing with secret events.

N

na·tion | **nā′** shən | *n.* An independent country.

nat·u·ral | **năch′** ər əl | *or* | **năch′** rəl | *adj.* **1.** Belonging to by nature; inborn; native: *Eddie has a natural singing voice.* **2.** Formed or made by nature; not artificial: *There is the famous natural bridge.* **3.** According to the way things happen; ordinary: *Tiredness is the natural result of hard work.*

nau·ti·cal | **nô′** tĭ kəl | *adj.* Relating to or having to do with sailors, ships, or navigation:

Because I like to sail, I enjoy books with a nautical theme.

nee·dle | **nēd′** l | *n.* **1.** A slender, pointed steel sewing tool with a hole or "eye" to hold a thread. **2.** A plain slender rod or a rod with a small hook at the end, used in knitting or crocheting. **3.** A device used by doctors and nurses to give shots. **4.** Any needle-shaped thing: *The ground was covered with pine needles.* —*v.* **nee·dled, nee·dling.** To tease or annoy.

neigh·bor | **nā′** bər | *n., pl.* **neigh·bors.** **1.** A person who lives nearby. **2.** A person, country, or thing that is near another: *Canada is our neighbor.* **3.** A fellow human being: *Love your neighbor.*

net·work | **nĕt′** wûrk′ | *n.* **1.** A system of arrangement of lines that cross: *a network of roads.* **2.** A chain of radio or television stations that carry the same programs.

news·pa·per | **nooz′** pā′ pər | *or* | **nyooz′-** | *n.* A sheet of printed paper, or many sheets folded together, containing news, pictures, advertisements, etc.

news·stand | **nooz′** stănd′ | *or* | **nyooz′-** | *n.* A place where newspapers and magazines are sold: *My father buys the newspaper at the same newsstand every morning.*

nick·el | **nĭk′** əl | *n.* **1.** A hard, silver-colored metal found in certain rocks; a chemical element. **2.** A coin in the U.S. that is worth five cents.

night·mare | **nīt′** mâr′ | *n.* **1.** A scary or bad dream. **2.** A scary or bad experience.

ninth | nīnth | *n.* **1.** Next after eighth. **2.** One of nine parts; $\frac{1}{9}$.

noise | noiz | *n.* **1.** An unpleasant sound. **2.** Any kind of sound: *The noise of the machine made study difficult.* —*v.* **noised, nois·ing** To tell or spread news: *He noised the rumor.*

no·mad | **nō′** măd′ | *n.* **1.** A member of a group of people who move from one place to another looking for food and water for themselves and their animals. **2.** A person who moves from place to place: *The nomad met many people in many different places.*

North Pole *n.* The farthest northern point on earth and the northern end of the earth's axis.

note·book | **nōt′** book′ | *n.* A book with blank pages for writing.

no·tice | **nō′** tĭs | *v.* **no·ticed, no·tic·ing.** To see; observe: *I notice that you have a new car.* —*n.* **1.** Attention: *He escaped notice.* **2.** A statement or warning of what one intends to do: *We gave notice that we would move out of our apartment.* **3.** Written or printed announcement or description: *There are several notices on the bulletin board.*

 Idiom. **take notice of.** To pay attention.

No·vem·ber | nō **vĕm′** bər | *n.* The eleventh month of the year. November has 30 days.

O

oak | ōk | *n.* **1.** Any acorn-bearing tree. There are nearly three hundred kinds of oak trees. **2.** The wood of these trees.

ob·ject¹ | ŏb′ jĭkt | *or* | -jĕkt′ | *n.* **1.** A thing that has shape and can be touched and seen: *The only object rescued when the car sank into the lake was a tire.* **2.** Purpose; goal: *My object in life is to be a surgeon.*

ob·ject² | əb jĕkt′ | *v.* **1.** To protest, to show disapproval: *Father objects to our walking barefoot in the living room.* **2.** To oppose; give reasons for disliking: *Do you object to our plan?*

o·cean | ō′ shən | *n.* The vast body of salt water covering three fourths of the earth's surface.

Oc·to·ber | ŏk tō′ bər | *n.* The tenth month of the year. October has 31 days.

of·ten | ô′ fən | *or* | ŏf′ ən | *or* | ôf′ tən | *or* | ŏf′- | *adv.* Frequently; many times.

O·lym·pic | ō lĭm′ pĭk | *adj.* Of or relating to the Olympics. —*n.* **Olympics. 1.** A festival of ancient Greece with contests in athletics, music, and poetry. **2.** Modern sports competition held every four years in a different country: *Athletes from many countries compete in the Olympics.*

o·men | ō′ mən | *n.* Something that is supposed to be a sign of a good or bad event to come: *When Kesha found a penny, she thought it was an omen of good luck.*

on·ion | ŭn′ yən | *n.* A plant grown as a vegetable having a bulb, a strong odor, and a biting taste.

or·bit | ôr′ bĭt | *n.* **1.** The path in which one heavenly body moves about another. **2.** A circle of influence: *A famous person will often have many people following in his or her orbit.* —*v.* To travel in an orbit: *The earth orbits the sun.*

or·chard | ôr′ chərd | *n.* A piece of land where fruit trees are grown.

owe | ō | *v.* **owed, ow·ing. 1.** To have to pay; to be in debt. **2.** To have to do something because of the law, a promise, or a duty: *owe an apology.*

oy·ster | oi′ stər | *n.* A soft-bodied animal that lives inside two rough half shells: *Many oysters have pearls.*

P

pack·age | păk′ ĭj | *n.* A container or box that holds something. —*v.* **pack·aged, pack·ag·ing.** To put into a container or box.

paid Look up **pay.**

pa·rade | pə rād′ | *n.* A public event for a special occasion: *the Thanksgiving Parade.* —*v.* **pa·rad·ed, pa·rad·ing. 1.** To march. **2.** To walk proudly: *to parade around in new clothes.*

par·ty | pär′ tē | *n., pl.* **par·ties. 1.** An entertainment or social gathering: *a birthday party.* **2.** A group of people acting together: *A search party was sent out to find the missing child.* **3.** A political organization: *In an election, each party has a candidate.*

pay | pā | *v.* **paid** | pād |, **pay·ing. 1.** To give money in return for things or work done. **2.** To give or make: *pay attention; pay a visit.*

peace | pēs | *n.* **1.** Freedom from fighting. **2.** Quiet; order.

pearl | pûrl | *n.* **1.** A small, round, white or grayish gem that is found inside the shell of certain oysters. **2.** Anything that looks like a pearl.

pe·can | pĭ kän′ | *or* | -kăn′ | *or* | pē′ kăn | *n.* An edible nut that has a thin, smooth, oval shell and grows on a tree.

ped·es·tal | pĕd′ ĭ stəl | *n.* The base or support on which a statue or column stands: *The statue stood on a pedestal made of concrete.*

pen·al·ty | pĕn′ əl tē | *n., pl.* **pen·al·ties. 1.** A punishment established by law. **2.** A disadvantage imposed by a referee upon a game player: *One more penalty and he's out of the game.*

pen·du·lum | pĕn′ jə ləm | *or* | pĕn′ dyə- | *or* | pĕn′ də- | *n.* A weight that is hung from a fixed support, so that it can swing back and forth: *Pendulums are used to regulate the actions of some clocks.*

pen·sion | pĕn′ shən | *n.* An amount of money that is paid regularly to a person who has retired from work or is disabled: *After teaching thirty years, Mrs. Mays retired and received a pension.*

per·fect | pûr′ fĭkt | *adj.* **1.** Without fault; exactly right: *He got a perfect score on the test.* **2.** Complete; whole; thorough. —*v.* | pər fĕkt′ | To remove all flaws from.

per·form | pər fôrm′ | *v.* **1.** To do or carry out: *to perform your obligations.* **2.** To act with skill: *She performed in the play.*

per·fume | pûr′ fyōōm′ | *or* | pər fyōōm′ | *n.* **1.** A sweet-smelling liquid: *a new perfume.* **2.** A sweet smell; fragrance: *The perfume from the roses is wonderful.* —*v.* | pər fyōōm′ |. To fill with a sweet smell.

per·haps | pər hăps′ | *adv.* Maybe; possibly: *Perhaps it will rain today.*

pe·ri·od·i·cal | pĭr′ ē ŏd′ ĭ kəl | *adj.* A magazine or other publication that is printed at regular intervals, such as every week, every two weeks, or every month: *I look forward to receiving my favorite periodical every month.*

per·mit | pər **mĭt′** | *v.* **per·mit·ted, per·mit·ting.** To allow. —*n.* | **pûr′** mĭt | *or* | pər **mĭt′** |. A written letter, license, or document giving permission.

per·son·al | **pûr′** sə nəl | *adj.* **1.** One's own; a private part of one's life. **2.** That which is done in person. **3.** Of a person's body or physical appearance.

pet·al | **pĕt′** l | *n.* One of the leaflike parts of a flower, usually brightly or lightly colored.

pi·an·o | pē ăn′ ō | *n., pl.* **pi·an·os.** A large musical instrument with steel wire strings that sound when struck by felt-covered hammers operated from a keyboard.

pick·le | **pĭk′** əl | *n., pl.* **pick·les.** A cucumber that has been preserved by soaking in salt water or vinegar.

pic·nic | **pĭk′** nĭk | *n.* Food that is packed and eaten outdoors; a meal eaten in the open air. —*v.* **pic·nicked, pic·nick·ing, pic·nics.** To have a picnic.

pin·na·cle | **pĭn′** ə kəl | *n.* **1.** A tall pointed peak, as on a mountain. **2.** The highest point: *Being a star in the movie was the pinnacle of his career.*

pi·rate | **pī′** rĭt | *n.* A person who robs ships at sea.

pitch | pĭch | *v.* **1.** To throw or toss: *to pitch a baseball.* **2.** To set or put up: *to pitch a tent.* **3.** To fall forward. —*n.* **1.** A throw to a batter: *a good pitch right over home plate.* **2.** A degree of highness or lowness in music: *You have perfect pitch for this melody.*

piz·za | **pēt′** sə | *n.* An Italian dish made by baking a pie crust covered with tomato sauce, cheese, sausage, mushrooms, etc.

plain | plān | *adj.* **plain·er, plain·est.** **1.** Something that is easy to hear, see, or understand. **2.** Simple; without any decoration. **3.** Not rich or too spicy: *plain food.* —*n.* Flat, treeless land. *These sound alike* **plane, plain.**

plane | plān | *n.* **1.** A flat, level surface. **2.** An aircraft flown by an engine; airplane. *These sound alike* **plane, plain.**

plan·et | **plăn′** ĭt | *n.* One of the nine celestial bodies that move in a circular path around the sun: Mercury, Venus, Earth, Mars, Jupiter, Saturn, Uranus, Neptune, and Pluto.

plas·tic | **plăs′** tĭk | *n.* Any of many chemically made substances that are molded by heat and pressure and then shaped.

pleas·ure | **plĕzh′** ər | *n.* **1.** A feeling of happiness or enjoyment. **2.** Something that causes a feeling of delight and happiness.

pledge | plĕj | *n.* A serious promise: *The friends made a pledge to stay together.* —*v.* **pledged, pledg·ing.** To promise.

po·em | **pō′** əm | *n.* Writing in verse, often imaginative and in rhyme.

po·lar | **pō′** lər | *adj.* Anything to do with a region around a geographic pole such as the North or South Pole.

po·lite | pə **līt′** | *adj.* **po·lit·er, po·lit·est.** Having or showing good manners.

pol·lu·tion | pə **loo′** shən | *n.* Contamination of the environment with waste.

pop·u·la·tion | pŏp′ yə lā′ shən | *n.* **1.** The number of people who live in an area. **2.** People as a whole.

pore | pôr | *n.* A tiny opening in the skin of an animal or on the surface of a leaf, through which gases or liquids may pass.

pre·car·i·ous | prĭ **kâr′** ē əs | *adj.* Dangerous; unstable: *a precarious position.*

pre·pare | prĭ **pâr′** | *v.* **pre·pared, pre·par·ing.** To get ready or to plan and make.

pre·sume | prĭ **zoom′** | *v.* **pre·sumed, pre·sum·ing.** To think to be true, even without proof; take for granted: *I presume that everyone will be on time.*

pret·ty | **prĭt′** ē | *adj.* **pret·ti·er, pret·ti·est.** **1.** Pleasing; attractive. **2.** Appealing; charming.

prime time | prīm′ tīm | *n.* In radio or television, the evening hours that have the biggest audience, usually between 8 and 11 P.M.

pri·or | **prī′** ər | *adj.* Before or earlier in order, time, or importance: *Although she is now a nurse, her prior job was teaching.*

prob·lem | **prŏb′** ləm | *n.* A confusing question or situation; something difficult to figure out: *Finding a babysitter is a real problem.*

pro·duc·er | prə **doo′** sər | *or* | -**dyoo′**- | *n.*
1. The person, place, or organization responsible for making something: *Brazil is a producer of coffee beans.* **2.** A person who manages the making of a play, movie, or show: *I know a famous movie producer.*

pro·fes·sion·al | prə **fĕsh′** ə nəl | *adj.* **1.** Having a special knowledge or education for a job: *A doctor is a professional person.* **2.** Making money by doing what most people do for fun: *a professional tennis player.* —*n.* **1.** A person who has special knowledge or education. **2.** A person who makes money doing what most people do for fun: *We watched the professional ski down the mountain.*

pro·gram | **prō′** grăm | *or* | -grəm | *n.* **1.** A list of what is to be shown or done in a presentation, ceremony, etc. and who is to take part. **2.** The ceremony or presentation itself. **3.** An organized series of events: *What's the camp program for today?* —*v.* **pro·grammed, pro·gram·ming. 1.** To plan a program: *A committee programmed the activities for the celebration.* **2.** To train to perform; to plan a series of operations: *The computers were programmed with the necessary information.*

prom·ise | **prŏm′** ĭs | *n.* **1.** A statement that one will or will not do something: *I gave a promise not to be late again.* **2.** A sign of future success: *She showed promise of becoming a good astronaut.* —*v.* **prom·ised, prom·is·ing. 1.** To make a statement that one will or will not do something. **2.** To give hope or reason that one may expect something: *The thunder promised rain.*

proof | prōof | *n.* Evidence; demonstration of truth.

prove | prōov | *v.* **proved, proved** or **prov·en** | **prōo′** vən |, **prov·ing.** To show to be true; to demonstrate, or to give evidence: *She proved she knew how to do long division.*

pump·kin | **pŭmp′** kĭn | *or* | **pŭm′**- | *or* | **pŭng′**- | *n.* A large, round, orange-yellow fruit grown on a vine and often used in making pies.

pur·pose | **pûr′** pəs | *n.* The aim; intention; desired result.
   Idiom. **on purpose.** Not by accident.

puz·zle | **pŭz′** əl | *n.* **1.** Something that is confusing; a problem. **2.** A game or toy: *a crossword puzzle.* —*v.* To confuse: *The magic trick puzzled them.*

Q

qual·i·fy | **kwŏl′** ə fī′ | *v.* **qual·i·fied, qual·i·fy·ing, qual·i·fies. 1.** To be fit or show ability in skill or knowledge: *They qualified for the football team.* **2.** To limit: *to qualify your comments.*

quan·ti·ty | **kwŏn′** tĭ tē | *n., pl.* **quan·ti·ties.** The number or amount: *Pens and pencils are needed in equal quantity.*

quar·rel | **kwôr′** əl | *or* | **kwŏr′**- | *n.* A fight with words; an argument. —*v.* **quar·reled, quar·rel·ing.** To have a fight with words.

ques·tion | **kwĕs′** chən | *n., pl.* **ques·tions. 1.** Something asked for an answer or information. **2.** Matter to be discussed; problem or proposal: *The question of the class party was never settled.* —*v.* To ask for information.
   Idiom. **out of the question.** Unthinkable.

quick | kwĭk | *adj.* **quick·er, quick·est.** Fast; rapid; done with speed. —*adv.* **quick·ly.** Rapidly.

quit | kwĭt | *v.* **quit, quit·ting. 1.** To stop: *quit work at five o'clock.* **2.** To leave; depart from: *quit college.*

quite | kwĭt | *adv.* **1.** Completely; entirely: *You are quite right.* **2.** To a considerable degree: *It is quite cold today.*

quiz·zi·cal | **kwĭz′** ĭ kəl | *adj.* Showing confusion or puzzlement: *Because the student hadn't heard the question, she had a quizzical look on her face.*

R

rab·bit |**răb′**ĭt | *n.* A soft, furry animal with long ears and a short, fluffy tail.

rac·coon | ră **koon′** | *n.* A grayish-brown animal with black, mask-like markings on the face and a long, bushy, black-ringed tail.

raise | rāz | *v.* **raised, rais·ing. 1.** To lift or move to a higher position: *to raise your hand.* **2.** To gather together; collect: *to raise money for charity.* **3.** To help grow or rear: *to raise children.* **4.** To bring up or ask: *to raise a question.* **5.** To build or erect: *to raise a barn.*

—n. An increase in amount, price, pay, etc.: *a raise in salary.*

ran·dom | **rān'** dəm | *adj.* Made or done without a definite plan or pattern: *I didn't know which package to open first, so I made a random choice.*

    Idiom. **at random.** With no method, purpose, or pattern.

rap·id | **răp'** ĭd | *adj.* Fast; quick.

rath·er | **ră***th***'** ər | *or* | **rä'** *th*ər | *adv.* **1.** More willingly; preferably: *I'd rather see a movie.* **2.** More properly; justly: *This gift is for Sally rather than for Robin.* **3.** Somewhat; to a certain extent: *a rather silly idea.*

raw | rô | *adj.* **raw·er, raw·est.** **1.** Not cooked: *a raw potato.* **2.** Not artificially treated or processed; natural: *raw lumber.*

ra·zor | **rā'** zər | *n.* An instrument with a sharp blade used to shave or cut hair: *Be careful not to cut yourself with the razor.*

rea·son | **rē'** zən | *n.* **1.** A cause or motive for acting or feeling a certain way: *I have a reason for being angry.* **2.** An explanation; an excuse: *Give me one good reason.* **3.** The ability to think logically and clearly: *Don't lose your power of reason.* —v. **1.** To think with a clear mind. **2.** To try to persuade; to attempt to change a person's mind: *I will reason with you.*

re·cede | rĭ **sēd'** | *v.* **re·ced·ed, re·ced·ing.** To move back or away: *After the flood the river water began to recede slowly from the field.*

re·cord·er | rĭ **kôr'** dər | *n.* **1.** Someone who takes notes. **2.** A machine that keeps sounds on magnetic tape: *My tape recorder can play the song.* **3.** A small musical instrument that sounds like a flute.

re·cy·cle | rē **sī'** kəl | *v.* **re·cy·cled, re·cy·cling.** To treat or process materials that might be thrown away so that they can be used again: *Our class project was to recycle newspapers, cans, and plastic bottles.*

ref·e·ree | rĕf' ə **rē'** | *n.* An official in certain sports and games who enforces the rules and supervises the play: *The referee ruled that the team had scored a goal.*

re·lax | rĭ **lăks'** | *v.* To become less stiff; to loosen up; to be at ease.

re·main | rĭ **mān'** | *v.* **1.** To stay behind after others go: *remain after school.* **2.** To be left: *So much remains to be done!* **3.** To continue as before: *She remained my friend.*

re·mem·ber | rĭ **mĕm'** bər | *v.* **1.** To think of again; to recall or cause to remind: *I can remember my homework from yesterday.* **2.** To keep in mind: *to remember an appointment.* **3.** To present with a gift or reward: *You'll be remembered on your birthday.*

re·mind | rĭ **mīnd'** | *v.* To cause to remember; to recall to mind.

re·source·ful | rĭ **sôrs'** fəl | *adj.* Able to deal with new, difficult, or different situations effectively or imaginatively: *On our picnic we had to be resourceful because we forgot our knives and forks.*

re·view | rĭ **vyoo'** | *v.* **1.** To study. **2.** To think back in one's mind. **3.** To write or tell about a book, movie, play, or event: *review a book.* —n. **1.** A time of studying. **2.** A report of a book, movie, play, or event: *I read the movie review in the paper.*

re·vise | rĭ **vīz'** | *v.* **re·vised, re·vis·ing.** **1.** To look over and change in order to improve: *to revise a story.* **2.** To change or make different: *to revise an opinion.*

rev·o·lu·tion | rĕv' ə **loo'** shən | *n.* **1.** A complete overthrow of government: *the American Revolution.* **2.** A sudden or dramatic change: *the industrial revolution.* **3.** Movement in a circular path: *It takes a year for the earth to make a revolution around the sun.*

re·ward | rĭ **wôrd'** | *n.* **1.** Something given in return for a service or act. **2.** Money offered for the return of something lost. —v. To give something in return for something done.

rid·dle[1] | **rĭd'** l | *v.* **rid·dled, rid·dling.** To make holes in: *Mice had riddled the house.*

rid·dle[2] | **rĭd'** l | *n.* A problem or question that is not easy to understand: *Try to answer this riddle.*

ride | rīd | *v.* **rode** | rōd|, **rid·den** | **rĭd'** n |, **rid·ing.** **1.** To sit on something in order to make it move: *to ride a bicycle.* **2.** To be carried on or by; to travel: *I ride the bus.* —n. **1.** A short trip on an animal or vehicle. **2.** A structure at the amusement park used for pleasure: *The Ferris wheel is my favorite ride.*

right | rīt | n. **1.** On the side opposite the left: *Her house is on the right.* **2.** Just; good: *the difference between right and wrong.* —adv. **1.** Straight on; directly: *He looked right at the object.* **2.** Correctly: *John guessed right.* —v. **1.** To set something in order: *We had to right the capsized boat.* **2.** To make something good, just, or correct: *to right an injustice. These sound alike* **right, write.**
    Idioms. **right of way.** The right to move first. **right away.** Immediately.

right·ful | rīt′ fəl | adj. Having a just or lawful claim: *Louis is the rightful owner of the house.*

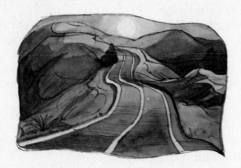

road | rōd | n. **1.** Pavement or cleared ground used to go from one place to another; a route or path: *Which road goes to town?* **2.** A direction toward something: *your road to success. These sound alike* **road, rode.**

roar | rôr | or | rōr | n. **1.** A loud, deep sound: *a lion's roar.* **2.** A loud laugh: *I could hear his roar next door.* —v. To make a loud, deep sound: *Please don't roar in my ear.*

roast | rōst | v. **1.** To cook by dry heat or over an open fire; to bake: *to roast a chicken.* **2.** To be extremely hot; to feel overheated: *You'll roast with your coat on indoors.* —n. A large cut of meat suitable for roasting.

rode Look up **ride.** *These sound alike* **rode, road.**

rook·ie | rŏŏk′ ē | n. **1.** A person who is a first-year player in a professional sport. **2.** A beginner who lacks training or experience.

room·mate | rōōm′ māt′ | or | rōōm′- | n. A person who lives with others in a room or apartment: *My sister's roommate at college is from another country.*

roost·er | rōō′ stər | n. A full-grown male chicken.

ro·ta·tion | rō tā′ shən | n. Circular turning on an axis: *The rotation of the earth takes 24 hours.*

rough | rŭf | adj. **rough·er, rough·est. 1.** Having an uneven surface; not smooth: *a rough road.* **2.** Violent; severe; not gentle: *rough games.*

roy·al | roi′ əl | adj. **1.** Anything belonging to or having to do with a king or queen: *a royal palace.* **2.** Made for or acceptable for a king or queen: *a royal welcome.*

rum·mage | rŭm′ ĭj | v. **rum·maged, rum·mag·ing.** To look for something thoroughly by turning things over or moving them around: *rummage through the closet.* —n. A thorough search.

S

sa·fa·ri | sə fär′ ē | n., pl. **sa·fa·ris.** A hunting trip, especially in Africa.

sail·boat | sāl′ bōt′ | n. A boat that travels by wind blowing against its sails.

sal·ad | săl′ əd | n. A combination of vegetables or fruit that is often served with a dressing.

sam·ple | săm′ pəl | or | săm′- | n. A small piece of something that shows what the rest is like. —v. To try a part; to test.

sand·wich | sănd′ wĭch | or | săn′- | n., pl. **sand·wich·es.** Two or more slices of bread with a filling of jelly, cheese, meat, egg, etc. —v. To fit between with little space: *Four of us were sandwiched in the back seat.*

sat·el·lite | săt′ l īt′ | n. **1.** A heavenly body that travels in orbit around another larger body. **2.** A man-made object that orbits the earth, the moon, or other bodies in space. **3.** A country that is under the control of a more powerful country.

Sat·ur·day | săt′ ər dē | or | dā′ | n. The seventh day of the week.

saw·dust | sô′ dŭst′ | n. The tiny pieces of wood that fall off during sawing.

scale¹ | skāl | n. An instrument used to find out how heavy something is.

scale² | skāl | n. **1.** Equally spaced marks on a line used to measure: *Your ruler is a scale.* **2.** Musical tones that go up and down in pitch: *to play the scales on the piano.* —v. **scaled, scal·ing.** To climb.

scale³ | skāl | n. One of the layered plates on the outer covering of a fish, snake, etc.

scarf | skärf | n., pl. **scarfs** | skärfs | or **scarves** | skärvz |. A piece of cloth worn around the head, neck, or shoulders for decoration or warmth: *Scarves are good for keeping your face and neck warm in winter.*

sci·ence | sī′ əns | n. **1.** Knowledge based on facts about nature and the universe. **2.** Any branch of knowledge about the universe: biology, astronomy, etc.

scold | skōld | v. To blame with angry words in an angry tone of voice.

score | skôr | or | skōr | n. **1.** A number of points in a game. **2.** A result on a test. —v. **scored, scor·ing.** To keep a record of points in a contest or exam.

score·board | skôr′ bôrd′ | n. A large board that shows the score and other important game or contest information to the spectators.

sea·son | sē′ zən | *n.* **1.** One of the four parts of the year: spring, summer, autumn, winter. **2.** A special time of the year: *Christmas Season.* —*v.* To give flavor to: *season food.*

sec·tion | sĕk′ shən | *n.* A separated part; a cut-off area of a whole. —*v.* To separate or cut into sections.

se·lec·tion | sĭ lĕk′ shən | *n.* The act of selecting or choosing.

self | sĕlf | *n., pl.* **selves** | sĕlvz|. One's own person separate from any other.

self·ish | sĕl′ fĭsh | *adj.* Caring too much for oneself and not for others.

sen·tence | sĕn′ təns | *n.* **1.** A group of words that expresses a complete thought. **2.** A decision by a judge in a court of law; a verdict.

Sep·tem·ber | sĕp tĕm′ bər | *n.* The ninth month of the year. September has 30 days.

serv·ice | sûr′ vĭs | *n.* A useful act. —*v.* **serv·iced, serv·ic·ing.** To provide or make ready for use: *I'll service your car.*

sew | sō | *v.* **sewed, sewn** | sōn | *or* **sewed, sew·ing.** To attach or fasten with a needle and thread.

shad·y | shā′ dē | *adj.* **shad·i·er, shad·i·est.** **1.** Sheltered from sun or light. **2.** Of questionable honesty or character: *a shady person.*

sham·poo | shăm pōō′ | *n.* A preparation for cleaning. —*v.* To wash and clean with soap or detergent.

share | shâr | *v.* **shared, shar·ing. 1.** To take part; join: *to share in the happiness.* **2.** To use, enjoy, or have in common: *to share the same room.* **3.** To divide or portion: *to share your lunch.* —*n.* Portion or part of something received, done, or enjoyed by a number of persons: *He took his share of the profits.*

sheet | shēt | *n.* **1.** Cloth used to cover a bed: *Fresh sheets are on the bed.* **2.** Thin, broad piece of something: *A sheet of ice is slippery.* **3.** A piece of paper: *Take out a new sheet of paper.*

shock | shŏk | *n.* **1.** A sudden or violent blow: *the shock of an explosion.* **2.** A sudden upset of the mind or emotions: *The bad news was a terrible shock to them.* **3.** Effect of electric current on the body: *a shock from a wire.* —*v.* To surprise, horrify, or disgust.

shoe | shōō | *n.* An outer covering for the foot often made of leather.

shore | shôr | *or* | shōr | *n.* The land at the edge of an ocean, sea, river, or lake.

shut·tle | shŭt′ l | *n.* **1.** The thread holder used in weaving to carry the threads back and forth through the yarn. **2.** A train, plane, bus, etc. that goes only between two places on a frequent and regular schedule. **3.** A space craft capable of carrying astronauts back and forth for short distances in space: *The astronauts took the shuttle from their spaceship to earth and back again.* —*v.* **shut·tled, shut·tling.** To move back and forth.

siege | sēj | *n.* The surrounding of an enemy town or fort and cutting off supplies to it for a long time in order to force a surrender.

sig·nal | sĭg′ nəl | *n.* **1.** A sign that warns, gives notice, or points out something: *a railroad signal.* **2.** An action that is used to start something: *a referee's signal to start the game.* —*v.* **sig·naled, sig·nal·ing.** To warn or point out.

sil·ver | sĭl′ vər | *n.* **1.** Soft, shiny metal that is easily shaped into jewelry, coins, etc. **2.** Coins; change: *to carry silver.* **3.** Forks, knives, and other tableware made with this metal; silverware. —*adj.* Having the color of silver.

sim·i·lar | sĭm′ ə lər | *adj.* Alike somehow but not the same.

sim·ple | sĭm′ pəl | *adj.* **sim·pler, sim·plest. 1.** A task that is easy to understand or to do: *a simple test.* **2.** Anything plain; not fancy: *a simple white shirt.*

since | sĭns | *adv.* **1.** From a certain time in the past until now. **2.** Ago; before now. —*conj.* Because.

sixth | sĭksth | *n.* **1.** Next after fifth. **2.** One of six equal parts; ⅙.

skate | skāt | *n.* A boot or shoe made with a blade or wheels on the bottom, used for moving on the ice, street, floor, etc.: *roller skate.* —*v.* **skat·ed, skat·ing.** To move by using a blade or wheels on the foot: *to skate home.*

ski | skē | *n., pl.* **skis** *or* **ski.** A long, thin piece of wood, plastic, or metal attached to a boot to glide on snow. —*v.* **skied, ski·ing, skis.** To travel on skis.

skill | skĭl | *n.* Knowledge or ability to do something well.

skin diving | skĭn′ dī′ vĭng | *n.* Swimming underwater for a long time by using a face mask, rubber flippers, and a snorkel.

skirt | skûrt | *n.* Clothing worn by girls and women, which hangs from the waist down. —*v.* To travel along the edge of: *The car skirted the puddle.*

smol·der *also* **smoul·der** | smōl' dər | *v.* **1.** To burn slowly with little smoke and no flame: *The coals will smolder for hours.* **2.** To continue in a hidden manner.

snack | snăk | *n.* A small amount of food eaten between meals; a light meal.

snake | snāk | *n.* A long, scaly, crawling animal without legs; serpent. —*v.* **snaked, snak·ing.** To crawl or twist like a snake.

soc·cer | sŏk' ər | *n.* A game in which two teams of 11 players each try to kick a round ball into the other team's goal. The arms and hands cannot be used for hitting the ball or stopping an opponent.

so·lar | sō' lər | *adj.* Of or having to do with the sun: *solar energy.*

sol·id | sŏl' ĭd | *adj.* **1.** Having a definite size and shape, not a liquid or a gas. **2.** Hard; firm; able to support weight: *solid ground.* **3.** Having a sound character; trustworthy: *a solid person.*

sol·i·tude | sŏl' ĭ tōōd' | *or* | sŏl' ĭ tyōōd' | *n.* **1.** The state of being alone: *The author needed solitude in order to write the book.* **2.** A place away from people: *the solitude of the mountain cabin.*

span·iel | spăn' yəl | *n.* A small to medium-sized dog with drooping ears, short legs, and silky, wavy hair.

sparse | spârs | *adj.* Not crowded; widely scattered: *Plants are sparse in the desert.*

spe·cial | spĕsh' əl | *adj.* Uncommon, unusual; that which is different from others: *a special day.*

speech | spēch | *n., pl.* **speech·es. 1.** The act of speaking: *to burst into speech.* **2.** Words; remarks: *Her speech is full of slang.* **3.** A formal talk delivered in public: *a graduation speech.*

square | skwâr | *n.* **1.** A figure with four equal sides and four right angles. **2.** Anything that has this shape: *a square piece of paper.* **3.** An open space in a town or city surrounded on all sides by streets: *Trees were planted in the city square.* —*adj.* **squar·er, squar·est. 1.** Having four equal sides. **2.** Measure of a surface area:

a square foot. **3.** Honest, direct, or fair: *a square deal.*

St. Abbreviation of **Street** and **Saint.**

stare | stâr | *v.* **stared, star·ing.** To look with open eyes for a long time. —*n.* A wide-eyed, fixed look held for some time.

starve | stärv | *v.* **starved, starv·ing. 1.** To become very ill or to die from extreme hunger. **2.** To be hungry: *I'm starving for chocolate chip cookies.*

sta·tion | stā' shən | *n.* **1.** A regularly scheduled stop on a train or bus route. **2.** A building used for such a stop: *a train station.* **3.** An assigned place or position for a certain person: *The lifeguard sat at his station.* **4.** A place that is used to send or receive radio or television programs: *How many television stations do you get?* —*v.* To put oneself at an appointed place: *The detective stationed himself nearby.*

steep | stēp | *adj.* **steep·er, steep·est. 1.** Having a sharp slope; almost straight up and down: *a steep cliff.* **2.** Very high: *steep prices.*

stom·ach·ache | stŭm' ək āk' | *n.* A pain in the stomach or abdomen.

sto·ry[1] | stôr' ē | *or* | stōr' ē | *n., pl.* **sto·ries. 1.** An account, oral or written, of something that has happened: *a newspaper story.* **2.** A tale of fiction. **3.** A lie: *Tell the truth, not a story.*

sto·ry[2] | stôr' ē | *or* | stōr' ē | *n., pl.* **sto·ries.** Any level or floor of a building.

stow·a·way | stō' ə wā' | *n.* A person who hides in a ship, airplane, or other vehicle in order to travel without paying for the trip: *The stowaway was found by the captain of the ship and made to buy a ticket.*

straw | strô | *n.* **1.** A narrow tube made of plastic or waxed paper used for drinking a liquid: *a soda straw.* **2.** Stems or stalks of grain that have been seeded and dried: *The animals in the barn sleep on straw.*

straw·ber·ry | strô' bĕr' ē | *n., pl.* **-ber·ries.** A sweet, red fruit with many small seeds on its surface: *Strawberries grow close to the ground.*

stu·di·o | stōō' dē ō' | *or* | styōō'- | *n.* **1.** An artist's workroom. **2.** A place where a film, TV, or radio program is made.

sug·ar | shŏŏg' ər | *n.* A sweet substance obtained from sugar beets, sugar cane, maple trees, fruits, etc. —*v.* **1.** To sprinkle sugar or to sweeten with sugar: *to sugar berries.* **2.** To make pleasant; make less disagreeable: *He sugared his criticism with a few flattering words.*

suit·case | sōōt' kās' | *n.* A flat, rectangular traveling bag.

Sun·day | sŭn' dē | *or* | -dā' | *n.* The first day of the week.

sup·pose | sə pōz' | *v.* **sup·posed, sup·pos·ing. 1.** To assume; expect; take for granted: *I suppose I'll see you at the party.* **2.** To imagine;

pretend: *The little girl liked to suppose she was a princess.*

sur·prise | sər prīz' | *v.* **sur·prised, sur·pris·ing.**
1. To take someone unawares; to come upon unexpectedly: *He surprised me with a visit.*
2. To cause to feel wonder or astonishment: *The mild man's fury surprised us.* —*n.* **1.** A catching unawares: *to be caught by surprise.*
2. Something sudden or unexpected: *a surprise for Mom.* **3.** A feeling caused by something sudden or unexpected; astonishment: *Imagine our surprise when we saw our new bikes!*

sur·vey·or | sər vā' ər | *n.* A person whose job is to measure land: *The surveyor will tell us exactly how big our property is.*

swal·low[1] | swŏl' ō | *v.* **1.** To transfer food or drink from the mouth to the stomach through the throat: *to swallow cake.* **2.** To perform the act of swallowing: *I feel as if there is a lump in my throat, and I cannot swallow.* **3.** To engulf; destroy. **4.** To believe easily: *They'll swallow anything you tell them.* —*n.* **1.** The act of swallowing. **2.** The amount swallowed at one time.

swal·low[2] | swŏl' ō | *n.* A slender, fork-tailed bird with pointed wings and swift, graceful flight.

sweat·er | swĕt' ər | *n.* Knitted or crocheted garment, with or without sleeves, for the upper part of the body.

sweat·shirt | swĕt' shûrt' | *n.* A heavy long-sleeved knitted pullover shirt usually made of cotton jersey.

swim | swĭm | *v.* **swam** | swăm |, **swum** | swŭm |, **swim·ming.** **1.** To pass through water by moving legs, arms, fins, etc. **2.** To cross by swimming: *The team swam the English Channel.* **3.** To be immersed in or covered by a liquid: *Their eyes began to swim with tears.* —*n.* The act or sport of swimming.

　Idiom. **in the swim.** Taking part in whatever is fashionable or current.

symp·tom | sĭm' təm | *or* | sĭmp'- | *n.* **1.** A sign in the body that is an indication of a disease or illness: *Tiredness was the first symptom that I had the flu.* **2.** A sign or indication of something.

sys·tem | sĭs' təm | *n.* **1.** A group of things that go together to make up a whole: *The trains, the tracks, the schedule, and the engineer are all parts of a railroad system.* **2.** A combination of parts of the body that

work together and are dependent on one another: *the circulatory system.* **3.** Orderly method of doing things; routine: *Hugh has a system for his day's work.*

T

ta·ble·spoon | tā' bəl spoon' | *n.* **1.** A measuring spoon equal to three teaspoons that is used for cooking. **2.** A large serving spoon.

tape deck | tāp dĕk | *n.* A machine that is able to play back magnetic tapes. It is used as a part of a high-fidelity sound system.

tar·dy | tär' dē | *adj.* **tar·di·er, tar·di·est.**
1. Not on time; late: *We were all tardy because of the storm.* **2.** Slow: *a tardy growth of plants.*

taught Look up **teach.**

teach | tēch | *v.* **taught** | tôt |, **teach·ing.** To give lessons; to help someone or something to learn.

teach·er | tē' chər | *n.* A person who teaches.

tear[1] | târ | *v.* **tore** | tôr | *or* | tōr |, **torn** | tôrn | *or* | tōrn |, **tear·ing.** To pull apart.

tear[2] | tîr | *n.* A drop of water from the eyes.

tel·e·phone | tĕl' ə fōn' | *n.* An instrument or system for sending and receiving speech and other sounds over electric wires. —*v.* **tel·e·phoned, tel·e·phon·ing.** To use this instrument to speak with someone; call: *Please telephone me.*

tel·e·scope | tĕl' ə skōp' | *n.* An instrument for making distant things appear larger, especially a large instrument of this kind for studying heavenly bodies. —*v.* **tel·e·scoped, tel·e·scop·ing.** To fit a smaller object into a larger similar object; nest: *Let's telescope these boxes to save space.*

tel·e·vi·sion | tĕl' ə vĭzh' ən | *n.* **1.** A system for sending and receiving moving pictures and sound. **2.** A machine that receives these pictures and sounds and presents them to a viewer.

ten·nis | tĕn' ĭs | *n.* A game for two players or two pairs of players who use rackets to hit a ball back and forth across a net.

their | thâr | *pron.* Of or belonging to them: *Their float won first prize. These sound alike* **their, there, they're.**

theme | thēm | *n.* **1.** A subject written or talked about; topic: *the theme of the discussion; the theme of a party.* **2.** Short essay: *Students write themes.* **3.** In music, a short tune or melody that occurs again and again in a composition.

there | thâr | *adv.* **1.** In or at that place: *Put it there, not here.* **2.** To or toward that place: *I can walk there in an hour.* —*n.* That place: *We came from there an hour ago. These sound alike* **there, their, they're.**

they're | thâr | The contraction for "they are." *These sound alike* **they're, their, there.**

think | thĭngk | v. **thought** | thôt |, **think·ing.** To use the mind to form ideas, opinions, beliefs, decisions, etc.

third | thûrd | adj. **1.** Next after second. **2.** One of three equal parts; ⅓: *He ate a third of the pie.*

thir·teen | thûr′ tēn′ | n. Amount or quantity that is one greater than 12.

though | thō | adv. **1.** In spite of the fact that; although: *We kept on working though it was very late.* **2.** Even if: *Start the job now though you cannot finish it.*

thought Look up **think.**

thread | thrĕd | n. A fine cord of twisted silk, cotton, wool, or similar fibers from which cloth is woven or with which things are sewed. —v. To make one's way through obstacles: *We threaded our way through the crowd.*

threw Look up **throw.** *These sound alike* **threw, through.**

throat | thrōt | n. **1.** The passage running from the back of the mouth to the lungs and stomach: *a sore throat.* **2.** A narrow entrance or passage: *the throat of a cave.*

through | thrōō | prep. From one end to the other: *to go through a tunnel.* —adj. **1.** Going or extending from one end to another: *a through street.* **2.** Finished: *I'm through with this work. These sound alike* **through, threw.**

throw | thrō | v. **threw** | thrōō |, **thrown** | thrōn |, **throw·ing.** **1.** To fling with a motion of the arm; hurl: *to throw a ball.* **2.** To cause to fall; cause to lose balance: *One wrestler threw the other.* **3.** To cast; project: *The lamp throws a shadow on the wall.* —n. A flinging; a casting: *a throw of the ball.*

Idiom. **stone's throw.** Short distance.

thun·der·storm | thŭn′ dər stôrm′ | n. A storm of lightning and thunder, usually with a downpour of rain.

Thurs·day | thûrz′ dē | or | -dā′ | n. The fifth day of the week.

tim·id | tĭm′ ĭd | adj. Lacking in courage; shy; easily frightened: *Frank was too timid to give his speech.*

to | tōō | or | tə when unstressed | prep. **1.** Toward; in the direction of: *on my way to school.* **2.** As far as: *going to Boston.* **3.** For the purpose of; for: *built to last; a key to the door.* **4.** Opposite: *face to face.* **5.** On; upon;

against: *There is a sign tacked to the door.* **6.** Until; till: *The play lasts to 10:30.* **7.** Before: *five minutes to six. These sound alike* **to, too, two.**

Idiom. **to and fro.** Back and forth.

toast·er | tō′ stər | n. An electrical device for browning and heating bread and rolls.

to·ken | tō′ kən | n. **1.** Something that represents something else, such as an event, special occasion, fact, object, or feeling; symbol: *The postcard is a token of our trip.* **2.** A piece of metal that looks like a coin and is used in place of money, as in paying the fares on buses or subways.

to·mor·row | tə mŏr′ ō | or | -môr′ ō | n. **1.** The day after today: *Is tomorrow a holiday?* **2.** The near future: *the world of tomorrow.* —adv. On the day after today: *I will give this to you tomorrow.*

tongue | tŭng | n. **1.** The muscular, movable organ in the mouth used in tasting and also, in human beings, for talking. **2.** A language: *Her native tongue is Spanish.* **3.** A manner of speaking: *to have a sharp tongue.* **4.** Anything like a tongue in shape or use, such as leaping flame or the piece of leather under the laces of a shoe.

too | tōō | adv. **1.** Also; in addition; besides: *You are invited to the graduation ceremony and the party, too.* **2.** More than enough: *There was too much food. These sound alike* **too, to, two.**

tore Look up **tear.**

tor·na·do | tôr nā′ dō | n., pl. **tor·na·does** or **tor·na·dos.** Violent, whirling wind that travels rapidly in a narrow path. It is seen as a twisting, dark cloud shaped like a funnel.

touch | tŭch | v. **1.** To be in contact: *Their heads touched as they whispered.* **2.** To feel with the fingers: *She touched the paint.* **3.** To strike lightly; tap: *He touched the glass bells.*

to·ward | tôrd | or | tōrd | or | tə wôrd′ | prep. **1.** In the direction of: *We sailed toward Hawaii.* **2.** Close upon; near: *We camped toward sundown.* **3.** About; regarding: *What is your attitude toward the candidates?*

track | trăk | n. **1.** A mark left by something moving: *The animal left its tracks.* **2.** A path or trail: *The track is two miles long.* **3.** The rails on which a train moves. **4.** A racetrack. —*v.* To follow by sight or scent.

traf·fic | **trăf′** ĭk | *n.* **1.** The movement of people, automobiles, planes, ships, etc.: *There was much traffic on the road.* **2.** The exchange of goods; buying and selling. —*v.* **traf·ficked, traf·fick·ing, traf·fics.** To buy or sell.

trans·por·ta·tion | trăns′ pər **tā′** shən | *n.* The means of moving anything from one place to another.

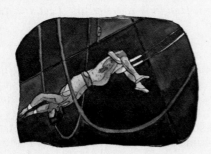

tra·peze | tră **pēz′** | *n.* A short bar placed between two hanging ropes, used by gymnasts and circus acrobats.

treas·ure | **trĕzh′** ər | *n.* Valuable thing or things such as jewels, gold, money, etc. —*v.* **treas·ured, treas·ur·ing.** To value; to think of very highly.

trem·ble | **trĕm′** bəl | *v.* **trem·bled, trem·bling. 1.** To shake from fright, cold, anger, etc.: *Your hand is trembling.* **2.** To move or quake: *I think the building is trembling.* —*n.* A shudder.

tried. Look up **try.**

trou·ble | **trŭb′** əl | *n.* **1.** A dangerous situation: *The police rushed to the scene of trouble.* **2.** Extra effort or bother: *Please don't go to any trouble for me.* —*v.* **trou·bled, trou·bling. 1.** To disturb or cause worry: *I'm troubled by your fever.* **2.** To bother: *May I trouble you for a minute?*

truth | trōōth | *n., pl.* **truths** | trōōthz | *or* | trōōths |. **1.** Something that is true; fact. **2.** Honesty or sincerity of speech and action.

try | trī | *v.* **tried** | trīd |, **try·ing, tries. 1.** To make an effort: *I tried to finish in time.* **2.** To test or experiment: *Try out your new skates.* **3.** To examine or investigate in a court of law: *The case will be tried in court.* —*n.* An effort.

Tues·day | **tōōz′** dē | *or* | -dā′ | *or* | **tyōōz′-** | *n.* The third day of the week.

tum·ble | **tŭm′** bəl | *v.* **tum·bled, tum·bling. 1.** To fall or roll over. **2.** To perform acrobatics such as leaps, headstands, etc. —*n.* A fall.

tu·tor | **tōō′** tər | *or* | **tyōō′-** | *n.* A teacher who gives private instruction to a student: *My English tutor helped me three times a week.* —*v.* To teach privately.

tweed | twēd | *n.* A rough woolen fabric made with two or more colors of yarn that is often used to make coats and casual suits.

two | tōō | *n.* One more than one; **2.** *These sound alike* **two, to, too.**

ty·rant | **tī′** rənt | *n.* A person or ruler who uses power in a cruel and unjust way: *The people were very upset because the king had become a tyrant.*

U

ug·ly | **ŭg′** lē | *adj.* **ug·li·er, ug·li·est. 1.** Unpleasant to look at: *ugly wallpaper.* **2.** Mean and disagreeable: *an ugly temper.*

ul·ti·mate | **ŭl′** tə mĭt | *adj.* **1.** Last; final: *Her ultimate goal is to be President of the United States.* **2.** Basic: *The ultimate cause of the accident was carelessness.*

um·pire | **ŭm′** pīr′ | *n.* A person whose job is to rule on plays in sports, especially in baseball: *The umpire called the pitch a strike.* —*v.* **um·pired, um·pir·ing.** To act as an umpire for: *Jill umpired the game.*

u·ni·verse | **yōō′** nə vûrs′ | *n.* Everything in existence: *the earth, the heavens, and all of space.*

up·roar | **ŭp′** rôr′ | *or* | -rōr′ | *n.* A loud noise caused by excitement or confusion.

up·set | ŭp **sĕt′** | *v.* **up·set, up·set·ting. 1.** To overturn or knock over: *The kitten upset the fishbowl.* **2.** To interfere or cause disorder: *The holiday crowds upset the train schedule.* **3.** To disturb or worry: *Did I upset you?* **4.** To unexpectedly defeat in a contest: *Our soccer team upset the champions.* —*n.* | **ŭp′** sĕt′ |. The act of overturning or causing a disturbance. —*adj.* | ŭp **sĕt′** |. **1.** Overturned: *an upset boat.* **2.** Disturbed; sick: *an upset stomach.*

u·til·i·ty | yōō **tĭl′** ĭ tē | *n., pl.* **u·til·i·ties. 1.** A company that supplies a service to the public: *The company that provides electricity is a utility.* **2.** Relating to such a company. **3.** Usefulness: *The utility of computers is well known.*

V

va·ca·tion | vā **kā′** shən | *n.* Time of rest from a regular routine; freedom from school or work: *a summer vacation.*

veg·e·ta·ble | **vĕj′** tə bəl | *or* | **vĕj′** ĭ tə- | *n., pl.* **veg·e·ta·bles.** A plant whose seeds, leaves, or roots may be used as food: *Carrots are my favorite vegetables.*

ve·loc·i·ty | və **lŏs′** ĭ tē | *n., pl.* **ve·loc·i·ties.** The rate at which something moves in a particular direction; speed: *the velocity of sound.*

vil·lage | **vĭl′** ĭj | *n.* A group of houses and businesses forming a small community, usually smaller than a town.

vir·tu·al | **vûr′** chŏŏ əl | *adj.* Being so for all practical purposes, though not in fact or name: *Kendall was the virtual star of the play even though she didn't have the biggest part.*

vo·cal | **vō′** kəl | *adj.* **1.** Relating to or made by the voice: *Because she had a sore throat, her vocal sounds were hoarse.* **2.** Relating to or made by singing: *I enjoyed the vocal music performed by the school choir.* **3.** Expressing opinions freely and often; outspoken: *She was vocal in her support of the new school building, making long speeches at every town meeting.*

voice | vois | *n.* A sound coming from the mouth made by speaking, shouting, singing, etc. —*v.* **voiced, voic·ing.** To give expression to: *He voiced his opinions.*

void | void | *n.* Empty space: *There was a void in the stadium after the teams and fans went home.* —*adj.* **1.** Empty. **2.** Worth nothing.

vol·ley·ball | **vŏl′** ē bôl′ | *n.* **1.** A game in which two teams try to bat a large ball back and forth across a net with their hands without letting the ball touch the ground. **2.** The ball used in this game.

vote | vōt | *n.* **1.** A formal expression of a choice: *a vote for student government.* **2.** The right or opportunity to express a choice: *I am too young to have a vote.* —*v.* To express a choice in an election.

voy·age | **voi′** ĭj | *n.* A long journey to a faraway place made by water or through space.

W

waist | wāst | *n.* **1.** The narrow part of the body between the ribs and the hips. **2.** Part of an object that is narrower than the rest of it: *the waist of a violin.* These sound alike **waist, waste.**

wal·low | **wŏl′** ō | *v.* To roll about in something such as mud or water: *Sometimes puppies will wallow in mud.*

wan·der | **wŏn′** dər | *v.* **1.** To roam without a particular purpose: *I wandered through the old gardens.* **2.** To get lost: *A search party was sent after the child who wandered from camp.* **3.** To ramble in speech or thought: *The speaker began to wander from the subject.*

warn | wôrn | *v.* **1.** To put on guard against danger; alert; caution: *The coast guard warned all ships of the hurricane.* **2.** To notify, signal: *Her look warned us it was time to leave.*

waste | wāst | *v.* **wast·ed, wast·ing. 1.** To squander; use without profit: *I am afraid that my brother wasted his allowance.* **2.** To destroy; spoil; ruin: *The forest was wasted by fire.* —*n.* **1.** Useless expenditure; profitless use: *a waste of opportunity.* **2.** Discarded material; refuse; something left over: *Factory waste pollutes our river.* **3.** Wilderness; desert: *Nothing grows in that desolate waste.* These sound alike **waste, waist.**

watch | wŏch | *v.* **1.** To look carefully; be attentive; be on the lookout: *If you watch, you may see how I do this trick.* **2.** To see; look at: *to watch a parade.* **3.** To keep guard: *We watched all through the night.* —*n.* **1.** Close observation: *Keep careful watch and you'll see a falling star.* **2.** Wakefulness for the purpose of guarding or tending to: *a mother's watch over her sick child.* **3.** A small timepiece, usually worn on the wrist.

weak | wēk | *adj.* **weak·er, weak·est. 1.** Lacking physical strength: *to be weak from hunger.* **2.** Likely to fail or break if placed under pressure, stress or strain: *a weak bridge.* **3.** Lacking in ability: *weak in math.*

wealth | wĕlth | *n.* **1.** A large quantity of money or possessions; riches. **2.** An abundance: *a wealth of ideas.*

wear | wâr | *v.* **wore** | wôr | *or* | wōr |, **worn** | wôrn | *or* | wōrn |, **wear·ing. 1.** To have on the body: *wear clothes; wear a smile.* **2.** To cause damage by long use: *wear a hole in a sock.*

weath·er | **wĕth′** ər | *n.* The atmospheric conditions at any place at a particular time: *The weather is beautiful today.* —*v.* **1.** To come through safely or successfully: *to weather a storm.* **2.** To become bleached, dried, etc. by the action of the sun, wind, rain, etc.: *The shingles of the old house had weathered to a beautiful silver gray.*

Idiom. under the weather. Not feeling well; ill.

Wednes·day | **wĕnz′** dē | *or* | -dā′ | *n.* The fourth day of the week.

week·end | **wēk′** ĕnd′ | *n.* **1.** The end of the week, especially the time from Friday night to Sunday night. **2.** A visit, holiday, or house party during this period: *a weekend at the beach.*

weigh | wā | *v.* **1.** To find out the heaviness of something by means of a scale or balance: *to weigh a parcel.* **2.** To have a certain weight: *He weighs 90 pounds.* **3.** To turn over in the mind; ponder: *She weighed another plan.*

weight | wāt | *n.* **1.** The amount a thing weighs: *the weight of a feather.* **2.** An object, usually metal, of specific heaviness used to balance a scale: *a set of weights from one ounce to five pounds.*
    Idiom. **pull one's weight.** To do one's part.

weight·less | wāt′ lĭs | *adj.* **1.** Having very little or no weight. **2.** Not affected by the pull of gravity: *The astronaut had to get used to being weightless in space.*

wheat | hwēt | *or* | wēt | *n.* **1.** A kind of grain. **2.** The seeds of this plant used to make flour.

wheth·er | hwĕ*th*′ ər | *or* | wĕ*th*′- | *conj.* **1.** If: *I don't know whether you're telling the truth or not.* **2.** No matter if: *The race is beginning whether or not you are ready.*

whis·tle | hwĭs′ əl | *or* | wĭs′- | *v.* **whis·tled, whis·tling.** **1.** To make a shrill, piercing sound: *The train whistled.* **2.** To make a shrill sound with puckered lips or between the teeth: *We whistled for a taxicab.* **3.** To move with a speed fast enough to make a sharp, shrill, or piercing sound: *The wind whistled in the storm.* —*n.* **1.** A sharp, shrill, piercing sound: *the whistle of a quail.* **2.** A sound made by forcing air through puckered lips: *You have some whistle!* **3.** A device used to make a whistle: *The traffic officer blew her whistle.*

whole | hōl | *adj.* **1.** Not broken; having all parts: *The vase was dropped, but it is still whole.* **2.** The entire amount or extent: *We had trouble with the car the whole way home.* —*n.* **1.** Entire amount with all pieces; sum: *The whole is equal to the sum of its parts.* **2.** A complete system; unity: *The organs of the body work as a whole.* These sound alike **whole, hole.**

whom | hōōm | *pron.* **1.** What person: *To whom am I speaking?* **2.** That (person): *This is the man whom I mentioned yesterday.*

whose | hōōz | *adj.* Possessive form of **who:** *the woman whose painting we bought.*

wife | wīf | *n., pl.* **wives** | wīvz |. A married woman.

wish | wĭsh | *n., pl.* **wish·es.** Something desired, needed, or wanted. —*v.* **1.** To crave; to want or feel a desire for. **2.** To express a hope for another: *I wish only the best for you.*

won·der·ful | wŭn′ dər fəl | *adj.* **1.** Extraordinary; remarkable; causing wonder: *a wonderful trip.* **2.** Admirable; excellent: *a wonderful idea.*

wore Look up **wear.**

wreck | rĕk | *v.* To destroy or to take apart: *The building was wrecked because it was a fire hazard.* —*n.* **1.** Damage or destruction caused by wind, an accident, etc. **2.** Remains of anything ruined or destroyed: *The wreck was hauled away.*

wrin·kle | rĭng′ kəl | *n.* A fold or ridge on a surface; crease: *a shirt full of wrinkles.* —*v.* **wrin·kled, wrin·kling.** To make a fold or to become creased.

wrist | rĭst | *n.* The joint connecting the hand and forearm.

write | rīt | *v.* **wrote** | rōt |, **writ·ten** | rĭt′ n |, **writ·ing.** **1.** To shape letters or words with a pencil or pen: *Write so that I can read.* **2.** To make up stories, poems, or books: *She writes stories.* **3.** To send a note or letter: *Write a thank-you letter. These sound alike **write, right.***

wrong | rông | *or* | rŏng | *adj.* **1.** Incorrect; false: *a wrong answer.* **2.** Not right; bad, wicked: *It is wrong to steal.* **3.** Unsuitable; inappropriate: *to do or say the wrong thing.* **4.** Out of order; amiss: *There is something wrong with my watch.* —*v.* To treat unfairly.

Y

yolk | yōk | *or* | yōlk | *n.* The yellow part of an egg.

Z

zone | zōn | *n.* **1.** Any of five regions on earth divided by climate. **2.** Any area that is set off from others. —*v.* To divide into special areas.

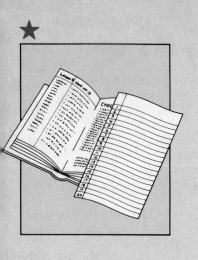

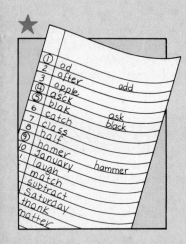

THE CHECKPOINT
Study Plan

When you have finished a Checkpoint page and you know that you have the correct answers, use the Checkpoint page and this Study Plan to test yourself.

★ Cover your answers to the Checkpoint page with a piece of paper. Number the paper 1 through 20. For each spelling clue, do steps 1, 2, and 3.

1 Read the clue and say the answer.

2 Spell the answer aloud.

3 Write the answer.

★ Uncover your first answers and do steps 4, 5, and 6.

4 Check your answers.

5 Circle the number of each misspelled word.

6 Write the correct spelling next to each incorrect word.

★ To study, cover your answers again, and fold the paper so that only the numbers show. For each circled number, repeat steps 1 through 6.

224